Praise fo

No Racial Elephants in the Therapy Room

"Dr. Rheeda Walker has built a career dedicated to improving the mental health of minoritized and marginalized populations, with a specific focus on Black people. *No Racial Elephants in the Therapy Room* takes her work to a whole other level by directly talking to those that need it most: white and other non-Black providers. True to Dr. Walker's form, she holds no punches and makes no apologies. She lays out the real-world and persisting consequences of systematic oppression and white supremacy on the mental health of Black people—providing readers with the necessary knowledge, strategies, tools, and tips to provide culturally adapted and sensitive care to Black people. *No Racial Elephants in the Therapy Room* has the potential to transform the mental health workforce in a way that no other book has been able to accomplish. It should be required reading for graduate students, the faculty who educate them, the clinicians who supervise them, and the existing providers who will one day be their colleagues."

—**Jason Washburn, PhD,** professor and chief of psychology at
Northwestern University Feinberg School of Medicine

"Dr. Walker provides a stellar resource for non-Black therapists who support Black folks seeking therapy in her book, *No Racial Elephants in the Therapy Room*. Her writing highlights the harm Black clients face when they seek out therapy, and she skillfully encourages providers to think more comprehensively and holistically about their clients. As a white therapist, I found this text to be helpful, validating, and honest, and many tangible pieces of support were provided within. The education she provided in these pages should be mandatory reading for all therapists and therapists-in-training."

—**Danica Harris, PhD, SEP,** co-owner, therapist, and somatic coach at
Empowered Healing Dallas, @theempoweredtherapist

"The stigma and taboo that surrounds mental health treatment in the Black community is a real issue. Well-meaning clinicians often feel uncomfortable discussing the challenges and disparities that Black people face daily. With her disarming candor and wit, Dr. Walker addresses this elephant in the room head-on, creating a safe space where Black people can be their authentic selves, explore their truths, and find the healing they deserve in treatment spaces."

—**Nedra Glover Tawwab, MSW, LCSW,** *New York Times* bestselling
author of *Set Boundaries, Find Peace* and *Drama Free*

"No Racial Elephants in the Therapy Room addresses the harsh reality of how racism presents itself within the therapeutic relationship, illustrating how it can manifest among well-intentioned white and even non-Black providers. Each chapter unravels tough truths, and Dr. Walker skillfully equips clinicians with the necessary tools and information to become culturally competent in supporting Black clients during pre- and post-intake while providing guidance on how to use certain therapeutic frameworks to support their needs. Many therapists enter this field with good intentions, but Dr. Walker's work serves as a reminder that good intentions cannot prevent harm. If white clinicians aspire to be allies to disrupt the cycle of trauma Black people encounter within the mental health industry, they must recognize and confront the elephants in the therapy room, including those they introduce from their own biases and deep-seated stereotypes. *No Racial Elephants in the Therapy Room* is an essential reading for all mental health professionals, especially white and non-Black clinicians."

—**Minaa B., LMSW,** author of *Owning Our Struggles*

"If you have ever wanted to have a frank conversation with an African American friend or colleague about working with African American clients, this book is for you. If you believe that you already understand all that you need to know, this book may surprise you. In *No Racial Elephants in the Therapy Room*, Dr. Rheeda Walker teaches us about the complexity of being Black in America, how it can impact mental health, and how a deeper understanding of its nuances can improve our ability to develop empathic and effective therapeutic relationships with the people who look to us for understanding and help."

—**Peter C. Britton, PhD,** associate professor, University of Rochester Medical Center, VA Finger Lakes Health Care System

"Written by one of the nation's leading authorities on Black mental health, Dr. Rheeda Walker's new book, *No Racial Elephants in the Therapy Room*, is a gift to the field. For clinicians who earnestly aspire to manage issues of race, Dr. Walker's direct and candid approach sheds light on key racial topics and the Black experience that can often be avoided. Dr. Walker has an uncanny knack for clarifying complex racial issues, and she provides thoughtful and informed guidance about what to do and what not to do about racial issues that can arise between clinician and client. Bottom line, this book is a superb and compelling guidebook for providing culturally competent and optimal clinical care for clients of color."

—**David A. Jobes, PhD, ABPP,** professor of psychology and associate director of clinical training, The Catholic University of America

"As a white therapist, I've wanted this book for years, and I'm grateful to Dr. Walker for writing it. It gives an unapologetic, educational, and rich insider view on the harm therapists can do if they avoid the racial elephant in the room. And it gives solutions— how to practice cultural humility and curiosity, explore racial identity development, beware of microaggressions, attend to racial trauma and systemic injustice, apologize for mistakes, and more. Every non-Black therapist should read this book!"

—**Stacey Freedenthal, PhD, LCSW,** associate professor, University of Denver Graduate School of Social Work, psychotherapist, and author of *Helping the Suicidal Person*

"*No Racial Elephants in the Therapy Room* offers a rare gift to therapists seeking to better meet the mental health needs of the Black clients whom they support. This book offers the insights therapists want to know—and their Black clients need them to know—regarding the unique experiences and struggles, frustrations and concerns, fears and hopes, all designed to help therapists to reduce rapport-damaging assumptions and avoid common reasonably intended mistakes, and instead offer informed empathy and more culturally considerate therapeutic value to their Black clients in the therapy room."

—**Lambers Fisher, MS, LMFT, MDiv,** author of *Diversity in Clinical Practice*

"Mental health disparities have persisted at least since they were identified six decades ago, and a major contributing factor is ignoring the 'elephant in the room'—namely, the impact of race in the lives of African Americans. Dr. Rheeda Walker draws on her wealth of research and clinical experience to offer inviting, accessible, and practical guidance on racial issues for therapists. Using a cognitive-behavioral framework, she explores cultural humility, spirituality and religiosity, and both client and therapist racial identity as ways to effectively address the elephant in the room, offering helpful case examples, self-assessment exercises, and methods to self-correct one's missteps. If all therapists followed the guidance in this book, mental health disparities would be reduced."

—**Gordon Nagayama Hall, PhD,** emeritus professor of psychology, University of Oregon, and author of *Multicultural Psychology* (4th ed.)

"At last, a comprehensive guide for delivering culturally affirming mental health care to Black families. Dr. Walker eloquently leads readers from the first therapy session to the last, offering valuable insight and guidance on cultivating culturally affirming skills. This is an essential read for every professional working with Black clients."

—**Sonyia Richardson, PhD, MSW, LCSW,** assistant professor, University of North Carolina at Charlotte

"Dr. Walker competently explores the chasm in the training and preparation of non-Black therapists to provide optimal mental health care to Black clients in *No Racial Elephants in the Therapy Room*. This timely guide is a powerful and practical resource to help non-Black therapists appreciate the heterogeneity and uniqueness of the Black experience, examine their personal and therapeutic identities, and navigate challenges on the journey. An important outcome of improved mental health equity is the increased acceptance of and access to therapy for Black folks, signaling the need for a competent behavioral health workforce, which is still predominantly white. Dr. Walker invites the reader to acknowledge their fears, utilize existing skills, and abandon comfort zones by adopting a lens of cultural humility and honing authenticity and empathy to more fully meet the therapeutic needs of clients who cannot ignore how race impacts their emotional and psychological well-being."

—**Brian McGregor, PhD,** owner, McGregor Research & Consulting, LLC, and adjunct clinical assistant professor, Department of Psychiatry and Behavioral Sciences, Morehouse School of Medicine

"This book should be required reading for all clinical programs. Dr. Walker has done a phenomenal job with this book. It has the perfect balance of introspective questions to challenge individuals to become better clinicians, while also including scripts to provide concrete examples to help trainees understand how to apply knowledge in practice and develop their therapeutic communication skills."

—**Raquel Martin, PhD,** professor, psychologist, and scientist

"This incredible book is an absolute must-read for white mental health providers. It powerfully lays out important ideas and information related to providing culturally affirming care with Black and African American clients, while also providing clear and specific recommendations for how to put these ideas into action in your clinical practice at each step of a client's care. The exercises within it are powerful ways to engage in the ongoing self-reflection needed for cultural humility, and the book provides an incredibly helpful framework and specific concrete strategies for applying CBT therapy with Black Americans in a culturally adapted manner within the context of systemic oppression, as well as incorporating acknowledgment of this sociocultural context. I will certainly be returning to this valuable resource in the future and encourage other providers to do the same!"

—**Jessica L. Maples-Keller, PhD,** assistant professor, Department of Psychiatry and Behavioral Sciences, Emory University School of Medicine

"Dr. Rheeda Walker is a leading voice in the field of psychology, especially when it comes to uplifting the rich and unique cultural experiences of Black Americans. Therefore, it is no surprise that in *No Racial Elephants in the Therapy Room*, Dr. Rheeda brings her distinct insights and expertise to elevating the issues that prevent many white clinicians from providing exceptional psychological care to Black clients. Dr. Rheeda guides the reader through ways to embody cultural humility, ways to use evidence-based practices without dismissing the realities of oppression, and ways to incorporate culturally relevant coping strategies, like spirituality, into care. Yet, this vital resource is not just a 'cultural competency checklist' but rather a timely and unapologetic call to action for every white clinician willing to do the hard work of ensuring that Black and African American clients receive the equitable care they deserve."

—**Natalie Watson-Singleton, PhD,** licensed clinical psychologist and co-founder of the Dialectical Engagement in Anti-Racism (DEAR) Project

NO RACIAL ELEPHANTS

in the
Therapy Room

An Unapologetic Approach
to Providing Culturally Affirming
Mental Health Care to Black
and African American Clients

RHEEDA WALKER, PhD

Foreword by Scott Waltman, PsyD, ABPP

NO RACIAL ELEPHANTS IN THE THERAPY ROOM
Copyright © 2024 by Rheeda Walker

Published by
PESI Publishing, Inc.
3839 White Ave
Eau Claire, WI 54703

Cover and interior design by Emily Dyer
Editing by Jenessa Jackson, PhD

ISBN 9781683737452 (print)
ISBN 9781683737469 (ePUB)
ISBN 9781683737476 (ePDF)

PESI Publishing
pesipublishing.com

To all the clinicians whom I have had the fortune
to accompany along the path to providing clinically
sound and culturally meaningful care.

Table of Contents

Foreword

There is much to be learned from *No Racial Elephants in the Therapy Room* and the application of the wisdom it contains. **Simply stated, this is the book I wish I would have used when I first started as a therapist**; I would have benefited greatly from it and so would my clients. I have long been a fan of Dr. Rheeda Walker, as I have found her pragmatic and unapologetic approach to be both interpersonally effective and disarming. In her seminal work *The Unapologetic Guide to Black Mental Health*, she reaches out to members of the Black and African American communities to have a pragmatic and frank discussion about mental health, as one would have with a close family member or friend. It is full of heart, candor, and a little bit of humor. She brings that same style to this book written for therapists who work with BIPOC (Black, Indigenous, and People of Color) clients—specifically focusing on how to work well with Black and African American clients.

Often, white clinicians are uncomfortable or unskilled at broaching topics of race with their clients. They worry about saying the wrong thing or, conversely, erroneously assume that a client's race is irrelevant. This attitude of colorblindness is one that many of us have been exposed to. The idea is that the color of someone's skin should not matter and that everyone should be treated equally. This can lead people to ignore identities and factors related to race, with the ideal of treating everyone the same. The challenge is, many Black and African American clients do not live in a world that is actually colorblind—only a world that periodically pretends to be colorblind. In order to connect with my clients on a human level, I have to be able to see and understand the world they live in. And I have to be able to have a conversation with them about what it is like to live the life they live with the identities they have. Wouldn't we all like to be more skilled at how to have these conversations?

That is what Dr. Walker has accomplished with this book. She focuses on taking a stance of *cultural humility* as opposed to focusing on cultural competency as something that can be checked off a checklist. In my experience as a white psychologist, when I'm working with individuals from diverse backgrounds, such as BIPOC clients, factors related to race, power, discrimination, and privilege are right in the room with us, though normally we're not able to address them until I myself call them out and broach the subject. Most of my clients have sadly been well accustomed to the phenomenon of *white fragility* and are often unsure if I will be able to understand, or even try to understand, where they're coming from. This book is geared toward calling out that specific elephant in the room. And Dr. Walker does a fantastic job of that.

She walks you through core concepts such as guided discovery and psychoeducation and their application. She gives suggestions for every step of the therapy process, from the first phone call to termination. She expertly discusses assessment, diagnosis, conceptualization, and treatment. This is a book I will read over and over again, as there is so much to be gained. She discusses the rich diversity and heterogeneity found within Black and African American cultures and makes helpful suggestions for integrating these cultural values into treatment. There is a treasure trove of example dialogues and, very importantly, example dialogues about how to recover when you make a misstep. In essence, she describes how to provide *culturally affirming* mental health care while learning to be humble and vulnerable.

Finally, I want to call attention to the highly nuanced and skillful way Dr. Walker addresses the use of cognitive behavioral therapy (CBT). This approach is one with decades of research support and power behind it and, at the same time, is one that has profound potential for being misused. Therapists who do not well understand CBT (or who are not culturally informed) can fall into the harmful pitfall of treating accurate views of societal interactions (e.g., racism, discrimination, microaggressions) as distortions or faults on the part of the client. Dr. Walker guides you on how to avoid these pitfalls with compassion, humility, and curiosity. This is the type of CBT that the world needs more of. This is the type of CBT that my clients need and that I myself need, though the themes and lessons of this book extend well beyond CBT.

I am so grateful for this book, as I am currently not aware of any other book that accomplishes what Dr. Walker has accomplished here. There is a critical gap in literature, and she has filled that gap. It is on us who do the work to read and apply the knowledge she has provided here, while we approach each individual with whom we work with cultural humility.

Scott Waltman, PsyD, ABPP

Clinical psychologist

Author of Socratic Questioning for Therapists and Counselors

President-elect, fellow, diplomate, and certified trainer/consultant, Academy of Cognitive and Behavioral Therapies

Board member, International Association of Cognitive Behavioral Therapy

Board certified in behavioral and cognitive psychology

Editor, Advances in Cognitive Behavioral Therapy Newsletter

Introduction

As a therapist, you know that the single most important predictor of success in psychotherapy is the therapeutic alliance. The alliance reflects your ability to relate to the client, your capacity to work collaboratively to achieve therapeutic goals, and the client's attitude toward you. The client understands the game plan and has confidence that it will work. The working relationship is key and more potent than your experience, your years of providing care, or the type of therapy you provide. You may have heard this referenced as one of the "common factors" of psychotherapy. There is an initial level of trust that you must develop with your client before you can achieve the deeper levels of trust that are needed in therapy. This is true for any client. But what if the alliance is weak because the client is Black and you are not, and you have not anticipated the challenges that may come to bear if there is inherent distrust and a healthy suspiciousness on the part of the client?

The reality is that many Black clients are not confident that white clinicians will be able to help them without exacting the very microaggressions and missed cultural cues that are often the source of the client's problems in the first place. There are valid reasons for their concerns, as many white providers are uninformed and ill-equipped to broach the topic of race and racism in therapy. Most graduate training programs are rooted in Eurocentric perspectives, with a few "multicultural" or "diversity" courses sprinkled in to satisfy degree and licensure requirements. The reality is that training programs have not traditionally centered the complex reality of African American individuals.

Though various businesses and industries in the United States, as well as mental health institutions, have *visited* with racial reckoning, there are still limited tools for moving the needle on mental health services for clients who are overexposed to social injustice. Very often, forward-thinking clinicians feel that they have no place to begin or no options to meaningfully improve. Despite efforts to rise to a level of "cultural competence," this persistently lethargic response to the emotional impact of injustice is more problematic than ever because it confirms what Black people already know—Black life doesn't *really* matter. Your inability to change society does not change the reality of how society impacts what goes on in the therapy room.

If you are a white provider, this may describe your experience. Perhaps you feel compelled to avoid certain questions from Black clients because of potential embarrassment about something you think you "should" know about racism or about "Black culture." Perhaps you fear that you will unintentionally do harm by saying something that is racist. Or perhaps you believe that if clients don't bring up the issue of race or race-related stress in therapy, then racism is not an issue at all. Although many Black clients will not zero in on the impact of racism in their lives, this does not mean that you should conspire to avoid integrating race-related stressors in your conceptualization of their concerns when it could be relevant. Doing so ignores the critical experiences that prompt most African American clients to seek Black therapists in the first place. Ignoring race leaves a very large elephant in the room.

I don't do elephants in the room. I especially do not permit elephants in the psychotherapy room. In this context, elephants are the seemingly polite but unsaid thoughts and unexpressed feelings. As a therapist, you must be willing to explicitly acknowledge these elephants if you want to develop a meaningful therapeutic relationship with your clients. Otherwise, these elephants will impede therapy progress. I adopted this perspective from the late Dr. Daniel Boroto, my inspiring former supervisor in the Florida State University doctoral program in clinical psychology.

Over the years, many "Boroto-isms" have carried over in my approach to clinical work. One elephant that persists is the uncomfortable subject of race. Perhaps because Black people do not have the luxury of *not* thinking about race, this elephant is in every room, and in the context of therapy, it grows ever larger when it is either ignored or presumed irrelevant by white practitioners. But for many African Americans, it is ever present. It is present because our very survival sometimes depends on our capacity to successfully navigate race so that *others* will feel comfortable. Many of these behaviors fall under the domain of "respectability politics" or the belief that Black people will earn certain benefits by conforming to mainstream narratives of acceptable behavior and "acting right." There is a tough divide that separates Black people from everyone else. Anyone who wants to bridge that chasm must begin with the racial elephant in the room.

It is for this reason that I decided to write *No Racial Elephants in the Therapy Room*, an uncompromising twenty-first century guide for non-Black therapists looking to bridge the disconnect between the clinical training they receive and the lived realities of African American clients. Formatted as a workbook and designed as an accessible reference, this book fills an undeniable void. Within these pages, providers will find useful language, tips, and instructions needed to care for individuals who identify as African American or Black.

In chapter 1, I discuss how you can be part of a paradigm shift in mental health care despite understandable apprehension among African Americans to seek mental health services. In chapter 2, I explain why one of your initial priorities is to adopt a disposition of cultural humility in lieu of prematurely checking the box for "cultural competence." Doing so will allow you to better understand why racism merits attention in psychotherapy. Chapter 3 expands on this discussion by specifically explaining how to intentionally navigate the first session with your client.

Although I thread strategies for navigating the client's experiences of racism throughout the book, chapter 4 is explicitly set aside for this conversation. I also take an important dive into diagnostic approaches to avoid missing well-disguised emotional distress (chapter 5), as well as strategies to approach cognitive restructuring in a way that empowers your client without minimizing the heinous impact of racism and structural oppressions (chapter 6). As part of intervention, I integrate spiritual and religious strategies, given their high value to Black identity (chapter 7). Too often, clients check these resources at the door to the therapy room, perhaps because of pervasively "secular" mental health training. And of course, I address Black identity (chapter 8) and white identity (chapter 9) because how the client sees themselves and how you see yourself are elephant-dynamics that play out in the therapy room via the client's experiences of daily events and your comfort with discussing race.

In chapter 10, I amplify some key topics that have been introduced in previous chapters, and review some important reminders of what *not* to do, including abandoning your clinical training, asking your client if they like rap music, and showing your white fragility. Before you know it, you'll be at the end of the book. Because the same is true for therapy, chapter 11 ends with consolidation, an important phase of therapy. In this chapter, I explore why we refer to the end as "consolidation" and not "termination."

Throughout the text, you'll notice that I use specific labels, some of which have more consequence than others. As an example, I use the terms *therapy* and *therapist* in reference to *psychotherapy* and *psychotherapist*, respectively. Hopefully, we agree that our goal is to advance psychologically oriented interventions via talk therapy—not other types of therapies like occupational or physical therapy.

In addition, my use of both *African American* and *Black* as descriptors for Black people and my capitalization of *Black* are intentional. Not all Black people identify as African American. Though some identify as Nigerian, or Afro-Puerto Rican, all share African ancestry and vulnerability to race-based discrimination and stress. Though your client appears to be Black, you cannot assume they identify as African American since it might be more appropriate, for example, for them to identify as Nigerian American. *I* capitalize *Black* because I know it to be synonymous with a robust system of cultural beliefs and historical context.

You'll find that my approach throughout this book is straightforward, to the point, and above all, unapologetic. Individuals who struggle with language such as white privilege and racism will not find solace in this text. I much prefer to speak plainly so that there are no misinterpretations. You cannot remove the elephant from the room if I leave "room" for you to interpret the elephant as acceptable, or if I create "space" for you to assume that maybe avoiding conversations about race isn't so bad. I recognize that it is important for you to receive valuable insights without calling in your ego defenses—and there is a time and a place to protect people from their insecurities, fragilities, and fears—but this is absolutely not that time. I have seen too much to give you a sanitized version of what really needs to take place in the therapy room.

With this in mind, please note that this book is only comprehensive to the degree that you are willing to do your own work with each client you encounter, as there is very little (if any) utility in seeking out a competency "checklist" for working with Black clients. In fact, if a therapist is looking for a box they can check off for competency, I'm actually more concerned about their capacity to provide culturally meaningful care.

Eradicating an elephant from the room can be a real challenge because so many elephants are part of our society. But you can do this! I am convinced that when you pursued your graduate training in counseling, social work, or psychology, you did so with the intention of helping all people. Although you may have become disillusioned in your practice by how much you have had to figure things out on your own, this book is here to serve as your guide. Let's get to work on being part of a progressive mental health force that genuinely meets Black and African American clients where they are.

Chapter 1

Much to Overcome

As a whole, Black people seek professional mental health services less frequently than white individuals. Black women in particular are said to subscribe to super-human beliefs about not needing outside help, but it's Black men who are even less likely to see a mental health professional. While some argue that access and income are the primary culprits, studies show that medication use and outpatient therapy access are not affected by income level (Substance Abuse and Mental Health Services Administration [SAMHSA], 2015). The reality is there are other factors at play that make Black people unlikely to seek care. This includes the mismatch between their own perceived need for help and their true level of impairment, the shame and stigma around seeking help, and the belief that no one has time to see a professional when there are real and more pressing issues at play, like dealing with stressful work managers or teachers who discipline our children more harshly and more often than their white counterparts.

Black people are also less likely to seek mental health care, in part, due to generational and personal mistrust of white people in general. Some scholars have suggested that part of *being* Black means to have a healthy mistrust of white people and white institutions (Terrell & Terrell, 1981). This includes educational systems, banking systems, health care, and of course, mental health. These entities are deemed to be "for white people." Given the way Black people have been treated in our society and in many societies around the world, it is no wonder that mistrust is considered healthy. A psychologically healthy Black person would not be so naive as to embrace anything that is rooted in white culture. If therapy is something that white people do, it might be assumed to be inherently not for Black people. An unfortunate consequence of these dynamics is the progression of more persistent, less treatable mental health challenges that lead to long-term, undesirable (and oftentimes involuntary) hospitalization. Indeed, it is a stark reality that Black people are unfortunately overrepresented in inpatient facilities.

Although many in the Black community have historically avoided seeking mental health care, the cultural milieu has started to shift, perhaps in response to celebrity transparency and Hollywood storylines about mental health struggles. Many popular television shows have humanized complex emotional pain and serious mental illness. Viewers saw this in HBO's *Insecure* when Nathan, played by Kendrick Sampson, revealed that he struggled with a new diagnosis of bipolar disorder, as well as when Yvonne Orji's character, Molly, attended regular sessions with her therapist to manage her life issues.

Perhaps even more compelling has been celebrity acknowledgment of mental health challenges. Lenard McKelvey, known as Charlamagne tha God, as well as Taraji P. Henson, Michelle Williams, and countless others have openly and shamelessly shared their struggles and how they eventually benefited from professional mental health care. These narratives have been powerfully important for shifting the narrative, given the weight of celebrity influence. As you may remember from Bandura's social learning theory, people "learn" from models who have power or status. When people see a "model" benefit from some novel behavior, they learn that they, too, can benefit from that same or similar behavior. This is especially true when the observer can identify with the model. Couple this context with the reality that African Americans are the largest consumers of television media and streaming audio (Nielsen, 2022).

Given these shifts in how we as Black people perceive professional mental health needs, this population is increasingly looking for therapists. However, they might not be looking for you and, frankly, they may be intentionally avoiding a therapist who looks like you. Despite their preferences, they may not have a choice. The overwhelming majority of psychotherapists or mental health providers are white (American Psychological Association [APA], 2022)—and primarily white women. In my discipline of psychology, 84 percent of active psychologists are white. Just over 4 percent are Black or African American. What makes this statistic even more eye-opening is that 62 percent of psychologists have indicated they "never, rarely, or occasionally" provide services to Black clients (APA, 2016). Those who do provide services to this demographic are, themselves, more likely to identify as Black, Hispanic, Asian, or multiracial. In sum, white psychotherapists are least likely to see Black clients, but there are relatively few Black therapists to meet the critical need.

In case you're wondering, this preference for a Black or African American therapist does not make African Americans racist or even paranoid (an assumption that can and has contributed to an overdiagnosis of schizophrenia among this community). The perspective of distrust and ambivalence among Black folks is a necessary part of surviving in a racially driven society. You are very likely aware that this country's history is rife with examples of neglect, exclusion, and mistreatment of Black people in what has been historically white-led institutions, particularly in medicine and health care. The care of Black people by non-Black practitioners must begin with a clear acknowledgment of this colossal elephant in the room.

And while it might be nice for a Black client to see a Black therapist, there aren't enough Black therapists to go around. This means that the ones who are out there are burning out. A recent *Forbes* article detailed the dual challenges that Black therapists face when it comes to providing care while also managing their own feelings about police brutality, white-supremacist violence toward Black people, and the lack of professional support (Gold, 2021). Many of these therapists came, and continue to come, into the discipline from a social justice perspective, recognizing the unmet needs of the Black community. In this context, once they become someone who can help, the inclination is to do more and give more, leading them to make self-sacrifices that can ultimately lead to their own distress.

Ideally, you are someone who can address this unmet need—by being a culturally sensitive therapist and also by identifying ways of directly or indirectly supporting your peers who are Black or African American. Speak up in a meeting when your African American colleague has been subjected to a racial microaggression. Offer them assistance on responsibilities that take time but offer little reward. If it's feasible, gift them with a two-year subscription that could help with an expressed need, such as the latest billing platform. If it could be of interest, consider paying their registration for a CEU training course or other training that you're attending. If you need to "fish" for their interests, you can ask, "Hey, there's an ACA-sponsored CEU training coming up about working with families. It's in a few weeks. Did you have in mind to attend? Did you register yet?" If there's an opportunity to get them registered, you can do so early and let them know (and always cancel for a refund if it doesn't work out).

You don't always have to make a grand gesture. Smaller efforts demonstrate that you recognize the pain in the community. For example, I have a colleague who makes amazing brownies with peanut butter filling. On occasion, she offers them to me. She doesn't say, "Hey, I know the racism is bad out there today, so what can I do?" We have sufficient rapport that she knows one of my favorite things is her peanut butter brownies, so she brings me some on random occasions—a small gesture that goes a long way. Therefore, if you can't take on a caseload, offer support in some other way. As you read through this text, think of not just your client load but the people around you who are more than likely carrying a heavy load. One elephant in the room is the assumption that all therapists are the same. But therapists in communities that are suffering unseen often experience the same kinds of unseen-ness as the broader community. We may simply carry it better and hide it more elegantly.

So if you are endeavoring to help African American clients, you must first ask yourself this: In your heart, are you comfortable seeing Black clients? Now that many clinicians actively use virtual platforms and can provide care outside of their immediate communities, are you promoting yourself as someone who is keenly aware of the needs in the Black community, including clients with intersectional identities, such as those who are Black *and* also gay or transgender? Do you have close relationships with someone who is African American or Black? Have you had more than one meal with that person? If not, can you consult with a Black professional for a candid conversation about expanding your sphere of clinical care? Are you willing to consider that you may very well be awkward around people who are different from you?

These are questions that you may have to begin to ask yourself. That is not to suggest that you harass your one "Black friend" into meeting with you for lunch every other week. Most of this individual work is up to you. Perhaps you can take the initiative to watch one of the many YouTube videos on healthy conversations about race.* You might review a video that implores white people to take more responsibility for talking about race.**

This is your invitation to be more individually accountable for how you show up in the world. There are no longer any excuses for engaging in "therapy as usual" if that therapy does not involve a conscientious effort to conceptualize and engage with Black and African American clients who exist in a very racialized world. Your personal proximity to the lived experiences of Black people is something to consider as you begin

---

* For example, watch Caprice Hollins's 2020 TEDxSeattle Talk at https://www.youtube.com /watch?v=7iknxhxEn1o.

** For example, watch Dwinita Mosby Tyler's 2020 TEDxMileHigh Talk at https://www.youtube .com/watch?v=VQSW5SFBsOg.

your journey to being a more inclusive mental health provider. Regardless of how you arrived here, it is important that you are committed to providing care that goes beyond the dismissive assumption that "all people are human."

How I Arrived Here

These realities of overwhelming and unaddressed need, non-inclusion, mistrust, and mental health stigma coexisted with my curiosity about the mental health of Black people and the noted absence on this topic in my undergraduate textbooks. As a professional of more than twenty years, I identify almost equally as a clinical psychologist, researcher, professor, and educator. Because I have been employed in university settings, my primary responsibility has been to train future clinical psychologists. As part of my training, I insist they not leave elephants in the room. Understandably, many struggle with this relatively atypical style, as it seems impolite. I guide and supervise treatment planning, review trainee videos, and watch live sessions on occasion. I role-play the part of the therapist, and if there is a crisis, I am called upon to be part of the session because therapists in training do not make final determinations on if a client could be in imminent danger. I appreciate this work. More importantly, I value the work of clinicians who see clients daily. We are living in increasingly challenging times where clients are reporting more stress and seem to have fewer external resources and internal coping strategies to manage.

Being in an academic setting also means that I use cultural and clinical insights to contribute to the science of our discipline. When you hear on the news about "a study at the University of XYZ," there are people like me who are engaged in asking curious questions, developing hypotheses, and designing experiments and other strategies to gather data and determine whether our hypotheses are supported, or whether the research findings say "not so fast."

The research I have been engaged in since I was a doctoral student is focused on the well-being of Black Americans. This was not easy to do, politically, for attaining scholarly publications. I encountered questions that you may have expressed in the past—questions like "Why do we have to think about race?" "Are people *that* different?" and "Aren't we all human?" Unfortunately, we're not all having the same human experience. Not everyone's humanity is respected. Even if you are a well-intentioned person, you may say and do things that affect others adversely. When these missteps happen, it's important to acknowledge how you deal with them. Do you tell the other person, "You took it the wrong way"? Perhaps this is your natural response outside of the therapy room, but would you use that off-ramp in a session with a client and still expect to be able to build that all-important rapport? In the long run, you want to ensure that your thinking and values both inside *and* outside of the therapy room are aligned in a way that benefits historically mistreated people. You can't build rapport with elephants in the room.

And when it comes to the outside world, there's more than an elephant. There's a whole zoo. As you know, there are many unique perspectives worth understanding in the world, and when you are able to value these different perspectives, it makes room to understand why Black people are culturally different and definitely not deficient, as much of our K-12 educational system would have you believe. Sadly, and from an early age, we have all been socialized in a system that perpetuates ideas of inferiority in the Black community. Even if you don't adopt these ideas yourself, the social hierarchy easily facilitates notions of deficiency and inferiority together with a comfortable dose of racial color-blindness.

My research qualifies as more racially "bold" than blind. I focus primarily on the interplay of risk factors and protective factors that are associated with suicide, as well as anomalies, in the mental health experience of Black people. As a researcher, I couldn't ignore it when the suicide rate was increasing for Black youth. Though I have studied suicide for years and could have predicted that our suicide deaths could begin to skyrocket, something about 5- to 11-year-old Black children killing themselves at a higher rate while the rate decreased for similar-aged white children left me dumbfounded.

Incidentally, there is also reason to believe that suicide deaths increased during the peak of COVID-19 infections for Black adults while decreasing for white adults. These are the types of anomalies to which I attend. It's also the reason we need more providers who are comfortable having racially nuanced conversations—not only Black providers who can presumably relate to the experiences of Black clients, but most importantly, culturally humble providers already in place who will pick up the slack and offset some of the load in the Black community. I presume that there are a lot of well-intentioned white therapists out there who are looking to help but are fearful about doing so.

But there is no time for fear. If patterns continue, we may arrive at a time in the near future when the suicide death rate for African Americans increases to mirror the tremendous level of psychological strain in the African American community. When you think about the kinds of risks that lead to death and the factors that amplify the chances that someone will take their own life, note that Black people are higher on just about every single index that seems to elevate risk. Yet, our death rates have historically been lower. I would expect more people to be in therapy. This is why I have studied both risk and resilience.

Going Beyond "One Size Fits All"

As a professor at the university level, I teach a required interventions course in addition to supervising clinical cases. In the interventions course, I model cultural consciousness in everything from case conceptualization to treatment planning. Students enrolled in my course understand what it means to evaluate how race (as well as gender, sexual orientation, language preferences, education, and income) impact the overall thinking about the client experience. When I was in grad school in the '90s, this wasn't much of a conversation. This may also be true for you—perhaps your training presumed a sense of "one size fits all" rather than acknowledging meaningful group differences. As an example, you may have been socialized to conceptualize men as being less connected to their emotions, but you may not have learned that Black and Latinx individuals are more likely to report physical symptoms of depression, such as sleep disturbance and physical pain, than cognitive symptoms, such as hopelessness or thoughts of suicide.

Even if you learned about group differences in clinical presentation, you might be wondering if you can just point them out to a client. I'd say yes, sort of. Imagine that your client is a 35-year-old African American woman who came to therapy because she is tired of feeling "overwhelmed all the time" and because her cousin suggested that she "talk to someone." She is married, employed full time, and raising two elementary school-aged children. Teachers say that one of her children likely has attention-deficit/hyperactivity disorder (ADHD). By your client's report, she was recently promoted at work and seems to do be doing well overall. You saw her for a full intake session but don't feel that her pattern of symptoms come together in a meaningful way. Though she reports anxiety and depression as her biggest challenges, she seems to be functioning just fine and doesn't present with much hypervigilance or worry that would be indicative of generalized anxiety, social anxiety, or any other anxiety-related concern.

THERAPIST: In our last session, you indicated that your primary care doctor assessed you as being in good physical health.

CLIENT: Yes.

THERAPIST: And you don't experience any physical pain that isn't accounted for.

CLIENT: I have headaches several times a month, but the doctor said it's likely stress.

THERAPIST: Do you ever feel like you have problems concentrating or with your focus?

CLIENT: No. I get distracted with my kids, but otherwise, I can focus pretty good.

THERAPIST: At work and at home?

CLIENT: Yes.

THERAPIST: Okay, tell me about your sleep.

CLIENT: I get in bed, but I don't fall asleep for hours. Nothing seems to help. I probably get four to five hours of sleep a night.

THERAPIST: Does this happen most nights?

CLIENT: Yes, probably six nights a week.

THERAPIST: You mentioned that you're active in a number of organizations, including at your church?

CLIENT: Yes.

THERAPIST: Do you enjoy those activities?

CLIENT: [*confused*] Well, sometimes I do. I should help whenever I can.

THERAPIST: On a 0–10 scale, what level of enjoyment do you get from volunteering at church, with 0 being the lowest and 10 being the highest amount of joy you can possibly imagine?

CLIENT: [*without hesitation*] 4.

THERAPIST: Okay, and how many hours do you spend each week in these volunteer activities?

CLIENT: Let's see, I'm there about four hours on Saturdays and two hours other days, so about six hours each week.

THERAPIST: Okay, tell me what you do that gives you joy of at least a 7 rating each week.

CLIENT: Well ... I don't know. I would have to think about that. Nothing comes to mind.

THERAPIST: It sounds like you work hard for your family and even in your volunteer activities but aren't getting much joy out of life. For some people, it's just normal. It's what they do, but it's good to have balance in life. We can talk about this further, but your mood sounds pretty low and suggests symptoms of depression. Depression can show up in lots of different ways. For some people, it shows up as disrupted sleep and reduced interest in things that they enjoy.

In this example, the therapist doesn't have to specify how different patterns of mental health challenges show up differently *due to race*. In fact, they may want to delay doing so if they do not yet have rapport with the client or do not understand the extent to which she identifies as African American. However, the therapist does need to use psychoeducation to get buy-in from the client. This woman may be highly accomplished and outgoing, but she also may be suffering silently because she is afraid to "fall apart," doesn't have time to fall apart, or a bit of both.

What We Know About Racial Matching

The research on racial matching has been relatively inconsistent with regard to therapy outcomes and length of time in therapy. For example, Dr. Thomas Joiner and colleagues (2022) found that clients remained in therapy longer given an ethno-racial match to the therapist. However, those clients did not seem to meet treatment goals any more effectively when same-race therapists were available. Of note, when African American clients receive services from a white therapist, they report a poorer therapeutic alliance than those who receive services from an African American therapist. Some African American clients even rank race as more important than a therapist's years of experience.

This means that even if a therapist markets themselves as having "multicultural advocacy" on their online profile, it does not make them any more "relatable" to African American clients. In the end, racial matching is often perceived as the only genuine path to connecting meaningfully with a mental health provider.

While I certainly sympathize with Black people's preference for same-race therapists, that does not mean that a white therapist cannot help a Black client meet their goals. A therapist does not have to personally identify with a client's every demographic to be helpful. They do, however, have to be mindful of these demographics. And multicultural competence cannot be the shortcut. Taking cultural competency courses for licensure is rarely sufficient. As I say to my clinical supervisees, therapy is a microcosm of the world outside of therapy. Because people of African descent are well aware of racial dynamics, therapists have to be well-informed and sensitized to racial differences and absent any stereotypical beliefs if they are to be effective in the therapy room.

And if we're honest, racial matching in therapy is not a guarantee of therapeutic rapport anyway, given the heterogeneity of Black people. This is understood among Black people who know that "all my skinfolk ain't kinfolk," as Zora Neale Hurston so eloquently stated. The quote acknowledges the tremendous variability in the level of assimilation and adoption of traditional beliefs and values in the Black community. If an African American therapist strongly identifies with the white majority, they will only be relatable to clients who similarly identify with the majority culture. That therapist could encounter challenges in developing a strong therapeutic alliance with Black clients who are less acculturated.

I hope it goes without saying that despite the title of this book, *Black people are a heterogeneous group.* Homogeneity would greatly simplify the task before you. You may already struggle with the idea that you might have to do anything differently at all. After all, you picked up this book for checklists of things to do differently. Imagine that you might have to do things differently with each of your clients who is Black or otherwise racially different from you. This may feel uncomfortable if, again, you want to believe that all people are the same—that people are people. You may even wonder whether it's "racist" to treat people differently based on race. If so, I'm so glad you raised this point so we can address it.

Acknowledging that there are group differences based on race (or religion, gender identity, nationality, or any other context that makes people different) is not racist. In fact, it allows us to live in a more inclusive society. The problem, however, is that we often assume bad things about people based on their race. We rarely assume good things. When someone says to a Black person, "You don't act Black," they aren't referencing the resilience that has allowed Black people to thrive in a dehumanizing world or the grace with which those same individuals present themselves despite having been demeaned. No. Instead, the reference point is the negative stereotypes that have been assigned to Black people as lazy, loud, hypersexual, and unintelligent, among others. To the degree that you believe that some Black people demonstrate these qualities any more than white people is indicative of work that you will need to continue throughout this book. It will be difficult for you to engage Black clients or other racially different people without getting your thoughts together.

When it comes to racial matching, Black and African American clients who have never been in therapy will often fall on a continuum—somewhere between being very comfortable with and being highly apprehensive about seeing a white therapist (and perhaps a combination of the two). Some are accustomed to and thus very comfortable navigating interactions with white people. These individuals may have been enrolled in schools where they were the only person in class who looked like them. They grew up in neighborhoods and perhaps even attended churches where white people were the overwhelming majority. They may or may not have had a positive experience in these environments, but either way, they are accustomed to being socialized around white people. And, importantly, they have received the same messages about the negative stereotypes that characterize Black people. The consequence is that while they might be Black, they are more comfortable with white people.

I say this to make the point that these individuals are likely to be comfortable seeing a white therapist. They may talk to you about being told that they "don't act Black," or it may be an issue they do not raise at all. We'll discuss this further in chapter 8, but I raise the topic now because you may argue that you have Black clients for whom race isn't an issue. And that maybe this "race thing" isn't a big deal. It is certainly true that it isn't an issue for every Black or African American client. However, it is important for you to realize that your clients will appear different based on their racial socialization. Just because a client does not have the language to communicate their struggle does not mean that their struggle has no dimension of race embedded in it.

Using Cognitive Behavioral Therapy in an Unfair World

Before I wrap up this chapter, I want to acknowledge that, even in an unfair world, I conceptualize my clients' problems and concerns through a cognitive behavioral (CBT) lens by looking at the connection between their thoughts, feelings, and behaviors. You are likely familiar with and may even use this approach to therapy. However, as I tell my students, it is important to explain your approach to your clients (including those who think they already know CBT) in case someone else's version is somewhat different from yours and so your clients can understand why you approach matters the way you do. Your understanding of my approach is important because there are several conversations and examples illustrated throughout this book that are informed by this perspective.

I appreciate the present-focused approach to CBT because it allows clients to connect their thoughts with their feelings and behavior so they can increase their sense of empowerment, especially in situations that are disempowering. Most clients seek therapy because they want something about their lives to be different. They are tired of worrying and feeling worthless. However, many clients do not realize that specific thought patterns that may have served them at one point in life, perhaps even childhood, are no longer serving them now. They're at the point where it's time for a new script. I am convinced that the first step to a better life can be achieved by addressing these less-than-helpful patterns of thought.

In CBT, change begins with the client. At the same time, for a lot of clients who identify as Black or some other racially minoritized group, the racialized demands and overt racism that exist in the outside world are real. It's not in their head. While the very existence of racism is not something that you can (or should) challenge in therapy, what you *can* challenge are the maladaptive thoughts and beliefs that are interfering with a client's mental health. For example, the brutality of chattel slavery in this country has led to a type of "superhero" coping style among Black adults that can be maladaptive. This coping style also leads Black folks to keep their struggles secret, normalizing quiet suffering. The recommendation that you "put on your own oxygen mask before helping others" isn't part of the cultural vocabulary in the Black community. This means you will sometimes have to be creative with the use of guided discovery to get your client *oxygenated*. I share a brief example here of a 41-year-old single mom of three. She decides to try therapy after hearing from some social media influencers who insisted that therapy changed their lives. She feels she could use something "life-changing" but is not sure where to begin.

THERAPIST: How have you been taking care of yourself?

CLIENT: I know I'm supposed to, but who is going to get everything done for my kids if I don't?

THERAPIST: Tell me more about that.

CLIENT: I'm not sure you would understand.

THERAPIST: Even if I could begin to understand on my own, it's important that I understand from your perspective.

CLIENT: In addition to going to work, I'm cooking every day and helping with homework as a single mom. I have to make sure that my boys stay on top of their grades and how they show up at school—they're the only Black boys in their classes. It's just a lot to manage.

THERAPIST: It sounds like a lot. [*pauses to acknowledge the weight of what the client has disclosed*] I wonder if there are ways that you can take occasional shortcuts, just to give yourself some breathing room.

CLIENT: I would feel like I'm failing as a mom if I do.

THERAPIST: It also sounds like you could be running yourself into the ground—maybe until you can't go anymore. I'm concerned that you wouldn't be physically able to be a good mom when that happens.

CLIENT: [*reluctantly*] You make a good point.

These types of conversations need to be happening more often—allowing clients to retain their values while gently challenging them in the interest of maximizing mental health. The often-discordant ways in which Black and white people are believed to see the world is one reason why Black people prefer Black therapists—someone who "gets it" without having to explain all of the details of their thoughts and fears. Of course, if you're engaged in CBT, you will have to ask the client to detail their thoughts. I'll say more about this later, but suffice it to say that you cannot skip steps in therapy because you're embarrassed about something you think you "should" know. However, from the client's perspective, you need to "get" their experience in order to be helpful.

This CBT approach may be counter to what you do as a therapist. For example, perhaps you adopt a more Rogerian approach in which you engage in empathic listening and fully accept and respect the person's perspective without judgment. I can appreciate the merits of more person-centered approaches as one strategy for assisting clients through their challenges. In fact, one of my first clinical supervisors was a Rogerian clinician who affirmed everything that I did in therapy. It was frustrating at the time because of my perfectionist worry that I wasn't getting therapy "right." Years later, though, I appreciated that he was simply trying to help me be comfortable in the therapy room and in my own skin. As we all know, it is important to establish rapport with clients, so we all gain from learning person-centered skills. However, the type of clinician that I am cannot stay here because my goal is to help clients challenge any thoughts that are interfering with their lives. If you are a therapist who identifies with the white population and—most importantly—looks like a member of this group, challenging a Black client's thoughts likely requires a more delicate approach than I, as a Black therapist, might take. This does not mean that it cannot be done.

Much to Overcome

As a Black woman, I see the myriad ways Black people have suffered, due in part to ongoing, systemic discrimination they have experienced, accompanied by fears of looking weak or crazy. While many argue that Black people should move on, Black folks won't get far with injured minds and pieced-together well-being. I do believe that's where we are. The need for healing persists for those who have been and continue to be systematically mistreated.

To establish a strong working relationship with African American clients, there is much for you to overcome as a white therapist. The goal may not be simple rapport-building. You also have to navigate the very nature of what your "whiteness" brings to any room—potential inauthenticity (e.g., acting like there's no elephant), belief in Black inferiority, fear of looking racist (and, in turn, avoiding race), and the privilege to not have to understand racism.

The reality is that the therapy room is a space that feels naturally inauthentic to many Black people, who are fighting to navigate life in a racialized world. This is a world that has historically omitted the stories of Black folks. If you're familiar with popular television shows like *Friends* and *Seinfeld*, you'll notice they were set in the very diverse landscape of New York City but somehow managed to omit stories that centered Black people. These omissions are of no surprise to those who are often marginalized. Cisgender, white, able-bodied individuals seem to comfortably sideline those who are dissimilar. This is one reason that many Black people are more likely to "let down their hair" in spaces that are less "integrated" and more homogenously familiar. Of course, this isn't the case for all Black people. However, it is certainly true for most.

As a result, some Black clients may habitually hide their true emotions and real self when seeking therapy, especially with a white therapist. It is often an agreed-upon thing that folks in the Black community do. Consider this exchange with a 20-year-old African American university student whose mother advised her to go to therapy. The mother fears that her daughter's anxiety is increasingly affecting her academic performance. The daughter is in her second session with a white therapist and seems slow to warm up to the therapist.

THERAPIST: Is it uncomfortable for you to share your thoughts about what you experience on campus?

CLIENT: No.

THERAPIST: [*pauses briefly for more discussion since anxiety is a presenting problem*] Do you have any discomfort when it comes to speaking up in class?

CLIENT: Some, but not much.

THERAPIST: If you *were* feeling uncomfortable discussing challenges in class [*pauses*] . . . would you tell me?

CLIENT: [*surprised by the follow-up*] I think so.

THERAPIST: I can appreciate your uncertainty. Can you tell me what would make you hesitate to share your fears with me?

CLIENT: I just don't know if you'd get it. Also, you might think something is wrong with me.

THERAPIST: That's fair. Has there been an occasion today or in our first session that I communicated something was wrong with you?

CLIENT: No.

THERAPIST: Or that I didn't understand?

CLIENT: No.

THERAPIST: Would you tell me if I did?

Notice that this therapist essentially takes a CBT approach by asking for evidence to encourage more authenticity in the relationship with the client. I'll talk more about CBT in chapter 6, but I highlight it here to show how you can handily use a CBT technique to reframe an unhelpful thought or presumption. The client aimed to look like there was nothing "wrong" with her, which is understandable because "fitting in" and being a team player facilitates success for Black people. However, it is important for you as the therapist to begin to dismantle assumptions that the client may bring to therapy. Such beliefs are highly ingrained, so change in therapy could take time, but you have to do your part so that the client can feel more comfortable opening up.

Again, there is much to overcome. But with key language and determination to avoid elephants in the therapy room, you can establish a solid working relationship, use evidence-based skills, and assist African American clients with humility and reasonable confidence.

Chapter 2

From Color-Blind to Culturally Humble

Have you ever said, "I don't see color" or "I just see you as human" to someone who you know to be Black? Have you insisted that "we're all God's children"?

On the surface, color-blindness may seem like an ideal human value. When Reverend Dr. Martin Luther King Jr. suggested that he wanted his children to be judged not by the color of their skin, wasn't he suggesting that we ignore race? To be honest, I don't think so. Many forget that Dr. King wanted his children to be judged instead by the content of their character. He did not want them to be judged by stereotypes. But as I discussed in the last chapter, "Blackness" is unfortunately confounded by stereotypical assumptions of being aggressive, lazy, unintelligent, and even subhuman. Too often, African Americans die before anyone can assess the content of their character because character is contingent on skin complexion. We live in a society where you as a helping professional will have to acknowledge that your client doesn't exist in a color-blind society. Black clients live in a color-*abrasive* society.

To get the most of this book, you will have to subscribe to the reality that Black people contend with being both invisible and hyper-visible. In a world where all humans strive to be seen and valued, Black people are invisible in white-dominated spaces where they are often perceived as unworthy of justice, health care, or other equal opportunities because of the color of their skin. This can be especially tormenting. At the same time, they are also hyper-visible in that they have the added burden of being expected to represent all Black people and having to demonstrate non-adherence to stereotypes, such as presumptions that they are unintelligent, criminal, or hypersexual.

For many, these pressures are par for the course. Middle-class Black parents have to decide between enrolling their children in schools that are more diverse but less "rigorous," and sending them to competitive schools that will prepare them academically to compete in a competitive world but where they may be bullied for being Black. The conversation of how to engage with the police is also not unusual. When melanated skin is an automatic indictment, how do Black boys and young men temper their fears and present themselves calmly so as not to excite a trigger-happy police officer? These are the regular, and often painful, conversations in Black households. And while other racially and ethnically marginalized families likely have conversations that are specific to their own cultural context, these conversations don't exist in white households. You have to understand there may be a reality to which you are not privy if you are not immersed in Black and other marginalized communities.

If you have apprehension about whether Black people have a systematically unique experience in the United States—not just with regard to disproportionate police brutality but also with regard to inequities in accessing health care, in teaching and schooling, in getting a loan for a new business, and in just about any domain that you can imagine—you will essentially have to work a bit harder to embrace the strategies and scripts that I will share in this text. Importantly, if you overtly deny your obligation to consider Black clients' context in the world, you will have "one foot in and one foot out" in a way that will undermine success in therapy with Black and African American clients.

As you reflect on any ambivalence you may be carrying about these realities, consider this self-reflective exercise:

In the space provided, describe how you identify yourself professionally (e.g., LCSW, counselor, psychologist).

What does it mean to you to identify as you do? That is, what do you see as your professional responsibilities?

_____

_____

_____

_____

_____

On a 0–10 scale (with 0 being "not important at all" and 10 being "very important"), how important to you are your professional responsibilities? _____

Some therapists feel better suited at developing rapport, while others are more skilled at identifying the source of a client's concern and developing a plan for intervention. Others still are most experienced at overcoming resistance in therapy. What are your particular talents in your work as a mental health professional?

_____

_____

_____

_____

_____

What are some circumstances in which you might fail to use your particular talents with a client?

_____

_____

_____

_____

_____

What would you do to ensure that you're using your talents with your clients consistently?

_____

_____

_____

_____

_____

Although you may have limited experience in working with African American and Black clients, your dedication to your professional obligations, your use of your unique talents, and the confidence that you will show up for *every* client will be critical to your work as a mental health provider.

Color-Blindness and the Elephant in the Room

We have arrived at a time in society where racism is mostly unacceptable. Progressive (and even non-progressive) individuals don't want to be called racist. Though we do not yet live in a state of equal justice for all, many aim to tolerate racial differences by ignoring race. If you subscribe to a color-blind world, doing so unfortunately permits the elephant to sit more comfortably in the therapy room. This "elephant behavior" occurs when your client likely knows that you're not Black—and you are pretty confident that the person in front of you or on the Zoom screen is Black—but you pretend as if they are no different from anyone else. Although that type of elephant behavior may be permissible in other contexts, it is not warranted in situations that require the therapeutic alliance. That's because most conversations in daily life don't bear similar weight to the conversations that occur in therapy.

As a mental health professional, I have always been fascinated by the notion of not seeing race, since not seeing race is arguably, at least in part, a distorted sense of reality—and a distorted sense of reality is associated with psychosis. I'm not suggesting that you are psychotic, but hopefully you see the connection to disconnecting from the reality of someone's race. The only solution is to be honest about who your client is so you can have the presence of mind to navigate any errant and inappropriate biases that you may have. It may feel like the right thing to do is to ignore a Black person's race so you can avoid the negative traits you would normally ascribe to them, but in doing so, you are also choosing to ignore the ill-effects on the client of the very pervasive assumptions you are trying to overcome in yourself.

Here, your color-blindness, though well-intended, will not help your client. In fact, it can be harmful. Not only does color-blindness keep your Black client invisible, but it also renders you less sensitive to racism, which means less effort to be inclusive. There already exists a built-in hierarchy in psychotherapy wherein you as the provider present as the expert and the client presents as someone with a malady to be "fixed." When you add unspoken race to the hierarchy—where the therapist holds the cards on what is discussed—it creates an unnecessary layer of complexity. Previous research has found that, in workplace settings, employees from minoritized racial and ethnic backgrounds are less committed to their work when the work environment leans more color-blind (Plaut et al., 2009). Though no study has examined clients' commitment to therapy goals in such environments, I wonder whether a therapist's color-blind disposition can affect a client's engagement in therapy. Common sense says it would. If an entire domain or a meaningful facet of a client's experience is being systematically ignored by a white therapist, it can be taken as dismissive or even racist. In contrast, when a client who identifies as African American or Black has a therapist of the same race, they are naturally less concerned about their therapist adopting a color-blind ideology.

The consequences of color-blindness have also been borne out by the work of counseling psychologist and professor Dr. Helen Neville, who has studied color-blindness extensively. In some studies, Neville and her colleagues (2013) found that color-blindness can undermine the capacity to generate empathy. Consider these brief but alternative exchanges that could occur early in therapy, perhaps in the second session, for a client who presents with symptoms of generalized anxiety disorder:

Scenario A:

CLIENT: [*reluctantly*] I feel pretty sure that my application for the apartment was denied because I'm a Black man.

THERAPIST: New York is a tough market. There are probably a lot of reasons for not getting an apartment.

CLIENT: Pft. Yeah, well, you wouldn't understand. I only brought it up because I just found out before I walked into our session.

Scenario B:

CLIENT: [*reluctantly*] I feel pretty sure that my application for the apartment was denied because I'm a Black man.

THERAPIST: That must be really very frustrating. What happened?

CLIENT: It's frustrating and exhausting. I thought for sure I'd be successful this time. I got through all of the online stages of the application process. But once I met the realtor in person, she seemed different. She wasn't as friendly as when we talked on the phone.

In scenario A, the client shuts down because he doesn't feel seen or heard. In scenario B, the client is heard and invited to share more about his experience, leading to an opportunity to further explore his frustration. In scenario A, the therapist minimizes the client's experience, perhaps with the intention of helping the client see that there could be "more than race" involved in the situation. While there could be other factors at play, this is not a moment for generating alternatives. With this recognition that the therapist must address the painful situation or risk alienating the client, let's consider how these scenarios might both play out, balancing problem-solving and empathy:

Scenario A continued:

CLIENT: [*reluctantly*] I feel pretty sure that my application for the apartment was denied because I'm a Black man.

THERAPIST: New York is a tough market. There are probably a lot of reasons for not getting an apartment.

CLIENT: Pft. Yeah, well, you wouldn't understand. I only brought it up because I just found out before I walked into our session.

THERAPIST: [*pausing briefly*] You're right. And I could have responded in a way that acknowledged your actual experience. Would you be okay with telling me more about what happened?

CLIENT: It's frustrating and exhausting. I thought for sure I'd be successful this time. I got through all of the online stages of the application process. But once I met the realtor in person, she seemed different. She wasn't as friendly as when we talked on the phone.

THERAPIST: It sounds like your meeting with her went much differently than you expected.

CLIENT: Right! Much different. And the only thing I can think of is that she switched up because I'm Black.

THERAPIST: Have you had something like this to happen before—that someone treated you differently than you would have expected?

CLIENT: It happens all the time. I actually try to do as little in person as possible, so people don't necessarily know I'm Black.

Note that in this instance, the therapist gains more insight into the client's strategy for daily life—a strategy that could contribute to his overall anxiety. If true, this insight provides a potential opportunity for the therapist to assess sources of anxiety and generate an effective treatment plan.

Scenario B continued:

CLIENT: [*reluctantly*] I feel pretty sure that my application for the apartment was denied because I'm a Black man.

THERAPIST: That must be really very frustrating. What happened?

CLIENT: It's frustrating and exhausting. I thought for sure I'd be successful this time. I got through all of the online stages of the application process. But once I met the realtor in person, she seemed different. She wasn't as friendly as when we talked on the phone.

THERAPIST: How was she on the phone?

CLIENT: She seemed easygoing and more energetic. She was almost chipper. But in person, she didn't make much eye contact and seemed to rush the meeting.

> And the next day, she left me an email that I didn't get the apartment. It just seemed like everything was going smoothly until we met in person.

THERAPIST: Her shift almost sounds like she was withdrawing from you? Especially given the outcome.

CLIENT: Yeah, exactly.

THERAPIST: If you would have gotten the apartment, her shift might not have mattered to you.

CLIENT: Do you think there could have been another reason I didn't get the apartment?

THERAPIST: We can't be sure, but it sounds like the thought maybe just entered your mind.

In both scenarios, the therapist uses guided discovery to end up at a place where they can work with the client to create solutions while simultaneously building a stronger relationship. We'll talk more about the collaborative process of guided discovery and appropriate problem-solving in chapter 6, but for now, it is important to be aware of using language that suggests problem-solving before you understand the client's full experience of their race-related situation. Don't put the cart before the horse. Even more, you don't want to cast a seeming judgment with a response of "this happens all the time" or that it could happen to "anyone" because it minimizes the client's burden of race.

Note that some clients will automatically diminish the role of race in scenarios such as this. That could be a relief for you because you're let "off the hook" and don't have to introduce the idea that race played a role in the matter. Whether or not it's on the client's mind or your mind, race could have affected the outcome. All of this is useful for you to keep in mind. The client might not bring up race because they think *you* are uncomfortable with discussions of race.

In this scenario, it is possible that the realtor received some bad news on her way to meet the client, or it could be that she was racist and surprised to discover that the client was African American. It is also possible that the property manager was racist and would be alarmed if the realtor had rented the property to a Black person. As the therapist works with the client to resolve anxiety symptoms, the reality is that they cannot be sure of where race shows up. It's best to assume it's there along with many other factors. I discuss racism throughout this text because how it contributes to your client's misfortunes is ongoing. Racism isn't something that is faced and resolved. The permutations of it are endless.

Before we go further, let's take a moment to assess your views on matters of individual responsibility using some items from the Color-Blind Racial Attitudes Scale (CoBRAS; Neville et al., 2000). Indicate the degree to which you honestly agree or disagree with the statements below (with 1 being "strongly disagree" and 6 being "strongly agree"). Note that there is no right or wrong answer, and it will help if you are as open as possible.

_____ 1. Everyone who works hard, no matter what race they are, has an equal chance to become rich.

_____ 2. White people in the U.S. are discriminated against because of the color of their skin.

_____ 3. It is important that people begin to think of themselves as American and not African American, Mexican American, or Italian American.

_____ 4. It is important for public schools to teach about the history and contributions of racial and ethnic minorities. [*reverse scored*]

_____ 5. Racial and ethnic minorities in the U.S. have certain advantages because of the color of their skin.

_____ 6. Race plays an important role in who gets sent to prison. [*reverse scored*]

_____ 7. Racial problems in the U.S. are rare, isolated situations.

When you're done, tally up your scores, which should range from 7 to 42. Be sure to score the items that are indicated as reverse scored with 1 being "strongly agree" and 6 being "strongly disagree." The higher your total score, the more unaware you are of race-related issues and how some people are racially privileged while others are disadvantaged. Some studies show that individuals who endorse higher scores on the full version of this questionnaire are also more likely to adopt racial prejudice and intolerance for racial differences (Neville et al., 2000). For perspective, if you scored higher than 14 on these seven items, I would advise that you take some time to read up on racial disparities in the housing market, the legal system, health care, and the economy. In recent years, I was introduced to the practice of *redlining*, a federal policy that led to a decrease in home value and home ownership for Black Americans. It is one concrete example of injustice that receives little to no attention in mainstream press or social studies texts.

Elephants Can Invite Microaggressive Behavior

Many believe that racism is a problem of the past and that people are simply too sensitive about race. It takes effort to be mindful of all that people are sensitive about these days, right? And it's painful sometimes. However, as a therapist, you are expected to make the effort to do so. You have to keep your radar on in the same way that you attend to suspected childhood physical and sexual abuse as a mandated reporter. If you are someone who believes racism to be a hassle in therapy, you are at risk for engaging in microaggressive behavior, which refers to "brief and commonplace daily verbal, behavioral, or environmental indignities, whether intentional or unintentional, that communicate hostile, derogatory, or negative racial slights and insults toward people of color" (Sue et al., 2007, p. 271). Dr. Chester M. Pierce and colleagues (1977) originally labeled microaggressions as a type of "put down" (p. 65).

I agree with Dr. Priscilla Lui and Lucia Quezada (2019), who characterize microaggressions as a subtle form of discrimination. I emphasize this perspective because it highlights the gravity of the circumstances. The alternative is to risk characterizing microaggressive events as minor, generally meaningless mishaps. However, available research has suggested that microaggressions can be more problematic than overt racism because those who experience microaggressions must expend energy assessing the nature of the slight (Salvatore & Shelton, 2007). Although clients know that they feel uncomfortable or put off, they are not quite sure of the source of the distress. And the more subtle the microaggression, the more insidious it can be. Since it can be hard for clients to put their finger on, you may have to trust their experience until you have more data. Know that their distress is associated with strong feelings of anxiety, anger, exhaustion, and even low self-esteem (Yeo & Torres-Harding, 2021).

If I had a dollar for every microaggression that I have ever experienced, well, you know the saying. I have no reason to believe that I am any more "articulate" than anyone else who has earned a PhD, but comments about how well I speak are routine from others in professional settings. Some years ago, I was floored when a student knocked on the (open) door of my office. As I recall, he told me he was looking for "Dr. Walker," though I was right in front of him, sitting behind my desk. No one else was in the room. I imagine that the student would have presumed that I was Dr. Walker if my race and gender were different, but any amount of time circling this idea illustrates why microaggressions are destructive. I choose when to tackle my invisibility. I speak up in meetings if I feel I cannot possibly sit on a question or comment. It is disheartening at best to attempt to contribute to a conversation but to somehow go unheard.

Unfortunately, people who perpetrate microaggressions are often unaware that their behavior is problematic. To step up your clinical game, you will have to be mindful of these perspectives and watch for your own microaggressive behavior. Otherwise, you risk compromising the therapeutic relationship. Microaggressions create a breach in the therapy alliance, the single most important predictor of therapy success.

Microaggressions wouldn't be so impactful for the Black community if they weren't built into mainstream society and thus occur on such a consistent basis. Your client has to navigate microaggressions regularly, especially if they are employed—or otherwise exist—in predominantly white settings. The last thing your client needs is to encounter microaggressions in therapy, a presumed "safe space." However, available estimates suggest that at least half (and as much as 80 percent) of clients have experienced racial microaggression in psychotherapy (Constantine, 2007). These estimates are alarming and likely mirror life outside of therapy. They may also speak to why African American clients prefer African American therapists. One of the most popular posts that I have shared on social media says, "Black therapists are so important. I just sat through my entire session taking out my braids and not once did she look at me crazy." The volume of responses to my post spoke to a client's desperate need for their therapist to meet them where they are and, at minimum, not look at them like they're *crazy* for taking part in behaviors that are cultural norms.

When the *Elephant* Is a Microaggression

Unfortunately, microaggressions can and do show up in therapy when a presumably well-intended therapist communicates something demeaning to a client. Remember that elephant in the room? This elephant can show up as unaddressed microaggressive behavior, which rides right on the elephant's back, in part, due to social norms about racial stereotypes and clinical discomfort with discussing race.

Research has shown that when microaggressive behavior is addressed, clients report a similar working relationship with their therapist as clients who have not experienced any microaggressions in therapy (Owen et al., 2014). But when it's not addressed, the elephant in the room just grows larger as the therapeutic alliance shrinks smaller. Consider this possible scenario between you and your Black client in the sixth session. In this fictitious but not out-of-the-ordinary dialogue, you diagnosed a 32-year-old client with adjustment disorder with mixed anxiety and depressed mood following the recent death of her younger brother due to COVID-19. After processing grief with your client for five sessions, the two of you decide to work on anger management.

THERAPIST: Did you have any opportunities to work on your anger management skills since our last session?

CLIENT: Yes, I suppose I had an opportunity yesterday, but it didn't go so well. It didn't go well at all.

THERAPIST: Okay, tell me about it.

CLIENT: I went to my favorite store, but I went to one on a different side of town than I usually go to. It's a good way to take a break from the monotony of the day and everything I have on my mind. It was the middle of the day, so there were just a few other shoppers in the store. I didn't need anything in particular, but I thought I'd pop in to see what they had in their housewares. I have a lot of deadlines coming up and they are stressing me out. Anyway, a salesperson approached me and asked if I needed any help, but I said no because I was just looking. I noticed that she walked by my aisle a few times and kinda looked in my direction. About the fourth time that she walked by, I asked if she needed anything. She said that another shopper thought she saw me putting something in my purse. I was livid.

THERAPIST: Is it possible another shopper thought they saw you putting something in your purse?

Let's stop here. Perhaps you already know that of all the possible responses you could have selected as a therapist, this is not the one that will offer empathy. It is not the one that will build rapport if you are still working on rapport. In fact, this response will likely elicit a very frustrated response from your client, who is wondering why you are taking the side of a stranger rather than empathizing with the client you know. In this situation, you have one of two possible responses: One demonstrates your capacity to self-correct. The other communicates your rigidity and single-mindedness. You may be thinking that you're adhering to the goals of CBT by helping the client develop "cognitive flexibility" in how they perceived the situation, but you want to be very mindful of how and when you choose to redirect to therapy goals. Now, let's resume the conversation:

CLIENT: Yes, it's possible, *and* they also would have been wrong in what they *thought* they saw! I need to be able to shop in peace without having to deal with someone else's bad eyes!

THERAPIST: You're right. I'm sorry. That was the least helpful thing that I could have said after hearing your experience. It's really sad that you were out shopping and really doing a good thing for your own well-being, but instead had to add on bias and a nosy shopper.

CLIENT: Exactly! Why can't people just mind their own business?

THERAPIST: It's terribly unfair when people impose their biases on others. As a white person, I can honestly admit that I don't know what it's like to walk in your shoes. With that being said, I want to help meet your therapy goals, recognizing that the things that are out of your control are going to be there more often than either of us would like. And I'm going to do my part to be much more mindful of that. Could that work for you?

This response attempts to right the ship of communication with the client. In essence, you must be absolutely sincere and apologetic and absent any condescension in tone. The alternative is something that occurs too often—the therapist "innocently" asks the client if another shopper may have seen them putting something in their purse; the client gets angry; and the therapist follows with defensiveness or a total loss for words. If you're the therapist, you may be thinking that *you* didn't accuse the client of anything. You weren't there. You simply want to help your client "see all sides" in the interest of increasing "flexibility" in their thinking. But if you get defensive or even worse, angry with your client, who is more in need of cognitive flexibility?

In these moments, you need to practice deep breathing or engage in another emotion regulation strategy to calm yourself down. Defensiveness or any amount of upset is problematic. Suggesting that the client was overly sensitive is not showing sufficient empathy for someone who is in pain. In case you are less than familiar with microaggression literature and research, telling someone or suggesting that they are being "too sensitive" in response to a difficult situation is problematic. As a mental health provider, you also have an ethical obligation to do no harm. It is, in all instances, your responsibility to be in control of your emotions and to act on them in a way that is not therapy-interfering.

Remember that microaggressive behavior is emotionally harmful for those who experience it. We'll discuss the impact of microaggressions more in chapter 4, but know that it is sometimes driven by the therapist's color-blindness, which can also lead to therapeutic recommendations that are woefully discordant with the client's beliefs and cultural worldview. If you realize your misstep after a client has departed, but your client shows up in the next session, address it then. However, if you can address it in the moment—before your client leaves—that is the best time to do so. The following vignette illustrates how both these scenarios may look in practice. In this example, you have been working with a 33-year-old Black woman on issues related to comorbid depression and anxiety. In today's session, you suggest that placing her grandmother in a group home could be a viable option to lessen the client's ongoing stress. However, you detect a deep sigh and noticeable shift in the client's disposition. After a short pause, your client responds with "that's really just not an option."

Here's how the conversation might go if you have an opportunity to address your possible misstep in session:

THERAPIST: When you talked about difficulties with being a caregiver for your grandmother, I suggested the possibility of sending her to a group home. Was my suggestion upsetting for you?

CLIENT: Actually, it was. Black people don't do that. They don't send grandparents and elderly family members off to homes.

THERAPIST: I apologize for being insensitive. I knew that you were apprehensive, but I didn't think about all the reasons why you might feel that way.

CLIENT: I know you were trying to help problem solve, but the situation is more challenging than you can imagine.

THERAPIST: I'll try to be more mindful of whether a suggestion is one that you can see carrying out and also try to think of all of the reasons why a suggestion might not work. If it's okay with you, I'll think about this between sessions, and we can revisit this at the beginning of our next session.

If you miss the initial opportunity but your client returns, you might begin your session like this:

THERAPIST: Before we discuss your homework and how your week went, there is something that has been on my mind since our last session that I'd like to check in with you about.

CLIENT: Okay.

THERAPIST: When I suggested that you consider sending your grandmother to a group home, you looked at me like I had lost my mind. I think I may have missed something. Was I being insensitive when I suggested that you consider sending your grandmother to a group home?

CLIENT: I was taken aback by it, but I figured you just come from a different reality.

THERAPIST: I really appreciate your sharing with me. I also appreciate you giving me the benefit of the doubt. I wouldn't want to make a suggestion that is off-putting or insensitive. It is crystal clear for me now that a nursing home cannot be an option. Can we add to the agenda to revisit alternative solutions that would actually make more sense for you? I understand that the situation with your grandmother is incredibly stressful, and it'd be even more upsetting to you to feel like you have abandoned your responsibility.

As these vignettes illustrate, when you can sufficiently address a microaggressive behavior you have enacted in session, it can potentially neutralize the behavior and salvage the therapeutic relationship. But it takes a certain amount of awareness and humility to achieve such a feat. If any of this seems overwhelming, that is understandable. Keep in mind that no more is being asked of you than is required of your clients on a daily basis. You have the presumed advantage of being a high-functioning individual who has tools and resources to navigate life. Even more, your life may not be rife with the kinds of microaggressions, put-downs, and systemic discrimination that Black clients encounter on a daily basis on top of their feelings of hopelessness, isolation, and occasional thoughts of suicide.

Cultural Competence Is One Goal

Drs. Derald Wing Sue and Gina C. Torino (2005) have explained that cultural competence is determined by core elements of awareness, knowledge, and skills. All three must be present. Awareness refers to having an understanding of your own assumptions and values—values that are too often presumed to be universal. I liken this to the assumption that everyone does or should speak English, even in other parts of the world. U.S. citizens travel to other countries and get annoyed that the people there do not speak English. It's fascinating. Your values are yours. Examine them closely.

The second element of cultural competence is knowledge, which involves familiarizing yourself with different cultures and people's different ways of making sense of the world. Two people can experience the same event differently due to differences in how they make sense of what they see.

Finally, the third element of cultural competence is skills that facilitate your proficiency to deliver culturally centered interventions. The process, however, has to be a fluid one in which you take what you know and use it to the benefit of your client. Therapy with your African American client is both what you say and how you say it.

Unfortunately, though, many psychologists are not, in fact, implementing multiculturally responsive recommendations in psychotherapy. In one study, approximately 30 to 40 percent of providers rarely or never followed through on plans to improve multicultural competence and rarely or never sought culture-specific consultation or referred clients to someone who might be more qualified to provide culturally informed care (Hansen et al., 2006). That the majority (60 to 70 percent) did is somewhat reassuring, but the proportion who did not is sizable, and this is enough to be concerning. Having earned a PhD, I understand the inclination to rely on years of doctoral training and continuing education, but there is no substitute for being prepared to meet the needs of clients who have not been the focus of your training.

Sit Down—Be Humble

Perhaps one of the reasons cultural competence falls short is because in an attempt to assess competence, scholars have developed checklists* to make the more abstract notion of competence discrete and measurable. The challenge with these types of processes is that competence is reduced to endpoints: Are you culturally competent? Did you earn a passing grade in your multicultural psychology course? Did you complete your continuing education hours for diversity? I doubt that most clinicians who answer "yes" to these questions would suggest they have "arrived" at the competence finish line. However, checklists often become benchmarks that are substituted for the necessary lifelong, humble commitment to competence.

It is for this reason that, in the late 1990s, Drs. Melanie Tervalon and Jann Murray-García (1998) promoted the distinction of cultural humility in lieu of cultural competence. They argued that cultural competence should not be defined by a discrete endpoint but instead reflect "a commitment and active engagement in a lifelong process that individuals enter into on an ongoing basis with patients, communities, colleagues, and with themselves" (p. 118). This ongoing commitment to self-reflection and self-critique is what cultural humility is all about.

According to Merriam-Webster's dictionary, *humility*, a noun, is the state of being humble, which is defined as "reflecting, expressing, or offered in a spirit of deference or submission." This is the disposition that I propose you adopt as a clinician. Adopting a state of *being* makes you less inclined to over-rely on checklists or think that three hours of diversity CEUs is enough training to count as growth. Instead, being humble amplifies awareness and fosters intentionality. You are more likely to be culturally responsive if you are humble because you are less likely to exact a sense of superiority and more likely to be respectful of diverse clients (Hook et al., 2016).

Because humility requires a willingness to look inward (and often critically), it is easier to look for a box you can check and move on. However, your failure to practice humility reinforces the unbalanced power dynamic with you as the expert on all things. This is unfair to the client. As you know, the therapist is only the expert on matters of mental health. The client is the expert on their life and life circumstances. By default, there is always something for the therapist to learn. Therefore, you will need to

---

* For example, see Dr. Richard H. Dana and colleagues' (1992) checklist for the examination of cultural competence in social service agencies at https://doi.org/10.1177/104973159200200208.

make a lifelong commitment to being culturally humble, recognizing that you are uninformed of the plight of Black people in the United States. With a strong sense of humility on hand, you are much less likely to make a mishap in therapy.

Further, without a sense of humility, it can be dangerous when clinicians can have just enough information from a "multicultural" course. For example, consider this session with a 52-year-old client with whom you've been working on issues related to depression. In the fourth session, he discloses that he was unable to follow through with your homework plan for behavioral activation. You learned in graduate school that Black people are generally very religious and inclined to pray about life struggles. However, you take for granted that your client's disclosure that he prays about his depression could be interfering with his completion of agreed-upon homework assignments.

THERAPIST: How did your activity for getting out of the house go this past week?

CLIENT: I had a plan, but it didn't work out. I ended up in my usual routine: going to work and then staying in my apartment, barely leaving my room all weekend.

THERAPIST: So when you left the session, you felt like we had a good plan in place, but it fell through? [*empathically stating an observation rather than questioning in a judging way*]

CLIENT: Pretty much. I usually try to hang out with friends on weekends when I'm up for it. It's just hard to get my energy going. I try to pray about it.

THERAPIST: After you prayed, were you able to make progress toward getting out of the house?

CLIENT: No, I just felt stuck.

THERAPIST: I wonder if prayer interfered with your progress.

On the one hand, it is important to consider barriers to a client's progress, but it is more important to be mindful of their cultural values. A more open conversation from a posture of cultural humility could go more like this:

THERAPIST: How did your activity for getting out of the house go this past week?

CLIENT: I had a plan, but it didn't work out. I ended up in my usual routine: going to work and then staying in my apartment, barely leaving my room all weekend.

THERAPIST: So when you left the session, you felt like we had a good plan in place, but it fell through?

CLIENT: Pretty much. I usually try to hang out with friends on weekends when I'm up for it. It's just hard to get my energy going. I try to pray about it.

THERAPIST: That's good that you pray. How helpful would you say that has been for you?

CLIENT: [*pauses*] It helps some.

THERAPIST: That's good to hear. I ask, in part, because we talked about another strategy to get you going so that maybe you had more energy . . . but I wonder if we're asking too much of you, especially when you get comfort from prayer.

CLIENT: It's possible. But I'm a man of God. Prayer has gotten me through a lot of mess. I don't know if I can trust the plan that we came up with, especially when I just don't feel like getting out most days.

THERAPIST: That's fair. I wonder if we can figure out a way to incorporate prayer into your homework activity for this week. Let's talk more about what prayer looks like for you and when it has been most helpful in your life.

I alluded to it earlier: Those of us who have graduate degrees may feel that we know more than we actually do. Also, those therapists who grew up in culturally diverse communities may make misguided assumptions. The most important dimension of being humble is what you do and what you do not do. In session, you may have to still yourself as you resist the urge to say something that will be offensive. Outside of session, you will have to engage in self-education and perhaps more continuing education to avoid making missteps. You may not be able to keep microaggressions from occurring in therapy, but with a strong command of cultural humility, you can limit the chances considerably. In chapter 9, I'll share more exercises that you can implement to address issues that could set you up for microaggressive mishaps.

Consider also that adopting a sense of humility won't be enough to meet the client's therapy needs, but your ingrained curiosity about your client's emotions, interpersonal relationships, and other life circumstances will help you meaningfully connect with your client and expand the overall therapy prognosis. In your curiosity, ask systematically thoughtful questions to better understand their experience. Perhaps you can employ some degree of cultural curiosity to avoid pretending like you "get it" when you don't. You might have to check in by putting yourself "out there" and asking self-deprecating questions that begin with "I'm not sure I fully get it, but do you think I'm on the right track when I say _____?" This process helps assure your client that you're more invested in understanding their experience than you are in being the expert.

Finally, keep in mind that being competent and *behaving* competently are two different, though related, things. While it's nice that you attended a CEU training in person and that it was led by a Black man, your CEU alone does not make you capable. Engaging in training ideally increases your awareness, but the "continuing" part of CEU highlights the importance of this being an *ongoing* process. My dad used to say, "When you know better, you do better." The expectation was that once I had knowledge and insight, I would act accordingly. The expectation is that you do the same.

While it's understandable that time-investment barriers may make it inconvenient to implement culturally responsive care, it is not an excuse to abandon the goal of cultural effectiveness altogether. You must remain dedicated to your work if you are to bridge the gap between this "inconvenience" and your duty to provide the clinical care that is helpful and not harmful to your African American clients. In the interest of practicing what you know, I hope that you gain important insights from walking through this book with me and that you will be motivated to maximize the integrity of your work consistent with your values as a mental health provider.

Chapter 3

The First Session

The best and first opportunities to avoid elephants in the room and set the appropriate tone for therapy is in your initial contact with a potential client. This contact is likely to occur in a screening call and more comprehensively in the first session. Though relatively little could happen in a screening call beyond logistics, preparation is key. In this chapter, I will discuss your intentions for that conversation and review what you want to be sure to address in the first scheduled session. Of course, consent to treatment and confidentiality are necessary components, but your attention will be on maximizing rapport-building as your first priority.

This may be a good time to disclose that, in my first book, *The Unapologetic Guide to Black Mental Health*, I inform Black clients that they can indeed get relief from their emotional and psychological difficulties with the help of a white therapist. I also say very plainly that they will have to be intentional about the process. However, I feel pretty confident that going to therapy, with a white therapist no less, is one of the very last options that Black folks are considering. This is especially true for Black clients who will have talked to everyone in their families with whom they are willing to share their business—as well as talking with their pastor and prayer circle, their ancestors and spiritual friends, and even conferring with their vision boards—before they turn, in desperation, to therapy. By the time the client is considering talking to you, they have exhausted their resources and are fed up with being miserable. You are their last resort.

Remember that mental health services aren't designed with Black people in mind. Traditional evidence-based interventions fail on two fronts: They ignore the myriad social challenges that accompany generational oppression *and* they ignore the rich creativity and soulfulness of Black culture. Both are integral in the lives of African

American and Black people. "Blackness" represents a complicated way of existing in the world—a way that is not shared with middle-to-upper class, heterosexual, white, European American individuals. It isn't your fault. No one blames you for your upbringing or your comfort with the status quo. However, if you want to truly meet African American clients where they are, you will have to be aware of the sometimes deafening, and surely distracting, sound of the elephant in the room.

In the same way that African Americans have to show up as "suitable" versions of themselves in countless areas of life, many assume that they will have to leave part of themselves behind if the therapist isn't Black. And the assimilated person—that is, the Black person who is considered "acceptable" by society—isn't usually the whole person. Though the assimilated person is successful at work, in the classroom, and at any other predominantly white institution where Black people have to "perform," success can come at a cost. This is why so many Black folks prefer, understandably, to leave that cost behind when going to therapy.

Recall our discussion in chapter 2 of your obligation to consider your African American clients' unique, racialized context and the importance of addressing any ambivalence that you may have about doing so. This is a good time to revisit your determination to engage your clinical expertise and talents to provide the best possible care for every client. As I said before, your dedication to your professional obligations, your use of your unique talents, and the confidence that you will show up for *every* client will be critical to your work as a mental health provider. With that in mind, let's discuss some hurdles you have to overcome to do this work.

Phone Screening

Let's assume you have a website or some representation of your practice online that demonstrates you're a licensed mental health professional who has the training and willingness to help navigate potential clients' distress. You receive a voice message or a completed online request form from an interested individual. The first consultation provides both you and this potential client with an opportunity to assess fit. You discuss fees, insurance, forms of payment, cancelation policy, issues of confidentiality, and perhaps briefly, your therapeutic modality. Of course, you aim to assess the client's specific needs while the client determines their comfort with you. Assuming you do not appear to be African American or Black, you will likely get an extra dose of scrutiny. And unless there is an obvious reason for the client to deduce your race or ethnicity, they will presume you are white, given the usual demographics. If you're prepared, an initial consultation might go like this:

CLIENT: Hello, I'm interested in services and wondering if you are taking new clients.

THERAPIST: Yes, I will be in a few weeks when two of my current clients end therapy. Can you tell me what you'd want to work on in therapy?

CLIENT: I went through a divorce a few months ago. My husband left me and my 10- and 13-year-old daughters, and I don't think I'm dealing with it very well. I need to talk to someone.

THERAPIST: I see. I can imagine that's been a huge adjustment for you and your daughters. [*Note: Observe here that the therapist acknowledges the family unit. Multicultural texts highlight the importance of the family among marginalized groups, and this client may have hinted at it with her presenting concern, so it's good to acknowledge. Since the client mentioned it, the therapist doesn't have to speculate and can instead demonstrate good listening skills and sensitivity.*]

CLIENT: It really has been. Can I ask you a question?

THERAPIST: Yes, please.

CLIENT: Have you worked with African American women in the past?

THERAPIST: It has been a few years since I had a client who was African American. I've worked with women who are going through life changes, but it's been a while since I had a client who was African American. [*pauses to see what the client says rather than preemptively filling in*]

CLIENT: I see.

THERAPIST: [*hesitantly*] Do you have concerns that I might not be able to help you better handle your adjustment to the divorce because I'm a white woman?

CLIENT: I don't know. Are you married?

THERAPIST: I am married, yes.

CLIENT: Okay.

THERAPIST: I can understand your reservation, especially if you are concerned that I can't relate to your experience. And for therapy to work, you have to be able to connect with your therapist, whomever they may be. Take some time to think about it. If you'd like to schedule a session, I'd be happy to do so. You can also come for a session or two and we can evaluate whether or not we are a good fit. Would you rather try and schedule or wait a while to think about it?

Even if you come well-prepared to the initial consultation, there are no guarantees in life, so you might still lose a client after the first screening. It is also worth mentioning that if your office staff is off-putting, you could lose a client before you even get to the phone screening. In any case, the best that you can do is to be upfront and honest with any potential client. There is no point in trying to sound like you're comfortable with African Americans if you're unsure about your own comfort. The reality is that those who have a central identity are quite adept at knowing when you're uncomfortable. You might as well be yourself. Nobody (including you and the client) has time for inauthenticity.

If you have been proactive in making yourself available to a more diverse clientele but are still struggling to connect with African American clients in your practice, you may benefit from consultation—either from colleagues who have been successful in reaching African American clients or professional consultants who can evaluate your practice and provide feedback.

How You Show Up to Therapy

You always want to be yourself. You also have to be able to read the room. Reading the room applies in numerous contexts, but here I'm talking about the basics of your style of dress. You may think that as long as you're providing competent care, it doesn't matter much how you present yourself. Unfortunately, that is not 100 percent accurate. If you work in a community health setting that provides care for underwaged individuals who are overrepresented by people of color, how you present can be a barrier to your client's capacity to connect with you.

I recall a fun conversation some years ago when a white male graduate student joined my advisees (who tend to be from marginalized groups) and me at a program-wide event. The student, who had been assigned to the community health clinic, happened to mention his difficulties getting clients to open up when he asked questions of them. I knew the student well and was familiar with his generally easygoing and affable style. I asked plainly, "Do you show up at the clinic dressed as you do when we typically see you?" He smiled and said he did. The best that I could describe his style was very "preppy." It was professional of course, but almost too professional. One of my male advisees shared some tips for how this student could switch things up a bit. When I asked the student some weeks later if there had been any changes, he acknowledged that he had noticed a considerable shift in how clients at the clinic responded to him. He was pleased with how things had changed but acknowledged that some clients still seemed leery when he approached them. Nevertheless, his small changes had a noticeable effect. In case you're curious, I think he substituted his button-down shirt and sweater vest for something more casual.

First Session Introductions—with Intention

Different disciplines and different providers within each discipline will have different approaches for how much to disclose about themselves in introductions to a new client. In clinical psychology, I find that we often err on the conservative side of disclosure. The challenge with only sharing, "I'm a clinical psychologist who has been practicing for seven years here in Wichita" is that it is very impersonal. More importantly, it invites an elephant wherein your client has to fill in the blanks as to why you might be so secretive, why you're not sharing more about yourself, or even worse, why you don't feel comfortable with them.

In *The Unapologetic Guide to Black Mental Health*, I emphasize to readers that therapists may share a lot or a little with their clients. Of course, you do not want to overshare or begin to make the session about you—in the initial conversation or thereafter. You *do* want to have your script ready after the fees are agreed upon, confidentiality is understood, and consent for treatment is signed. Consider an introduction that looks like this:

THERAPIST: Thank you for coming in today and also completing your consent. I thought we might begin with a bit more introduction. As you know, I'm a licensed mental health counselor. I moved to Detroit fifteen years ago from Kansas for college and then graduate school. I loved the city so much that I stayed. Most of my family is still in Kansas, but I spend a lot of time here with my friends and two dogs that I rescued from a shelter. In my professional work, I enjoy working with adults and teenagers to find solutions for whatever is giving them the most difficult time. If you're ready, I'd like to hear more about you and what brought you to therapy.

You don't have to leave the door open in the beginning to answer questions about yourself. As you know, the session is for the client. You will check in later for questions or concerns they may have about you.

Explain Your Approach to Therapy

You'll find in this book that I'm generally disinclined to advise you on how to do the mechanics of your therapy. There are merits to multiple forms of therapeutic intervention to which I do not have expertise. However, I do insist that whatever your chosen modality or however you make sense of your client's challenges—and however you go about walking them through instituting change in their lives—it is important that you explain this to them in the first session. You might integrate it as part of your introduction to yourself, or you might use the client's presenting concern (regarding divorce, for example) to illustrate how you might think about your work with them.

Increasingly, television series and movies are improving and expanding how therapy is portrayed. Nevertheless, new clients have little insight of what to expect from therapists. Many of us have seen a primary care physician and dentist since we were children. These professionals follow relatively similar approaches to care (e.g., using specific instruments to check our temperature, to listen to our heartbeat, to check our gums, and to remove plaque from our teeth). We know the routines. Therapists are all trained in empathic listening, but there is otherwise considerable variability in the manner we deliver care. For that reason, you will have to be very clear in explaining your approach to therapy.

First Session Assumptions About Working Together

One thing that I always advise students to do in the first session is to not assume they are a good fit for the client. Avoid being presumptuous. Remember that the client may have finally scheduled a session with you because they think you are their only option! Nonetheless, the client may feel more empowered, and thus more at ease, if you remind them that they *do* have choices, even if their insurance and the long waitlists say otherwise. Think about it: You want to create a climate in the first session (or even in the first phone call) where your client feels more empowered than they do in other domains of their life—on the job with their dismissive manager, at the gym that morning where someone was disrespectful, and maybe even at home where they are caring for their father-in-law and two toddlers. You want to set a totally different expectation for a client who often feels disempowered, minimized, and invisible in life. When you acknowledge in the first session that it was *their* decision to work with you, it abdicates less responsibility to you and elicits more collaboration and potentially invites assertiveness. You also set the tone that you trust the client to make the best decision for themselves.

THERAPIST: I appreciated the opportunity to get to know you and better understand the challenges you have been dealing with. I imagine it took a lot for you to get to a point of seeking therapy.

CLIENT: [*nodding affirmatively*] It took an *awful* lot to get to this point.

THERAPIST: And I hope you've given yourself credit that even though it took a lot, you're here. A lot of people are still struggling because they haven't realized they could use some help, but you did it.

CLIENT: I guess you're right. I can see that.

THERAPIST: That's good to hear [*smiling*]. And like I said, I have enjoyed getting to know you. I also want to share, in case you didn't know, that the match between the therapist and client is important for the client to get the most out of therapy. So if you have any questions for me now, I am happy to answer them. [*pausing*] Or if you go home and decide that maybe we're not a good fit for any reason, I completely understand. The ball is in your court on whether you want to move forward with us working together.

CLIENT: Oh, okay, that makes sense. I don't think I have any questions. The conversation with you today has been helpful.

I advise trainees to have this disposition regardless of the client's background. If it helps you, be sure to tap into your humility as we discussed in the last chapter. Why? Because clients don't know what to expect, and it is your responsibility to let them know the options. Though most clients understand, intuitively, that they have to like their therapist to be comfortable sharing their deepest fears and greatest sources of pain, they do not necessarily know that the working alliance—that is, their capacity to work collaboratively with you—is of the utmost importance for success in therapy. This means that it is up to you to create space that encourages honest feedback and that invites a responsible end to therapy rather than premature termination.

Since I mentioned trusting the client, I have a brief afterthought about that point that I want to share before moving on: It is important to trust your client as part of the therapy process because the alternative is to distrust them and create a conflictual relationship with someone who already has conflict in life. Trusting your client models for them to trust themselves, which can, in turn, generalize to your working alliance.

When "What Brings You to Therapy?" Elicits an Unexpected Response

Once consent for treatment and fees are established, a typical next step is to ask what brought the client in for therapy. For fun, let's imagine a worst-case scenario. Instead of the client beginning with a description of recent life stressors, they respond with "Well, I've been hesitant to come to therapy because I couldn't find a Black therapist." To be sure, I imagine this would happen on a rare circumstance, but it really is the most elephant-like place a client could begin.

If your fears don't kick in and get in the way, this conversation is a veritable goldmine for rapport-building. I say this because Black and African American people are generally savvy about how uncomfortable non-Black people, especially white people, can be with Black folks in most settings. They do not assume that the therapy setting will be an exception. They know that one of the fastest and sure-bet ways to make a white person uncomfortable is to mention race, so if it does come up, you need to do two things: (1) be really prepared, and (2) treat the disclosure as an opportunity to maximize rapport and get off to an impressively strong start with a client who has taken a chance on you (and may even already trust you to some degree). An ideal in-person conversation with a 30-year-old Black male client could go something like this:

THERAPIST: It sounds like you preferred a Black therapist, but you've been struggling with your situation for so long that you decided to see the first available person?

CLIENT: I did. I figured I would be more comfortable with a Black therapist, but yeah, I've been overwhelmed.

THERAPIST: I appreciate your sharing this with me. I can understand how working with someone who has shared experiences would be more comfortable to talk to. If it's okay with you, I would like for us to talk more about that. I also want to hear more about what you've been struggling with.

CLIENT: Well, we can start with what I've been struggling with. It's a lot.

THERAPIST: Okay, let's start there.

CLIENT: I'm just overwhelmed. I want to start up a new business, but it's been hard to find a mentor. I'm also exhausted all the time because of sixty-hour workweeks. To add, my mother is elderly and living alone forty minutes away. I think I've been feeling depressed.

THERAPIST: That *is* a lot. And you said you've been carrying this for a while. Tell me, what does "feeling depressed" look like for you?

CLIENT: I just feel sad a lot. I hate to say it, but I cry a few times a week. I just don't feel like myself.

THERAPIST: How long would you say it's been since you felt like yourself?

Notice that, in this example, the therapist didn't force the issue by talking about the client's hesitation with seeing a white therapist. When you trust the client, it's okay to follow their lead.

Working with Understandably Apprehensive Folks

As I've said on multiple occasions, people of African descent are immensely diverse. This diversity can look like growing up in rural Alabama versus Los Angeles; having street knowledge or a graduate degree (though sometimes both); and growing up in the Bible Belt versus in a family that is more spiritual or even agnostic. Some clients abide by decades of age-old wisdom, while others swear by TikTok insights when it comes to solving any and every problem under the sun. The levels of diversity are innumerable.

I highlight the variability in perspectives because there are some clients who will show up in therapy perhaps more apprehensively than others. As I discussed in chapter 1, much of this apprehension is rooted in shame, stigma, and mistrust in the systems and providers that are linked to care. Religiosity is also associated with diminished mental health care, as church folks are a particularly apprehensive group. Although attitudes are shifting to the belief that God does send mental health professionals, there remains a lot of apprehension about seeing a professional. One study revealed concerns about confidentiality and privacy, with apprehension about even being seen walking into a mental health facility (Wharton et al., 2018). Because this particular study included older adults, I was not surprised that study participants expressed concerns about professionalism and the therapist being too "familiar."

This study raises an important point for how you address Black clients, as there is often a preference for more formality, especially among older African Americans. As a provider, you will need to be willing to address Black clients more formally (e.g., Mrs. Cecilia Brown may have to be Mrs. Brown and definitely not Cecilia), especially if the client is 60 years or older. Respect for elders is a cultural norm and expectation in the Black community. This is understood in a way that isn't observed so much in our majority society. While some may see these norms as odd, they are real, and it would be a misstep to ignore them in the first session. The simple question "Would you prefer for me to call you Mrs. Brown?" is an easy solution.

Creating Connection and Building Rapport

You may have noticed that there are awkward moments that can come up simply because we have learned in our society that there are appropriate and inappropriate things to say to Black people. Walking on eggshells—or watching the elephant trample on eggshells—can make things worse. You may recall that I mentioned in the introduction that not all Black people identify as African American. We live in a society in which the melting pot has washed away some identities, but not all.

I recall one scenario in which a student therapist was assigned to a Nigerian American female client. The student therapist knew this because the client was certain to emphasize her Nigerian ethnicity during the initial intake. However, the therapist did not address the client's identity right away because they felt that doing so could show their "ignorance" and because they didn't know what to "do" with the information. For the therapist, it also wasn't clear that the client's Nigerian background was consequential for her presenting concerns, so they left well enough alone.

To help the therapist build rapport and learn more about their client's presenting problem, I advised the therapist to ask the client what it meant for her to identify as Nigerian. The inquiry gave the client an opportunity to describe familial expectations for her success, including the legacy of doctors and scientists in her family that she was expected to uphold, despite the fact that she preferred to pursue her interests in art. This led to the therapist's conclusion that the client bought into the cultural milieu for much of her life, but she struggled with letting her family down, especially given that her parents had made many sacrifices for her. Initially, it seemed that the client only struggled with the family's seeming imposition, but in reality, she struggled with her own beliefs and identity of what it meant to be Nigerian.

In the end, the therapist's sincere inquiry about what the client's identity meant to her facilitated rapport-building, as it provided the client with some novel space to think deeply about her ambivalence—wanting to honor her family but struggling with their seemingly rigid expectations. By taking the time to dig a bit deeper, the student therapist was able to obtain more nuanced insight about what the client's identity meant to her and also why she was in therapy. The client appreciated the revelation that the struggle was as much internal as it was external. When a therapist is comfortable in the room and able to resist the urge to "not look ignorant," they can ask unforced questions that lead to increased authenticity and insight with clients.

In thinking about your own practice, would you anticipate having concerns about your capacity to develop rapport with a potential client who is a second-generation Nigerian American woman who approaches you for help with "family problems" as she sees it? Can you be honest with yourself if you are unsure? I can imagine that your brief progress through the first two chapters of this book may have compelled you to question how you have engaged with Black clients in the past. That is understandable. The best that you can do now is to be mindful of your current and future approach.

You don't have to be so paralyzed that you forget all of your clinical skills. In the scenario that I proposed, you can tell the client, "I'd like to hear more" in reference to her family problems. One of our favorite therapeutic prompts—"tell me more"—is quite handy here. For example, you might say, "I would like to hear more about your experiences with your family—as much as you feel comfortable sharing." You have acknowledged that the client does not have to tell all of her business right away for you to be helpful.

And here's a bonus that you likely already figured out: Given that this client is a second-generation young adult, the issue she is most overwhelmed by is partly a communication issue wherein she fears communicating with her parents that she prefers to pursue a career in fine arts. Asserting such a disposition could be perceived as disrespectful. A lot of second-generation young adults are navigating multiple identities and demands, including "living their best American life" while solidifying a "respectable" career that would make immigrant parents proud. If being an engineer satisfies "the best life," there is no conflict, but for many second-generation young adults, there is a discrepancy between what they desire and what parents expect. You want to do your homework on common concerns so you can develop working hypotheses. While they may or may not apply to your client, testing your hypotheses is part of the process.

At some point in the session, be sure to also acknowledge your client's strengths. Be particularly attentive to ones that you might infer as part of African or African American cultural values but that the client may not have expressed explicitly—the importance of family and community, of thriving despite overwhelming obstacles, and of persevering by using one's natural talents and gifts. Though a client may zero in on impenetrable family frustrations, make sure to highlight that they struggle, in part, because the importance of family is rooted in who they are. Prompt them by asking about times when their family came through for them or how it made a difference just knowing that their family had their back at a tough time. Because clients lose sight of the good times when they are overwhelmed, they only need to identify one good occasion for it to be impactful. On other occasions, a client may minimize the spiritual values that have kept them going, but you can find out about their faith and perhaps related talents by asking, "How did you get through all of that?" If they say, "I'm not sure," prompt them to take a moment to think about it—because it's worth it to do so. Attending to strengths is as important as acknowledging sources of difficulty.

Near the end of the session, ask the client if they have any concerns about working with you. This is a key question to build rapport. Doing so invites the client to share any thoughts, questions, and genuine concern they may have about you. At minimum, you communicate that you are open to disclosing something about yourself. When I was in training, the most notable response I received from a client when I asked this question was that I reminded her of her daughter. She went on for a while talking about her daughter and when she stopped, I prompted again with "I can tell you value your relationship with your daughter. Is there a concern you have about working with me to address your sleep problems?" Her reassuring smile and "no" response suggested that she didn't even recall why she was talking about her daughter. I advised that if any concerns did come up, I hoped she would let me know. As I recall, she came to therapy consistently and made good progress until we agreed that she had met her goals and could consolidate therapy.

By the end of the first session, the client has a sense of your style. Perhaps they have some lingering questions from your early introduction. In any case, you want to allow space to check in near the end.

Added Time for Discussing Confidentiality

I could have jumped into confidentiality much sooner in this chapter, as nothing can happen until your client agrees to therapy and understands the limits to confidentiality.

However, since there are some important considerations that come along with confidentiality for Black clients, I thought it best to wait until we considered other assumptions.

Ethically, confidentiality is already a standard part of your repertoire that you do not gloss over. However, concerns about confidentiality warrant more reassurance with Black clients because of the context of "mistrust." I have worked in various settings with primarily white therapists who seemed too casual about confidentiality. I understand how confidentiality works, but for someone who could have mistrust issues, a casual, routine explanation about confidentiality could leave unanswered questions that the client is reticent to ask. To be sure, I don't think any client deserves a "this is mere protocol" introduction to their right to privacy. When I observe students deliver their explanation, meaningfully, clients (of all backgrounds) nod in gracious appreciation.

As a suicide expert, I devote a lot of time to trainees on when and how to disclose and also what to do if a client could be in a suicide crisis. Unfortunately, you have little to no rapport with your client in the first session, which makes this challenging but important work. You have to assure them in this first session that you will not disclose anything about the content of your work together without their written consent *unless* you believe them to be a danger to themselves or others, or if you're made aware of abuse or other danger to a child, elderly person, or someone with disability. In the instance of a possible suicide crisis, consider the 30-year-old male client I referenced earlier in this chapter who presented with feelings of depression and expressed a preference for a Black therapist:

THERAPIST: I have to ask you about something, given how unlike yourself you've been feeling.

CLIENT: Yes?

THERAPIST: When some people feel overwhelmed and just tired but they're still trying to keep everything going, they may feel like life isn't worth living. They may even feel like they don't want to live anymore.

CLIENT: I have felt that way at times. But I haven't thought about suicide or anything like that.

THERAPIST: I see. Have you thought about how you would die?

CLIENT: [*pauses*] Honestly? I have thought about driving my car off the road on occasion.

THERAPIST: Hmm . . . when was the last time you had that thought?

CLIENT: It's been a while. Maybe four or five months ago? It was the summer.

THERAPIST: Do you remember what was going on at the time?

CLIENT: I do. I was already overwhelmed and my mom was giving me a hard time about not coming over to help her. I was doing a lot, but she didn't appreciate any of it. My sister wouldn't even help and she actually lives closer to my mom!

THERAPIST: How did you resolve the situation?

CLIENT: It wasn't good. One day, I just went off on my mom. I felt awful about it. She backed off and apologized, but I felt awful. I went and saw her a couple days later. I think I took off from work.

THERAPIST: It really does sounds like you've been holding everything together the best that you could. I know you felt bad about your mom because you love her and don't want to hurt her. At the same time, it doesn't sound like there is anyone who is there for you when you need help.

Notice the therapist does a brief reframe here by acknowledging the important value that is the client's relationship with his mom. Anyone could break under the circumstances that the client described. Nevertheless, the therapist may want to consider creating a safety plan with the client in the event that he gets to a similar place of being so overwhelmed.

THERAPIST: If it's okay with you, I'd like for us to work together to create a safety plan for times when you could feel like driving your car off the road, or like life isn't worth it anymore.

CLIENT: Do you think I need that?

THERAPIST: Well, a safety plan is helpful because when a situation begins to get very stressful, it can be hard to come up with a plan when you're already very upset. So if we put a plan in place for you, that lessens the chances that there will ever be a time that I have to break our confidentiality. Does that make sense?

CLIENT: Okay, I see what you're saying.

THERAPIST: Now, if I believe you to be a danger to yourself, I will have to get help for you, acknowledge that I'm your therapist, and share the nature of your crisis.

Regarding confidentiality, it is your job to assure your client that even if their family member or best friend were to call your clinic first thing on a Monday morning to ask how the client is *really* doing, you would have to inform the caller that you cannot even confirm or deny if the person they're calling about is a client of yours. Let the client know that is how important privacy is to you.

Now, if the client indicates that they want you to talk to their spouse or daughter—and they sign a consent form allowing you to do so—then maybe you can do that. Recognize that an African American client may feel more comfortable by including their loved one in session, as this grounds their personal experience while they work with a therapist who does not share their values. But before that happens, you and your client need to get on the same page about the goals of this third-party meeting, what the client hopes to get out of it, and how you will set it up. This is important because it is the client's therapy—no one else's.

Rarely will clients request to have someone join a session, but when they do, I recommend using the better part of a session to discuss what will happen in that third-party meeting. Honestly, I think the confidentiality policies are a useful way to reinforce to the client that they have someone in their life (you) who has prioritized them, their feelings, and their preferences.

In Other Awkward Moments

As therapists, we are trained to match each client's language as much as possible. I agree with this practice to a point. If a client uses language or slang or colloquialism in the first session (or beyond) that you do not understand, you're going to have to ask. Perhaps when you think the client is transitioning to another thought or when there is a natural pause, just say, "Can I pause you there for a sec? I can probably deduce from the context that when you say, 'Don't want no smoke' you mean that you don't want any trouble, but I don't want to miss something important. Is that about right?" The client will most likely appreciate the confirmation that you're attending to their words and that you care enough to get it right. Some clients will avoid using any slang or colloquialisms with you. That's fine too.

Depending on the client's level of acculturation and immersion in mainstream society, they will use varying levels of African American Vernacular English (AAVE) or Black English. AAVE is not indicative of inferiority or laziness and is not the same thing as slang. It is "a systemic rule-governed variety rooted in the history and culture of the speakers. While its origins date back to the earliest of days of language contact brought about by the Atlantic slave trade, it remains today a vibrant symbol of African American kinship, creativity, and survival" (Weldon, 2021, p. 1).

As an example, your client may share that a close family member "be gettin' on their nerves," which indicates that the family members annoy them *all the time*. This understanding is important for assessing frequency and burden of distress. The absence of the "g" is also a representation of AAVE. Both the absent "g" and the use of the verb "be" are readily explained using identifiable rules of grammar. The overwhelming majority of Black people are well-versed in AAVE. However, those who are middle class and upwardly mobile are often proficient in code-switching, which allows us to alternate our language use based on the environment. Because standard English allows Black people to fit in and seem less threatening, your client may intentionally employ standard English in therapy. On the other hand, they may only use standard English regardless of the setting. There is no way for you to know. Your only role in your client's use of AAVE is to let it unfold (or not) when they are comfortable and not to comment on their language unless you need clarification or if they have intentionally raised the topic.

If your client is local and you live in a community of 100,000 or less, you might run into them at the grocery store, at a movie theater, or really anywhere. This presents another possible awkward moment to navigate. Recognizing that you already know how to navigate public encounters with your clients, just be mindful that your working relationship with your African American client may warrant an even higher level of sensitivity. Without an agreement, you cannot acknowledge them in public if you see them out and about, but your client may not know that. Consequently, they may add their own interpretations to the experience, which would be problematic for your therapy alliance.

As an example, Black people commonly experience the sentiment that "we all look alike" to white people, so if you ignore your client and there isn't an "understanding" in place, they may believe that you didn't recognize them as your client but as just another Black person, belying your "true" worldview on Black people. The best approach is to have the conversation upfront and shortly after discussing confidentiality, such as:

THERAPIST: Your privacy is so important to me that if I saw you out and about in [*wherever the client lives*], I wouldn't speak to you or acknowledge you in any way.

CLIENT: Okay, but is it okay if I wanted to speak to you?

THERAPIST: Yes, of course. If you initiate contact, I would definitely respond. If you're by yourself, I'd wave hello. Would that be okay?

CLIENT: Yes, I think so. But if I don't say anything, you won't either, right?

THERAPIST: Exactly. I'd follow your lead. I wouldn't want you to think I was intentionally ignoring you. I wouldn't do that. Again, your confidentiality is what's most important. And even if you were with someone else and introduced me as your therapist, I would smile and say, "Hello, nice to meet you" and not much else.

These kinds of conversations come to mind as I think about when I was growing up in Savannah, Georgia. My mom was a labor and delivery nurse who cared for new mothers. I didn't understand as a child, but I know now that my mom was amazing at her job. It wasn't unusual for women to approach her in the mall or in a restaurant and introduce everyone who was with them to her because they wanted everyone to meet the nurse who took such good care of them. I don't imagine such scenarios for therapists, but it's best to address the matter before an awkward situation leaves your client in a panic when they see you and wonder what's wrong with you—or them—that you didn't acknowledge them.

Other Expectations

The overwhelming majority of African Americans do not know anyone in therapy (except maybe if they are living in New York City or Los Angeles) and have no point of comparison of what to expect. And although dynamics are shifting as more African Americans seek therapy, they still don't know what to expect from *you* until you tell them. This includes how long they can expect to be in therapy.

Be clear about how long therapy could take. Your client may have the impression that they will be in therapy for years! I will discuss this topic at greater length in chapter 11, but I feel so very strongly about clients not being in therapy for their entire lives that I advise students to begin consolidation, or the end of therapy, in the first session. This is achieved by communicating to the client that "the goal of therapy is to not be in therapy." That is, you recognize that the client comes to therapy to address specific concerns, and you aim to help them address those concerns. You can let them know that some concerns eventually unearth other concerns, which is understandable, but your goal is to help them best understand their struggle, gain new insights about themselves, and employ new tools and strategies they can use even after therapy ends.

On the other side of the spectrum, some clients will expect you to heal them in a few short sessions. For someone who has long-standing, years-long challenges, be sure to let them know that it is unlikely that a deeply embedded concern can be fully managed in a few 50-minute sessions.

Notetaking is another courtesy that you will want to talk to your client about. An easy comment might be "I like to take occasional notes during session to help keep up with details that you might share and that might help me think about how best to help you. Is that okay with you?" While concerns about notetaking are universal, the nature of those concerns may be more pernicious with African American clients who have concerns about privacy. And of course, make sure that your notes would not be off-putting for your client should they ever have cause to see them.

Final Considerations

Although the first session presents the best opportunity for you to make a positive first impression with your client, you may get other chances to fix any mishaps you make, provided that you commit to confronting potential elephants in the room. It is true that some clients may not return for a second session if an unaddressed, unpleasant moment occurs in the first session. But some will. While you want to make your best effort in your first conversation to avoid these missteps, with a bit of determination and commitment to your work, you can always take a deep breath and check in with your client—in the same way you would check in with them about how an activity went between sessions or what it is that they are feeling when you see their mood shift in therapy.

Checking in about a potential elephant is the same thing. The only difference is that you must grapple with any fears you may have, or with your own internal thoughts, about what the client may be thinking about you as someone who could never "get it." The big elephant in the room may always be how different you are, racially. The smaller elephants will arise based on what you tell yourself about what this difference means and how you choose to address it. In all cases, your honesty about how you feel regarding these differences and your willingness to address them with authenticity will make all the difference.

Chapter 4

The Elephant in the Room

Racism can't be that big of a deal, right?

The very idea of what folks complain about—when students reenact plantation life for a school assignment, when a white colleague mistakes one Black coworker for another, when an NFL owner uses the N-word because Black people use it all the time—is that even racism?

Aren't these just faux pas complained about by highly sensitive people being highly sensitive?

If these thoughts have ever come to mind, know that they are undercover elephants because, to be sure, all these incidents *are* "that big of a deal." They do not occur in isolation. Instead, they systematically and regularly remind Black people that the system that denigrates some and privileges others isn't going away.

Alternatively, you may have avoided any real consideration of the impact of racism because it is almost too overwhelming to consider how prevalent it is. Even as someone who has achieved a relatively high level of career success, I can say without a shadow of a doubt that I've experienced my share of race-based encounters. More than anything, racism isn't about professional stature or income level. It is about the dehumanization of people based on skin color and African ancestry.

I do not share any of this to inspire guilt or shame in you as a therapist. It does not do your clients any good for you to bring white guilt or paternalizing energy to your sessions. It's inauthentic, and it undermines rapport-building. Instead, a more productive approach is to aim to be clear about the impact of racism so that you can: (1) access the necessary empathy that your client will need when they share a troubling experience, like what the overt racist at work did; (2) introduce what your client may be missing if they are not aware of the role of racism in their distress; and (3) help problem solve the situation in therapy.

This may be a good time to revisit the self-reflective exercise you completed in chapter 2. Recognizing that your clients will be required to shift their behavior and perspective to achieve their goals, you are doing the same—developing a muscle that will engage your work with clients in ways that you may not have considered in the past. Your ultimate goal is to provide the best possible care. You must do so in ways that may even seem foreign to you. Nevertheless, if you don't want your blind spots to undermine your well-earned expertise, you must be determined.

Look over your answers from chapter 2 and make note of what you identified as your single most important professional responsibility. Has your answer changed since then? Be as specific as possible.

_____

_____

_____

On a 0–10 scale (with 0 being "not important at all," and 10 being "very important"), how important to you are your professional responsibilities? _____

Since chapter 2, have you identified any additional notable talents that you hold as a mental health professional? Be sure to indicate those here.

_____

_____

_____

How can you use your strengths to demonstrate cultural humility?

_____

_____

_____

Since chapter 2, have you observed any new barriers to implementing your talents? If so, list them here.

_____

_____

_____

Based on what you have read thus far, is there anything different you could do to ensure that you're using your talents with your clients consistently?

_____

_____

_____

The Impact of Racism, Race-Related Stress, and Racial Microaggressions

I was a doctoral student in Tallahassee, Florida when Dr. Rodney Clark and colleagues' (1999) landmark biopsychosocial model of racism as a stressor was published in *American Psychologist*, one of the top journals in psychological science. To this day, it may be the most widely cited conceptualization on racism's egregious hold on Black people. Too often, these conversations have been relegated to less visible scholarly outlets, so for me as an emerging scholar, the paper was immensely affirming. Importantly, it led the way to addressing the complex but direct ways that racism affects well-being. If you're not familiar with the paper, you would likely benefit from reading it.

In basic terms, Dr. Clark and his colleagues emphasized the physiological and behavioral responses that occur when someone experiences a racist event, among other contextual factors that influence how they respond (e.g., socioeconomic status, the frequency and chronicity of the racist event). Because the subjective experience of racism is stressful, the physical body responds by kicking into gear via the sympathetic nervous system. In this state of fight or flight, individuals can experience a variety of stress-induced changes in immune system functioning that make them more susceptible to negative health outcomes. Importantly, an individual's coping behavior in response to racism, such as whether they seek support from others, can help to mitigate these negative outcomes, but repressing or ignoring racism-related distress can lead to myriad emotional responses, including depression, prolonged anger, hopelessness, thoughts of suicide, or all of the above.

Another study of 1,000 Black women in the United States found that racism was related to changes in DNA structure, which is the part of DNA linked to age-related disease and death (Lu et al., 2019). Imagine that—racism literally gets under the skin. That means if a Black person isn't killed by a direct act, their life is literally shortened by the experience of racism. It is mind-blowing to think that racism impacts individuals at the molecular level, but Black Americans endure undue exposure to this risk. Importantly though, the results of this study were only true for women who kept their experiences of racism to themselves and didn't discuss with others. This isn't surprising and is very much consistent with what Dr. Clark and his colleagues reported years before. That is, healthy, adaptive behavior can help offset the impact of race-related stress.

Given the benefit of social support and that openly talking about racism can increase well-being and reduce morbidity and mortality, it is important for you as a therapist to talk to your clients about their experience of racism. If you do not identify with the Black community (and even if you do!), you will have to rely on a strong dose of empathy to carry this out effectively. If you don't, you risk presenting as disingenuous. For example, imagine that a female therapist has been working with a 33-year-old client for issues related to generalized anxiety disorder. The client begins the session by expressing frustration that her 10-year-old son is being regularly singled out in the classroom—and not in a good way. In this conversation, the therapist aims to understand as closely as possible what the client heard from her child:

THERAPIST: Something seems to have really upset you today.

CLIENT: I picked my son up from school not too long before our session. He said that the teacher called him out again today for no reason. This same teacher is always giving my son a hard time.

THERAPIST: Oh my, what did your son say happened today?

CLIENT: He said that another student was kicking his desk during class, and when my son told the student to stop, the teacher told him to be quiet. When my son tried to tell him what was going on, the teacher told him to stop talking back. He didn't even give my son a chance to explain.

THERAPIST: That sounds awfully aggravating for you and for your son. And the teacher has done stuff like this before?

CLIENT: Oh yeah. My son is one of the few Black kids, and the only Black boy, in the class.

THERAPIST: That sounds like it could be a lot to manage. Was your son upset when you picked him up?

CLIENT: He was, but honestly, I think I was more upset than he was. I just get tired of this stuff.

THERAPIST: We have talked over the months about how tiring it is just to deal with all of your responsibilities, and it sounds like dealing with this teacher just adds on.

CLIENT: It really does. Though it helps for me to talk about it here.

THERAPIST: Absolutely. Do you think that situations like these add to your anxiety?

CLIENT: Probably! I felt my chest getting tight when my son started telling me what happened. I was angry the teacher wouldn't let him explain himself.

THERAPIST: You're a very dedicated mother, so I'm not surprised that the situation escalated your anxiety.

CLIENT: Yeah, but I know I need to get better control of it.

THERAPIST: Tell me what you did in the moment.

CLIENT: [*laughing*] I came and talked to you! I was hot!

THERAPIST: Well, let's do something now. Can we practice deep breathing? Breathing doesn't take away the teacher's behavior. However, breathing allows you the space to get your wits about you so you can problem solve on behalf of your son. Does that sound okay?

Notice that the therapist let the client tell her story. She did not go directly to problem-solving by asking the client, "Could your son have stopped talking?" It's possible that the client's son could have stopped talking, but that isn't the point of the client's distress. Eventually, the client can schedule a conference with the teacher, but planning the conference would be premature if the therapist hasn't fully heard the client's frustration.

The therapist also acknowledged that the situation was difficult for the client as a dedicated mom, but she did not fill in how the client "should" feel. Though this therapist also happens to be a mother, she did not insert herself to show solidarity or to say "I know how you feel" as a way of empathizing. If a therapist isn't Black, they cannot convincingly share their feelings with a Black client. And even if a therapist is racially matched to a client, they cannot skip steps in the conversation by assuming they know what happened, how the client is feeling, or what was most upsetting about the situation. In this scenario, the teacher could be Black. Imagine that! The reality is that a teacher from any racial background could mistreat a Black student because we are all socialized in the same system—a system that embodies the preschool-to-prison pipeline, that is overly punitive to Black boys *and* girls, and that can be generally hostile to students who aren't white.

It is an understandable, knee-jerk reaction to want to offer clients a "when I went through" response if you also identify as a woman, a gay person, a non-Black Latinx individual, or any other identity that your client shares. Though this could work in some instances, it is more likely to create distance rather than bridging a connection or demonstrating empathy. *Maybe*—and I say that with considerable emphasis—maybe if you have been working with a client for months, and they ask how you would deal with something as a [*fill in the blank with your particular identity*], then it sounds like they may trust your perspective as someone who can relate. More importantly, it suggests that there is good rapport. However, if shared experiences of racism have not yet come up, as it likely would if a Black client has a Black therapist, you cannot insert yourself in the conversation. Your responsibility is always to be resolute in your determination to listen and access every bit of your emotional intelligence to hear your client's story from their own mouth.

While it is appropriate to respond that a situation sounds awful, you want to resist the urge to add on artificial empathy. Tap into the sadness that you would feel if someone close to you were hurt and feeling powerless. Let the client know that you cannot begin to imagine the scenario they have described, and ask how you can be most helpful right now. When the client has someone to talk to—whether that listener be their therapist, a friend, or a sympathetic coworker—it allows their body to be restored, relieving itself from fight-or-flight mode. If you know that you are not (or are not yet) that person as their therapist, direct the client to others who can relate. It is okay to ask, "Do you know other moms who can relate to these experiences? If not, maybe we can figure out how to create that network or find an online group." In any case, there is a solution that you and the client can generate together.

Racism Is More Than Just a Few Bad Apples

For some clients, racism is tied up in their experience. This is what I and others mean when we talk about systemic or structural racism—the persistent web of practices and policies that keep Black people on the bottom rung of every metric. In light of recent events, you may know that Black people experience more police violence than white people. But you may not know that Black people are more likely to be stopped and searched by police, more likely to be placed on death row, and more likely to be wrongfully convicted of a crime than white people (Selby, 2021). Beyond the criminal "justice" system, the additional disparities in housing, health, employment, and income persist. Black people with college degrees are twice as likely to be unemployed compared to their white peers (Ross & National Journal, 2014). Unfair treatment in schools have long-term effects on African Americans (Winerman, 2021). These are real life issues that place immense burden on African Americans, and the stories are too many to share here.

To help you understand how racism is embedded at every level of our society, even in our health care settings, imagine this session with a Black client who was diagnosed with prostate cancer while undergoing surgery following an automobile accident:

THERAPIST: I understand that you came in for therapy because you were in an automobile accident and now feel uncomfortable driving.

CLIENT: Yes, I was banged up pretty bad. The car was totaled, so now I don't have a car. Fortunately, I can walk to work, and my girlfriend can drive me sometimes, but it's been stressful.

THERAPIST: I can imagine it's been tough to deal with all of this. How long ago was the accident?

CLIENT: It's been about four months now.

THERAPIST: Okay, so four months ago you were in an accident. Your car was totaled, and you were banged up in the accident too. Were you hospitalized?

CLIENT: Yeah, I was in the hospital for about three weeks.

THERAPIST: Three weeks is a long time. Have you fully recovered from your injuries?

CLIENT: For the most part. Honestly, I'm more afraid to drive than anything.

THERAPIST: I see. Have you driven at all since the accident?

CLIENT: I tried once, but I couldn't do it. I was just too afraid.

THERAPIST: That's understandable. You went through a situation that would have been difficult for anyone to come through and just go back to driving. You were brave to come to therapy to work through this.

CLIENT: Honestly, I think one of the hardest parts of all of this was finding out that I have cancer.

THERAPIST: After your accident, you were diagnosed with cancer?

CLIENT: Something like that. I was in the hospital for the accident, and just as I was going under for surgery, I heard the doctor say that I have prostate cancer. I'm pretty sure they didn't know that I was still awake when they were talking. I was getting ready to go under, but I heard the docs as clear as day. They were really comfortable and casual about it. I woke up groggy, but it was the first thing on my mind. I have cancer?!

THERAPIST: That was an awful way to find out. Just awful. How have you been managing all of this?

CLIENT: I haven't. I've just been angry and sad—sad that I can't drive and have to rely on my girlfriend, and angry those doctors treated me that way. When I woke up, I asked a nurse about the cancer. She sent a doctor in to talk to me and he was just matter of fact, like I should have known I had cancer or something like that. I had all kinds of questions, and he was just cold. He didn't care at all.

THERAPIST: [*tentatively*] I want to ask you something that may or may not be off base, but do you think he would have treated you that way if you were a white man?

CLIENT: No, absolutely not. And that's part of what makes me angry. How am I supposed to go back there or anywhere for help? Those white doctors don't care.

THERAPIST: When the people who are supposed to help are part of the problem, it's hard to know what to do or where to turn.

CLIENT: It really is. I was already freaked out by the accident. I could have died. And then to have to deal with racist doctors. It's a lot.

THERAPIST: It *is* a lot. And I'm glad you shared this with me. It sounds like there is a lot for us to work through.

CLIENT: I don't even know where to start.

THERAPIST: The first step will be for us to make a list of everything you're dealing with and figure out if we can prioritize where it makes the most sense to begin. We can think about your biggest source of stress. It could be anger at the white doctors. And to be sure, your anger is understandable. We can evaluate how your anger could be affecting other parts of your life. The priority could be your fear of driving and maybe your lack of independence. Or it could be any fear about the cancer and how to manage that, recognizing that it could be helpful to work through going into a medical setting.

In this scenario, the therapist explicitly asked the client whether he thought he was being treated poorly because he wasn't a white man. While this may sound like an unfortunate one-off event, the history of racial mistreatment is pervasive in the United States. A landmark report by the National Academy of Medicine revealed that Black people receive inadequate care for many health-related concerns, including cancer, heart-related illness, stroke, and AIDS among others (Smedley et al., 2005). The health care system is replete with racial mistreatment due to racial bias. In 2016, a study found that 40 percent of medical students believed that Black people had thicker skin, less pain sensitivity, and blood that coagulated more quickly than that of white people (Hoffman et al., 2016). Medical students are not unintelligent people, so what is the source of such foolery? Your implicit acknowledgment of racism helps to affirm these jarring realities. Your client has to feel heard by you if you hope to move the elephant out of the room.

As a white therapist, you might be hesitant to mention the racism aspect of this scenario for fear that you are planting an idea that might not previously exist. While it may seem far-fetched that a Black client would encounter a callous doctor in the midst of receiving life-changing information, it is neither odd nor unusual. Take my word for it. African Americans commonly encounter cruel health care providers. Some cite the Tuskegee experiment as the reason Black folks often avoid doctors, medical establishments, and even life-saving vaccines. Though the Tuskegee "participants" who were directly impacted by the experiments weren't given syphilis, which is the common misunderstanding, they also weren't given the treatment that would have saved lives. The Tuskegee study is synonymous with the ways in which Black people are mistreated at the hands of presumed health care professionals. The fact that the maternal mortality rate for Black mothers is three times that of white mothers is one of many sources of evidence (Hoyert, 2022). Some would conveniently argue that education and income are to blame, but quality of care and structural racism are systemic issues that needlessly impact maternal health, morbidity, and mortality in the Black community.

Racism Is More Than Stress

In my research over the years, I have examined the connection between racial discrimination and thoughts of suicide and symptoms of depression. Early on in this work, peer reviewers, who are presumed experts in the topic area, criticized that I was not adding to the literature because we already know that stressful situations are related to thoughts of death. We certainly know that stressful life circumstances are related to feelings of depression and dysregulated mood, so in the reviewers' minds, discrimination was just another "stressor."

To show that it isn't, I used statistical strategies that others had failed to employ to demonstrate that the experience of racial discrimination is a distinct type of stress. More complex statistical analyses such as these permit us to take into consideration when one variable is independently related to some outcome. And this is what I have consistently found in my research. When I consider multiple other types of stressors, such as divorce, job loss, grief, and so on, racial discrimination is related to greater levels of depression and thoughts of suicide *even after* considering the possible role of other types of stressors. Racism is inescapable because it is enveloped in our culture, but it can be mitigated in open, sharing relationships, including in the therapeutic relationship.

My own thinking about this is that when you consider the isolation and hopelessness that is inherently built into racial discrimination, it isn't surprising that individuals can become overwhelmed when subjected to unfair and unjust treatment, categorization, and sometimes, dehumanization based on a characteristic that is out of their control. For some, it can be hard to overcome such that they internalize a hopeless disposition.

"Fitting In" Is Hard Too

In the United States, many have comfortably subscribed to the idea of our society as a melting pot, where many cultures come together as one big homogeneous group. To come together, however, means that those who are immigrants are expected to assimilate to the majority white culture and give up their cultures of origin. Doing so has detrimental consequences, given that a person's culture is synonymous with how they survive. Culture is more than food and music preferences. Culture is a way of life and how we see the world around us. In a racially and culturally stratified society, those who relinquish their inherent culture and strengths are more vulnerable. Grandparents and parents teach the next generation that "this is what you do to live and thrive and follow your life's purpose, harmoniously." What works for one community may not work for others.

A key concept that I have considered in my research is the concept of *acculturative stress*, which is the strain associated with having contact with majority society while sustaining connectedness to your culture of origin. Acculturative stress isn't discussed at all in everyday conversations. It was first introduced in the scholarly literature as an experience that is observed among Mexican immigrants in the United States. Though many presume that Black people have very little to acculturate, this could not be further from the truth. Strong familial connection and spirituality, for example, are cultural patterns that Black people have been forced to compromise in the bid for assimilation. Naming traditions are another cultural example that was abandoned generations ago, and even in contemporary times, "Black-sounding" names like Lakisha and Jamal are linked to fewer job and housing opportunities than names like Emily and Greg.

Perhaps most importantly, on a daily basis, Black people relinquish the right to be authentically who we are, dimming our talents so as not to threaten others in professional spaces and resisting calling out injustices for fear of retaliation. You may be familiar with references to "respectability politics" wherein Black people are advised to "behave" with the hope of garnering respect from empowered white people. In the name of fitting in and keeping the peace, the focus is too often shifted away from the injustice and inhumanity levied against Black people.

What's more, higher levels of acculturative stress are related to more frequent thoughts of suicide. In particular, my research has found that adapting to mainstream culture with greater exposure to non-affirming environments and less positive cultural identity is linked to wanting to die (Walker et al., 2008). For some people, acculturation isn't a stressful process, but for those who experience some strain as they attempt to adopt a different—and sometimes hostile—culture, they may be more prone to mental health crises.

We tend to think of racism as a series of negative external events. In the absence of such events, however, the pressure to fit into a different cultural context where there are real consequences of not assimilating (e.g., getting passed on a job promotion) is incredibly stressful. Most of us have felt the stress of trying to fit in at some point in our lives. Adolescence may have been the worst of times! But for Black people who may be more or much less acculturated, the strain is prolonged and sometimes deficient in support.

Because acculturation occurs at the group level and increasingly over generations, the phenomenon of the frog in the hot pot emerges. One generation strives to acquire mainstream education in order to be seen by the majority culture, but this education is absent their core cultural values. Consequently, subsequent generations lack identity. This is why "values" work is so important—and not just the values that someone "thinks" they should have, but the values that truly resonate. For example, the Black community places a strong value on faith in God and family, especially elders. If you are a therapist who subscribes to acceptance and commitment therapy (ACT), ensure that you are clear on which values are central to your client's cultural history and experience.

Heterogeneity of Experiences

Though African Americans have a variety of perspectives on racism, most feel pretty confident that it exists and does harm, while others are not so sure. There are then others in between, who know that racism exists but aren't convinced that it has the power to affect daily life and success. Recently, I was at a networking event where a young Black man and woman asked about my book *The Unapologetic Guide to Black Mental Health*. The young man asked what I thought was the biggest challenge for mental health among Black people. I responded that it was depression and anxiety brought on, in part, by the burden of racism. It's like air, I told the couple. The young woman nodded her head, but the young gentleman asked me if I thought racism "still existed." It was a fascinating follow-up to my point. The woman, surprised, asked him, "Is that a real question?" I knew it was.

In response, I asked him if he'd heard about the recent complaints that the new Ariel character in *The Little Mermaid*, played by Halle Bailey, was Black. He did. I asked why he thought there was so much anger and vitriol about a fictional character. He responded, "Well, people just didn't think she should be a princess." He was sincere in his response and didn't seem to take issue with the fact that a Black woman couldn't be a princess. He paused when the woman with him said, "So a Black woman can't be a princess?" The young man didn't respond with words, but his nonverbals suggested he thought it could be a fair point. Hopefully, you see the inherent problem if the young man co-signed that a Black woman could not be a princess. It is one thing for a white person to be angry. It's a whole other situation for a Black person to agree that Black people do not belong in certain spaces.

These are the kind of Black people who can experience a "breakdown" when they venture to realize that they have been mistreated because of the color of their skin. Imagine that you are at the beginning of your eleventh session with a 49-year-old Black male client who is in middle management at a Fortune 500 company. He presented to therapy because his primary care physician said that he might need to talk to someone about his stress and difficulties sleeping, given his chronic hypertension.

THERAPIST: Tell me, did you have an opportunity to speak to your manager about the contributions you make to your team?

CLIENT: [*chuckling*] I did. But it didn't go at all as I'd hoped.

THERAPIST: Tell me more about that.

CLIENT: Well, I summarized all of the work that I've done since my last promotion six years ago. I highlighted how my input has made tremendous change in our clients' portfolios, leading to greater revenue for them and for us. I included graphs and charts and even comparisons to others who were promoted with even less success and fewer accomplishments.

THERAPIST: It sounds like you put together a very impressive presentation.

CLIENT: I did! I spent a lot of time on it, but it doesn't seem to matter. That's part of what's so exhausting. Some days, I feel like the situation at work is hopeless. I know I do good work, and I put in a lot of effort to show for it. Other days, I feel like I shouldn't complain. I make good money. We live in a great neighborhood. My sons go to private school while my wife is able to take care of our home and coordinate philanthropic activities. I mean, I shouldn't let this promotion situation bother me.

THERAPIST: I can appreciate your willingness to reframe the situation. You've probably done that a lot to make sense of situations that otherwise make no sense at all.

CLIENT: I have to. I'd probably lose my mind if I didn't.

THERAPIST: That's an interesting thought. Would you say that, over the years, you've developed a natural strategy of reframing to be able to motivate yourself to keep going?

CLIENT: Yes, for sure.

THERAPIST: What do you think would happen if you didn't do that—if you didn't reframe situations like the one we've been working through over the last few weeks?

CLIENT: [*mood shifting somewhat*] I'd be angry. I'd be resentful.

THERAPIST: And as you think about the situation now, part of you feels angry and resentful?

CLIENT: Yes.

THERAPIST: What other feelings come to mind?

CLIENT: Hopeless. I feel hopeless . . . like nothing I do matters. But what good is it for me to feel like that and talk about that? I'd just end up like a lot of folks—feeling sorry for myself—and I have nothing to feel sorry about.

THERAPIST: I agree that you don't have anything to feel sorry about. You work hard and take care of your responsibilities at work and at home. It does seem, however, that you may be carrying some frustration just below the surface. And you may not be aware of just how much that frustration is affecting you. When you first came to therapy, you mentioned having a lot of stress and that it was affecting your sleep. You've made some adjustments and seen improvements in your sleep, but I wonder if the root of your aggravation and stress is still here.

CLIENT: Maybe, but I'm not sure I know what you mean.

THERAPIST: Well, you mentioned you don't see the point in talking about your feelings because then you'll feel sorry for yourself when you have nothing to feel sorry about.

CLIENT: That's right.

THERAPIST: But dismissing your feelings may be keeping us from uncovering the clues of what's been getting to you. I can understand your motivation for avoiding your feelings. I imagine this avoidance has served you well at times. But I think we're going to need to sit with them to get some work done.

CLIENT: Okay, how do we do that?

THERAPIST: Let's go back to your feelings of anger and resentment and your real concern about going "there." Can we do that?

CLIENT: Sure.

THERAPIST: Take me back to your recent situation at work—where you shared your very detailed presentation of your contributions and expected your manager to be as impressed with you as you are.

CLIENT: And he basically responded with "keep up the good work," though I explicitly stated that my level of performance is not commensurate with my job title.

THERAPIST: And when he seemed to dismiss your request and instead responded with "keep it up," how did you feel?

CLIENT: To be honest, I was confused at first. I felt dismissed. And for a moment, I was livid. So, I thanked him for his time, and I went back to my office to check email.

THERAPIST: You were livid, so you went to check email. Where did that anger go?

CLIENT: What do you mean?

THERAPIST: When you say you were livid, that's a pretty strong emotion to bottle up. Did you send someone an email about what happened? Did you reach out to anyone? Did you go for a walk at some point?

CLIENT: No, I just basically went back to work.

THERAPIST: [*quietly, as client stares blankly*] Wow. By chance did you get one of your headaches?

CLIENT: Actually, I did. Later that afternoon, I had a really, really bad headache. I think I even went to bed early that night.

THERAPIST: I'm going to venture a guess here. I could be wrong, but I think we may need to rule something out. Do you think that your identity as a Black man has impacted your progress at work?

CLIENT: I don't know. It's possible.

THERAPIST: The other folks in your comparison chart—were any of them Black?

CLIENT: [*laughing*] No, there aren't even any other Black people in my division.

THERAPIST: Oh, I didn't realize that.

CLIENT: Yeah, it's just how things are. I was fortunate to get in there at all.

THERAPIST: It sounds like your position in the company is a real opportunity on the one hand, but on the other hand, I wonder if your headaches and chronically high blood pressure are a result of your work environment.

CLIENT: It could be, but high blood pressure runs in my family.

THERAPIST: I see. Have you tracked your blood pressure on stressful days at work? It may help for you to keep a blood pressure monitor nearby. You can keep a chart on your phone with the date, what's going on, and your blood pressure at the time. And then throughout the day, you can track what's going on and your accompanying blood pressure. Is that something that you can do?

CLIENT: I can do that. It seems like you think part of my blood pressure and headaches and stress are brought on by my being a Black man in corporate America. I can't change who I am, but I will be mindful of how it's affecting my health.

This conversation eased the client to a place of acknowledging his context (even if he questions it) and attending to his well-being by expressing willingness to gather empirical data. He is right that he cannot change who he is. However, he can begin to problem solve with the therapist once he understands the impact on his health.

In the next chapter, I will address diagnosis in more detail, but one of the ways that scholars have conceptualized emotional health challenges in Black people is the idea of *John Henryism*, in which Black people work themselves to death, in part, to overcome stress, which compromises their physical health in the process. Dr. Sherman James (1994) summarized how these prolonged cognitive and emotional coping efforts have deleterious consequences for Black adults. As we work to overcome mental health stigma in the Black community, I am convinced that addressing health concerns (e.g., hypertension, cardiovascular disease, diabetes) through psychoeducation is one way to motivate African American clients to think differently about mental health. When clients are uncomfortable discussing mental health, they may be more inclined to acknowledge physical health-related consequences. It's more accessible for them to say, "I'm not going crazy, but I may be at risk for serious heart problems if I don't make some different decisions."

In the case of this client, he will have to decide how he responds to his circumstances and with full awareness that race may be playing a role. He can remain where he is and accept that management is unwilling or unable to see his true value, or he can continue to fight at the expense of his health (including his emotional health). But by pretending that the environment is not affecting his well-being, he is essentially permitting the elephant to settle in. And that's not helpful. He can only be bumped and disrespected by the elephant so many times before it's impossible to ignore. The situation is a recipe for ongoing and unnecessary stress if the client internalizes that something is wrong with him and that he must work harder to earn the promotion when others have been promoted with fewer accomplishments.

In all cases, the therapist must assess the impact of the client's potentially racialized climate. Clients do not always have the awareness of how various circumstances affect them. As a therapist, you must discuss the impact of racism and microaggressions with the client to highlight this very real experience, even if you are not someone who has personally experienced it. Doing so gives both you and the client more insight into the severity of the issue and the need for therapeutic intervention. Fortunately, there are measures to assess racism and related stress in the same way that there are scales to assess depression and anxiety. Options include the short form of the Index of Race-Related Stress (IRRS-B; Utsey, 1999) and the Inventory of Microaggressions Against Black Individuals (IMABI; Mercer et al., 2011), which assesses microinvalidations and microassaults—actions that downplay racism.

A woman said to me recently that she knew she was frustrated and felt angry at her job, but she did not know why. When I labeled her experiences as microaggressive and explained what that meant, she gained a sense of perspective and relief that "it wasn't just her" going crazy. It is not unusual for Black and African American individuals to feel strong emotions but have difficulty explaining the source of these emotions. Having some language to identify and quantify microaggressions can be impactful. It is okay to trust your client's experiences and to help them gain insight on the impact of those experiences on their life.

Like I discussed in chapter 2, as a therapist, you will also have to be mindful about correcting any mishaps when it comes to discussing race. And you will have to do so in a way that is sincere and genuine. As an African American woman, I can say things to my African American client that you cannot say if you're not African American. As an example, when I use "us" or "we" to affirm an experience in therapy, I am more likely to further the therapy alliance with the client, whereas the same words could be perceived as disingenuous coming from you. If that ever happens, the therapy will be short-lived. And as I will discuss further in chapter 6, if you, as a white therapist, nudge a client to "reframe" racially offensive behaviors and other microaggressions, you will earn of level of suspicion that you don't want from your client. You might as well be part of COINTELPRO, which undermined much-needed social progress and ruined the lives of many Black and African American people in the 1960s and 1970s. When the assumption for many is that white people cannot be trusted, remember to bring your most authentic and wise self to each encounter.

For Black people who venture to develop a working therapeutic relationship, the pull to "shapeshift" to be more acceptable to white people is ever present. At minimum, Black people are adept at code-switching so we're not misinterpreted as "ghetto" or other stereotypes that often result in our words or behaviors being dismissed as invalid or ignorant. You might have to hedge your observation a bit more so that you don't come across as judgmental, but doing so is worth the effort, especially when race-related stress and trauma show up in the therapy room.

I've said it before—racism is going nowhere. It's helpful for you to be aware of the very nuanced ways in which Black people are affected. That Black people chronically live on high alert is a truth that must be acknowledged. Race is linked to innumerable inequities, but the therapy room can be a retreat from those inequities.

Chapter 5

Expanding Your Thinking About Assessment and Diagnosis

You may be aware of the long history in the United States dating back to the nineteenth century of pathologizing adaptive behavior among Black Americans. Enslaved persons who tried to escape brutal slave masters were diagnosed with *drapetomania*, a "disease" they claimed resulted in the uncontrollable impulse for captive persons to run away. Proponents of chattel slavery argued that keeping Black people enslaved was necessary for their "well-being." During this same time period, the physician Samuel Cartwright introduced the diagnosis of *dysaesthesia aethiopica* to explain the so-called "laziness" among (mostly free) Black people—claiming that laziness was the result of the freedom to be idle. This is not to mention that Black people in the Antebellum period were believed to lack the mental capacity to suffer psychologically. That is, psychological disturbance was thought to require a certain level of sophistication that enslaved Africans were too "primitive" to possess (Jarvis, 2012). It is worth noting that these sentiments linger in the dehumanization of Black people that persists in contemporary times. Another historical stereotype was that enslaved persons were cheerful, easily excitable, and "prone to mania." Despite earlier assumptions regarding mania, Black and African Americans even now are more likely to be misdiagnosed with schizophrenia and underdiagnosed with bipolar disorder, which has a better prognosis.

Some years ago, I shared a panel discussion with a six-time all-star of the Women's National Basketball Association who spoke openly about the many years of personal and professional chaos that she experienced because mental health professionals failed to recognize her bipolar disorder. This nonsense hasn't just gone away. Because the system has been skewed from the beginning, color-blindness seems to be the furthest to which the mental health profession has evolved rather than embracing the inclusive society that marginalized people deserve.

Recall in chapter 2 that I discussed the dangers of adopting a color-blind lens—that such an approach to mental health care can be harmful for rapport and compromise the provider's capacity to provide care that meets the client's needs. Some assume, understandably, that color-blindness is admirable in the interest of treating everyone with fairness. However, it is actually in your best interest (and in your client's best interest) to practice the opposite of color-blindness by acknowledging your client for who they are—and conducting yourself accordingly.

Consider the ways you are able to seamlessly acknowledge and respond to other characteristics of your clients. Imagine you encounter a senior person in a wheelchair shopping alone at the grocery store. You happen upon them every so often in different aisles of the market. They seem to be happily navigating their shopping. Do you make any assumptions about that individual? If you see them reaching for groceries that are surely out of reach, do you feel inclined to help them? Now, imagine you encounter a professional in the grocery store—someone wearing a nicely fitted suit and stylish shoes. They're taller than the average person and seem to be in good health. Do you imagine having a natural inclination to help that individual as they engage in their lunch-hour shopping? I present this scenario as an illustration of how we respond to individuals based on what we assume about them—in this case, a healthy working-aged businessperson versus a wheelchair-bound older adult. The reality is that we treat people differently based on how we see them.

The same is true for the assessment and diagnosis process in therapy, even if you prefer to assume objectivity is an option. You will have to intentionally consider context for your African American clients. Although it is beyond the scope of this chapter to revisit every aspect of assessment and diagnosis, I will highlight key areas for consideration, including expanding your thinking about anxiety, depression, and suicide; introducing race-based trauma as a source of posttraumatic stress disorder (PTSD); and discussing unique concerns that have plagued people of African descent for centuries, particularly in the United States. Given the historical and persistent contemporary realities, it's not racist or unethical to take race, ethnicity, and culture into consideration when making sense of the client's distress and developing a meaningful case conceptualization. In fact, the APA's (2017a) multicultural guidelines insist that you do.

How I Think About Conceptualization and Why Diagnosis Is Important

A client's psychological distress typically emerges under the umbrella of anxiety or depression, the two most commonly diagnosed psychological disorders. Many clients do not meet full criteria but are struggling with adjustment to a life change or with a subsyndromal concern, wherein anxiety is elevated or depression symptoms are disruptive to daily life. Still, they don't meet the diagnostic threshold. Regardless, you need a starting point to begin to make sense of the client's concerns. I encounter a fair number of therapists who take the approach of offering strategies without the due diligence of developing a conceptualization and diagnosis. They don't ask questions like "How did the client's distress come about?" "Does the client have a treatable pattern of symptoms even if they do not meet criteria for a disorder?" As I indicated in chapter 1, I believe in the importance of evidence-based care and develop this approach with doctoral student trainees and in case consultation.

Consider a scenario in which your 40-year-old African American client presents for therapy because she is frustrated that her life has changed since she contracted COVID-19 six months ago. She tells you that she has difficulties remembering how to complete work-related tasks, and sometimes, she's just in a fog. She decided to come to therapy because her depression about her situation is getting the best of her. Her adult children and her friends are very supportive and encouraging, but she is starting to feel worthless. Your first step for such a client (and for any client, really) is to assess the last time she had a physical. In this case, you want to know what a neurologist has indicated about her condition and that there are no other preexisting concerns. As you know, clients sometimes experience physical health conditions that impact their emotional health. While that may be distressing for them to accept, you can agree on how they can maximize their daily life, recognizing that there are physical limitations and without piling on self-limiting beliefs such as "I'm never going to be the person that I used to be."

Once you and your client understand her limitations, you can develop a game plan to avoid prolonged depression symptoms and also to get her active again—both at work and in her personal life. The aftermath of COVID-19 is understandably distressing, but what your client says to herself about who she is—that is something she can control.

Whether you have been providing mental health care for one year or twenty-one years, you've likely adopted an approach to assessment and diagnosis that is comfortable for you. Moving from a place of comfort, even in the interest of being an even better provider, can be inconvenient at best. However, this is an opportunity to tackle a sneaky elephant in the room. Your ultimate goal is to maximize the chances that you can facilitate change in the lives of your clients regardless of their racial or ethnic background. You have to decide whether doing so is worth the temporary inconvenience and maybe even the unease that goes with making change. Consider your past training and continued education about culturally informed approaches to diagnosis and case conceptualization.

What lessons did you learn in your graduate training and later in your continuing education about psychological or psychiatric diagnosis with persons from different racial or ethnic groups?

_____

_____

_____

_____

On a 0–10 scale (with 1 being "not helpful at all" and 10 being "the highest level of helpfulness you can imagine"), how helpful have those lessons been for you? If you did not receive or do not recall any lessons, indicate 0. _____

If you scored a 7 or higher, indicate the ways in which that training was most helpful.

_____

_____

_____

_____

If you scored a 6 or lower, indicate the ways in which that training was less than helpful.

_____

_____

_____

_____

What areas would be helpful for you to commit to getting "uncomfortable" in your pursuit of more inclusive diagnosis and assessment?

_____

_____

_____

_____

What barriers to enacting effective diagnosis and assessment for your Black clients do you anticipate?

_____

_____

_____

_____

Common Problems with Uncommon Pathology

Though anxiety disorders are the single most commonly occurring mental health disorders, African Americans are less likely than white Americans to be diagnosed with or meet criteria for anxiety disorders. Sleep paralysis, a symptom that is typically linked to panic disorder, is one exception that is more common among Black than white Americans. Otherwise, anxiety disorders occur with similar or less frequency for

Black people. What is particularly intriguing about anxiety is that for Black people, the associated somatic symptoms (e.g., shortness of breath, sweating) are attributed to health conditions such as hypertension, heart disease, and so forth. Physical health abnormalities are a default explanation due, in part, to awareness of health problems in the community.

Black Americans are also less likely to be diagnosed with major depressive disorder compared to white adults but are more likely to experience persistent and debilitating symptoms and impairment (Bailey et al., 2019). Dr. Francis Baker (2001) introduced a useful conceptualization of depression in the Black community that may explain this underdiagnosis. According to Dr. Baker, there are three alternate presentations of depression among African Americans that are not reflected in the *Diagnostic and Statistical Manual of Mental Disorders* (DSM) criteria for major depressive disorder: the "Stoic Believer," the "Angry One," and the "John Henry Doer."

The Stoic Believer is someone who asserts that their faith keeps them going despite pain and hardship. You wouldn't necessarily know that they are suffering because they don't show it and don't complain. The Angry One is best characterized as someone who seems to have gone through a personality change or presents as abrupt and irritable without provocation. They may have been pleasant at one point in life, but at some point, they shifted. The third profile is that of the John Henry Doer, who takes on more and more at the risk of taxing their physical health, presumably because they can accomplish the tasks better than anyone else. Unlike the Believer, the Doer will complain that others aren't doing their part.

Anecdotally, when I speak to audiences that are primarily African American about these profiles, the nonverbal (and sometimes verbal) affirmation of Dr. Baker's approach is evident. Folks who hadn't thought of depression before are receptive to these three distinct profiles of depression.

In all three instances, Dr. Baker advises clinicians to be aware of African American clients who have multiple illnesses or chronic stress, especially if they live in large, urban cities or experience ongoing work or family-related struggles. She also advises clinicians to attend to clients with low energy levels, sleep and appetite disruptions, and difficulties looking positively toward the future. Otherwise, they risk overlooking severe emotion dysregulation.

In chapter 1, I introduced you to a 35-year-old African American woman who reported feeling "overwhelmed all the time." She is married, works full time outside of the home, and has two elementary school-aged children. At first glance, she seems to be doing well. She arrived at the session early, was professionally dressed, was open to answering questions, and presented as quite engaging and affable. She indicated that she has several close friends, though she doesn't see them as often as she likes. Though she reported feeling overwhelmed, she did not report excessive worry, hypervigilance, or even "depressed mood." With more discussion, though, she begins to disclose her poor sleep pattern and reveals that she has headaches, which her primary doctor attributes to stress. Let's revisit the conversation where you suggest that she could be depressed:

CLIENT: I don't feel depressed.

THERAPIST: When you say you don't "*feel* depressed," can you tell me more about what that would look like for you?

CLIENT: Well, depressed people don't want to move or get out of bed and certainly can't do everything that *I'm* doing. I take care of my family and I get my work done. In fact, I just got a raise last month. And like I said, I volunteer with three different organizations. I'm stressed out a lot, but that's not depression. I'm doing too much to be depressed.

THERAPIST: I think I follow you. And you *do* accomplish a lot, for sure. I want to be sure that we're seeing the whole picture so we can come up with an effective approach to therapy for you and so we don't create any unnecessary stress for you. [*pauses for client acknowledgment*].

CLIENT: I appreciate that.

THERAPIST: Tell me this, [*hesitantly*] because I also want to be sure that we're having as complete a conversation as possible. Is there a part of you that would be upset to consider . . . that you could be experiencing some depression?

CLIENT: I don't know. Maybe. I just don't think that's who I am.

THERAPIST: I can appreciate that. When we talk about depression in everyday language, it sounds like a . . . defect. Like something is defective about the person, and that's who they are—a defective person. Maybe even someone who can't live a full life?

CLIENT: Exactly. And my life is very full!

THERAPIST: It is very full. I also want to point out, if I can, that you previously said your enjoyment level with some of your volunteer activities is at a 4 on a 0–10 scale. And that you spend a big chunk of your Saturdays on those activities and some time during the week too?

CLIENT: Yes, but like I was saying, it's good to give back.

THERAPIST: I agree. It is good and important to give back. We especially need more people to be giving to communities so the work burden doesn't fall on the few who are willing.

CLIENT: [*nods, reflecting*] Yeah, I wish.

THERAPIST: My only concern is that you may be doing too much right *now*. You came in because you're feeling overwhelmed. I imagine that you've tried to figure out how to not be overwhelmed, but that hasn't worked out. [*smiling*] I'm pretty sure that coming here was a *last* resort. Unfortunately, you have so much on your mind that it keeps you from falling asleep at night. You're very likely sleep deprived. And to add, it seems you're starting to have physical symptoms of being overwhelmed and sleep deprived, given the unexplained headaches. Let's talk about how some people have symptoms of depression that *can . . . be . . . managed*, and how those symptoms say more about the person's lifestyle than it does about who they are or their character or their capabilities. How does that sound to you?

CLIENT: That makes a lot of sense. I hadn't thought of it that way. It's just the idea of being depressed kind of scares me.

THERAPIST: I can understand that. And we use different labels and language, so to speak, in our profession to help figure out how to address a client's concerns. As you know, depression and other mental health concerns are highly stigmatized, so that adds extra weight to what you're dealing with. But it doesn't have to be that way. We're all managing a lot without having to add on extra interpretation about what something means.

Also, notice that I said you have *symptoms* of depression, so we're going to focus on those symptoms rather than the label of "depression." We don't want the label to be an unnecessary distraction that prevents us from addressing your very real sleep problems, lessening your feelings of being overwhelmed, and identifying activities that you enjoy (at maybe a 7 or higher). How does that sound?

CLIENT: That sounds good to me.

In many ways, someone who just keeps moving no matter what, tries to compensate for others' shortcomings, or is irritable in a way that is off-putting to others, may be coping with sad and empty feelings—so much so that they do not recognize the feelings. This does not mean that the feelings aren't there. In any case, depression can be like whack-a-mole. If it doesn't pop up as low mood, it will eventually pop up somewhere—whether it shows up as sleeplessness in the quiet hours of bedtime, as a dysregulated stress response system, or as irritable mood. I share these insights because it may be helpful for providers to attend to symptom patterns when generating a plan of action rather than attending to the overall diagnosis of depression or anxiety.

The Cultural Formulation Interview: A Useful Tool for Avoiding Misdiagnosis

I recall an occasion in grad school that both surprised and saddened me. I was working in my local hospital outpatient practicum in a small office adjacent to the waiting area, which is where all the student trainees worked. When I wasn't meeting with a client, my door was open, so I overheard all sorts of conversations. On one particular morning, I overhead an African American man chatting with his family member. They were talking about responsibilities that needed to be addressed later that day, joking about another family member, and otherwise waiting patiently. Nothing about the conversation was remarkable.

In the team meeting later that day, one of my peers summarized the client's overall presentation in session, provided a preliminary summary of findings, and suggested a rule-out diagnosis for schizophrenia. At that point, my ears perked up. Schizophrenia? Feeling curious, I asked my peer what they observed or found that suggested possible schizophrenia. The response was that the gentleman endorsed an item on the Minnesota Multiphasic Personality Inventory-2 (MMPI-2; Butcher et al.,1989) that indicated seeing and hearing things that weren't there. In the case of the MMPI-2, the output contains ready "critical items" that a clinician can follow up about. Even if there aren't critical items, a therapist can get additional information before settling on a "possible schizophrenia spectrum concern." I asked if the therapist had followed up on these critical items. They had not. If they had, they may have realized the client endorsed this item due to his belief in the afterlife and his feeling that a deceased grandparent who helped raised him was still with him.

Though it is helpful to be aware of culturally relevant factors when conducting an evaluation, you do not need to know everything about different racial or ethnic groups to form a solid conceptualization and diagnosis of what could be impacting a client. You can use the Cultural Formulation Interview (CFI), associated with the DSM-IV, to help you integrate or acknowledge a client's cultural context while formulating diagnoses. The interview is broken down into four domains that emphasize: (1) how the client makes sense of their emotional distress from a cultural perspective, (2) what they see as the cause of this distress and in what circumstances their concerns are less upsetting, (3) how culture has informed their coping and help-seeking decisions, and (4) how culture affects future help seeking. With this information in mind, you can organize a working formulation of the client's presenting concerns.

Imagine you were the therapist interviewing the African American client for whom my peer was attempting to rule out schizophrenia. Let's assume the client is a 26-year-old African American male student who works part-time at a restaurant:

THERAPIST: Now that we've completed all of our paperwork, I'd like to hear more about what prompted you to come to therapy.

CLIENT: Well, my girlfriend said that I needed to see someone. I know I haven't been myself, but I just have a lot going on right now.

THERAPIST: Tell me more about what all is going on.

CLIENT: I just went back to school to get my MBA. I'm also working part-time because I need the money. My family would help me financially, but I'm too old to be asking for money, so I have to work. Juggling all of it is a lot.

THERAPIST: I see. Your family would support you, but you feel it's time for you to stand on your own.

CLIENT: Yes, absolutely.

THERAPIST: I see. And you said that you haven't been yourself. Tell me more about that.

CLIENT: Honestly, I just don't want to be bothered with people. I used to enjoy being out and spending time with my friends, but I have too much to do. So I've kept to myself, which isn't me. I used to be the life of the party, but my friends don't understand how I'm grinding right now to get ahead and build my future. I feel like no one understands. Honestly, I feel angry a lot—I'm trying to get ahead, and it feels like people are trying to hold me back.

THERAPIST: That must be very frustrating. Is there anyone other than friends who have been holding you back?

CLIENT: No, I guess not. But no one is helping me either.

THERAPIST: Who would you want to be helping you?

CLIENT: I don't know. Ugh! Sometimes it's hard for me to even think!

THERAPIST: Let's take a moment to pause . . . Is it hard to talk about what you've been experiencing?

CLIENT: Yes. Part of it is the idea of talking to a stranger. And I don't want you thinking I'm crazy.

THERAPIST: That's completely understandable. And I appreciate you sharing that with me. You know, there are a lot of assumptions about what it means to be in therapy and what happens in therapy. My goal is to best understand your experience so we can create a strategy to help you feel better and reach your goals for therapy. It does mean that I'll ask you a lot of questions, especially here at the beginning. You're the expert on you. I have some skills to share with you, but I wouldn't have any reason to declare that you are crazy. You're someone who could use some better tools and skills for life. How does that sound?

CLIENT: That sounds good to me. Thank you for that.

THERAPIST: You're welcome. Is it okay if I ask some more questions to understand what all could be going on?

CLIENT: Yes, we can do that.

THERAPIST: You'd mentioned that your girlfriend was the one who suggested you see someone. What made her suggest that to you?

CLIENT: Well, she's tired of me being mopey and in a bad mood. She says I've been super sensitive too—like I have snapped at her and at my mom a few times. I've been drinking much more than usual, but I don't see it as an issue. One night she said she heard me muttering in the bathroom and she could tell I wasn't just talking to myself.

THERAPIST: Do you remember that night and what was going on that you were muttering?

CLIENT: Yes . . . I was talking to my grandmother . . . my grandmother who passed away last year. I felt like I was hearing her voice. I know it sounds crazy.

THERAPIST: Was it comforting for you to hear her voice?

CLIENT: It kind of was. I mean, I know she wasn't *there* there. But sometimes I feel like I hear her voice saying, "Everything's going to be okay." It doesn't bother me at all, but I think my girlfriend thought I was losing it a bit that night in the bathroom. Maybe I am losing it.

THERAPIST: It sounds like there may be a part of you that questions if you're losing your mind.

CLIENT: It's just that my grandma and I were really close. When she passed away, it came out of nowhere and hit me pretty hard.

THERAPIST: That's understandable that your grandmother's passing took a toll on you. It sounds like you've felt connected to her even if she's no longer here with you physically. That doesn't make you crazy. It means you are grieving.

CLIENT: [*Pauses with a deep sigh of relief. Finally, someone sees the gravity of his loss. Even more, he's reassured that he isn't losing his mind and that his "condition" is likely temporary.*]

In this scenario, the client was engaged in normative behavior. He wasn't distressed by his grandmother's voice but instead found a sense of peace and connectedness. Because we live in a society where "voices" are synonymous with psychosis, it is important to reframe that for the client so that he resists overpathologizing his experience. Hearing voices is a potential marker of schizophrenia, but it is critical for the therapist to gain insight into the client's perspective.

Using the CFI, the therapist can also get at the client's definition of the problem by posing questions such as:

> *People often understand their problems in their own way, which may be similar to or different from how doctors describe the problem. How would* you *describe your problem?*

The therapist can use the CFI to explore how the client's social network perceives the problem as well:

> *What do others in your family, your friends, or others in your community think is causing your* [withdrawal and occasional snapping at people you love]?

Finally, recognizing that the client has some strengths (and even when it's not obvious that they do), it is always useful to use the CFI to assess what they have done to address their concerns:

> *Sometimes people have various ways of dealing with problems like* [feeling overwhelmed]. *What have you done on your own to cope?*

The CFI is designed to center the client's perspective. Therapists can practice the specific prompts on the CFI as they develop their expertise in working with Black and African American clients. You can find the full CFI in the appendix at the back of this book.

Assessing Suicide

Suicide can be an especially intimidating topic for therapists to address. I have encountered therapists who didn't want to be "rude" and who preferred to wait for just the right time to ask about current thoughts and history of suicide. But for the African

American community in particular, suicide warrants even more discussion than what we currently see in the mainstream, seeing as the death rate due to suicide has been steadily increasing among Black folks. Though homicide deaths exceed suicide deaths in the Black community (and the opposite is true in our overall society), suicide is still a top-five cause of death for Black adults and youth.

The increase in African American deaths due to suicide began well before the COVID-19 pandemic, persisted through the pandemic, and continues at the time of this writing. Part of what's notable is that deaths for white folks decreased during the height of the pandemic. High-profile deaths of Black folks, such as Stephen "tWitch" Boss, former Miss USA Cheslie Kryst, and actress Regina King's son, Ian Alexander Jr., have likely been categorized as anomalies, especially in the Black community. Based on my decades of research, however, I see these deaths as part of an unsettling trend that warrants attention at the national level. While suicide deaths are preventable, my concern has always been the limited support for persons who could be in crisis. Beliefs about suicide may be shifting with younger generations, including among younger generations of Black people, but there remains a common assumption that suicide is much more of a concern for white people.

In a suicide risk assessment, we ask several key questions regarding the intensity and frequency of suicidal ideation. Has the person had any thoughts about killing themselves or being better off dead? Have they ever had a suicide attempt? Do they have a plan and access to means? We also assess for a family history of suicide. But assessing family history may require additional inquiry with African American clients, as it is fraught with the impact of heightened stigma and misreporting. In work that I've done, suicide deaths in the Black community are more likely to be misreported as "undetermined" (Rockett et al., 2010). Even if a family member is suspicious of the circumstances in which their loved one died, they may not disclose a possible family history of suicide. It is also important to realize that when persons are in danger of hurting themselves, calling the police is often the last (very last) option, given the danger that law enforcement can pose for Black people.

Some years ago, I interviewed an African American dad who was experiencing considerable psychological and emotional pain. He was extremely clear that he was an especially proud and protective father and was staying alive for his children despite his otherwise very trying life circumstances. He readily endorsed thoughts of suicide, but when I asked if he had a plan for taking his life, he denied having one. I consider myself to be an astute interviewer and asked if he would tell me if he had a plan. He assured me he would. He also disclosed an occasion when a close friend came over to check on him and removed the client's gun from the home. Much later in the interview, and much to my surprise, he casually shared with me how he imagined he would (accidentally) die when his time comes. The certainty of his insight wasn't lost on me. I now advise clinicians to ask clients, "Do you feel like you know how your life will end?" or "Do you know how you will die?" And as I typically do for difficult conversations, I add, "Would you tell me if you knew?"

My experience with this African American client is consistent with research showing that individuals who identify with a racial or ethnic minority group are more likely than white people to be labeled as "hidden ideators" in the context of disclosing suicide ideation (Morrison & Downey, 2000). It also comports with findings that Black adults report having more reasons to live than their white and Hispanic counterparts even when they reported higher suicide ideation and previous, non-lethal suicide attempts (Richardson-Vejlgaard et al., 2009). Interestingly, the researchers observed that one of the dominant reasons for living was a moral objection to suicide—consistent with some of my own research findings—in which study participants believed that God (and not the individual) is responsible for life (Walker et al., 2006).

In *The Unapologetic Guide to Black Mental Health*, I introduce the idea of "low key suicide" to acknowledge habits that can lead to premature death among African Americans. Our expert definitions of suicide, which insist that an individual must intentionally engage in self-destructive behavior to end their life, fly in the face of someone who doesn't believe they are in charge of life. Long ago, Drs. Kevin E. Early and Ronald L. Akers (1993) described how suicide is perceived to be "a white thing." They found that Black folks distinguish "real suicide" from "slow suicide" and that those in the community may be inclined to acknowledge the latter as an understandable and thus acceptable form of premature death. Understandable forms of slow suicide include behaviors that might jeopardize someone's health, like routinely binging on alcohol, using illicit substances, or chronically driving while under the influence.

Other types of behaviors are more passive, but they are problematic nonetheless. If your client presents to you for work-related social anxiety—but they have unmanaged type 2 diabetes and high blood pressure while eating poorly and refusing exercise or a medication regimen—you may want to have a conversation with them about their health behaviors once they are feeling more effective at work. Helping your client gain relief from their initial concerns will better prepare both of you to address more serious issues such as health behaviors and daily trauma. In any event, you want to proceed with caution, just as you would anytime you introduce a potential concern that the client did not present to therapy with. Bringing up concerns that do not reflect the client's initial presenting problem can be perceived as judgmental.

Race-Based Trauma—Not Yet in the DSM

The manner in which Black people experience the world can be traumatizing. Although scholars initially made the case that racism represents a form of stress, others have begun to make the finer point that this type of stress is trauma-inducing (Carter, 2007; Williams, Printz, & DeLapp, 2018). As mental health professionals, we typically associate trauma with military combat, sexual assault, domestic abuse, physical childhood abuse, motor vehicle accidents, and so on. I wonder if racism is so integral to our society that labeling it as traumatic may seem non-sensical for some. There is also the reality that Black people are keenly aware of racism in ways that others are not. For example, a 2019 Pew Research Center poll found that Black people are considerably more likely than white people to acknowledge that Black people are mistreated when it comes to:

1. Dealing with the police (63 percent of white people vs. 84 percent of Black Americans)

2. The criminal justice system (61 vs. 87 percent)

3. Hiring pay and promotions (44 vs. 82 percent)

4. Applying for a loan or mortgage (38 vs. 74 percent)

5. Going to a store or restaurant (37 vs. 70 percent)

6. Voting in elections (30 vs. 58 percent)

7. Seeking medical treatment (26 vs. 59 percent)

This contemporary poll is one illustration of how mistreatment flies below the radar in mainstream society. Although discrimination is more observable in instances regarding the police and the justice system—perhaps given the availability of camera phones—in other areas, mistreatment hides in plain sight. Nevertheless, the reality is that when Black people experience mistreatment in multiple, unavoidable areas of life, these experiences compound and can escalate risk for trauma.

This means race-related trauma is another area in which you want to think critically about case conceptualization. In fact, Dr. Monnica Williams and her colleagues have made a strong conceptual and empirical case for adding race-based trauma to the DSM (Williams, Metzger, et al., 2018). As you know, trauma diagnoses presume that after an individual has experienced a traumatic event, they experience "intrusions" and some shifting of their cognitive and emotional state of mind together with a sense of hypervigilance and heightened reactivity to various stimuli. To screen for these possible symptoms in the context of race-related trauma, you can use measures such as the 21-item Trauma Symptoms of Discrimination Scale (Williams, Printz, & DeLapp, 2018). As Dr. Williams explains, the measure is intended to assess "uncontrollable distress and hyperarousal, feelings of alienation from others, worries about bad things happening in the future, and perceptions that others are 'dangerous'" (p. 8)—all of which are consistent with DSM-5 criteria for PTSD. The following are some selected items from the scale, to which respondents are asked to indicate *never, rarely, sometimes,* or *often*:

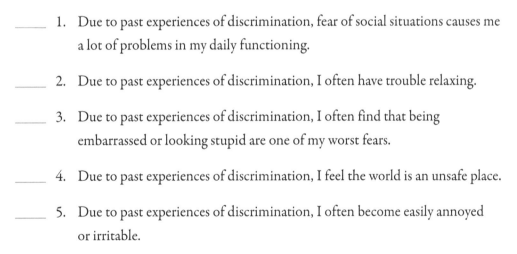

_____ 1. Due to past experiences of discrimination, fear of social situations causes me a lot of problems in my daily functioning.

_____ 2. Due to past experiences of discrimination, I often have trouble relaxing.

_____ 3. Due to past experiences of discrimination, I often find that being embarrassed or looking stupid are one of my worst fears.

_____ 4. Due to past experiences of discrimination, I feel the world is an unsafe place.

_____ 5. Due to past experiences of discrimination, I often become easily annoyed or irritable.

Screening for possible trauma symptoms is a worthwhile exercise when clients indicate that they have experienced a particularly upsetting racist event or events. The pain of persistent discrimination accumulates over time, and when clinicians can diagnose race-related trauma, the prognosis for their African American client is improved in ways that the client may not have imagined possible.

When Being "Strong" Can Be an Issue

As I discussed in chapter 1, Black folks often subscribe to a "superhero" coping style where they endure their struggles quietly. This is especially prevalent in Black women. However, I am intentionally hesitant to dwell on the "Strong Black Woman Schema" or "Superwoman" phenomenon as a concern. For one, this disposition among Black women has been protective and adaptive in a hostile society, and I'm not keen on pathologizing strengths. Second, while many women are beginning to recognize that they are taking on too much with little to no regard for their well-being, I doubt many would actually show up for therapy to address this reality. Given my first concern, it could be best to leave it be. Because we're addressing conceptualization, however, and the language of "being strong" resonates with so many Black women, let's discuss.

For many Black women, being "strong" is synonymous with being a Black woman. Despite both racism and sexism, Black women are assigned to overcome and succeed against all odds, take care of everyone else, and resist showing emotions or vulnerability (by not asking for help). This kind of strength is noble, but it has been linked to symptoms of anxiety and depression. Consider this continued conversation with the 41-year-old single mom I introduced in chapter 1. Recall that in the session, she indicated that she would be a bad mom if she took shortcuts:

THERAPIST: Who told you that you'd be a bad mom if you were to take some shortcuts to catch your breath a bit?

CLIENT: It's just understood. My grandmother worked hard and put herself last while she took care of her younger sisters and brothers growing up, and then later her own children. Then my mom worked hard as a nurse and also at home. My dad worked too, but my mom did it all for my brothers and me. It's just how it is.

THERAPIST: I understand that you feel it is important to be there for everyone. There has been a long history of sacrifice in your family, including sacrifices so that you could be successful. Is there any part of you that wishes things could be different somehow?

CLIENT: Yes, but it's also not fair for me to complain.

THERAPIST: Okay, tell me more about that. What would complaining look like?

CLIENT: Well, I'd be acting like I'm ungrateful for all of the sacrifices that have been made.

THERAPIST: Are you ungrateful . . . or are you just tired?

CLIENT: Good question.

We'll talk more about this in the next chapter, but notice that the therapist attempts to find evidence for the client's assertion that she is ungrateful. More importantly, the therapist reminds the client of what brought her to therapy (i.e., the feeling that she is running herself into the ground). They will have to work together to figure out how to maintain the delicate balance between what it means to be who she is as a strong Black woman and how she will maintain her sanity while doing so.

A Word on Sharing the Diagnosis

In any of these circumstances, you may wonder whether it is helpful to share your evaluation, your diagnosis, or whatever you're trying to uncover with your client. If the information is an unnecessary distraction and the client will be disturbed in assuming they have some deficit, why not withhold that information? I can understand your reasoning. And of course, I leave the decision to you, but I will say this: Always remember the context. If your client is someone who has overcome, or is overcoming, mistrust of white people or anyone who isn't Black, but they *find out* that you've been "treating" them for depression, it won't look good. At best, you'll have to do some "repair" work. At worst, they could leave therapy altogether with evidence that white people cannot be trusted. Again, that is up for you to decide. By sharing the diagnosis, you can demonstrate that you can be trusted with tough conversations and that you won't take the easy road. Also, if you make a good effort at psychoeducation, your client will be better informed in knowing to how to address their symptoms if they recur in the future.

I suspect that some people resist going to therapy for the same reason they avoid seeing a primary care physician: avoidance of bad news. Understandably, we all prefer the good news to the bad—"bad news" meaning a potentially scary diagnosis or a necessary commitment to change. But if a client is seeing a professional for some strain or distress, the odds are pretty good that they will get some undesirable news. The news will warrant some lifestyle changes that they will be asked to deal with on top of everyday life. None of this is easy. Most would rather just leave well enough alone. However, a devoted therapist can make the effort much more manageable.

Chapter 6

Cognitive Behavioral Therapy without Challenging Racism

It may not seem fair to have to think about things differently for various groups of clients. After all, humans are humans. However, humans are also enormously complex. In the same way that biological siblings who grow up in the same home are often very different from one another, differences show up among all groups and subgroups of humankind. And while the principle of unconditional love applies to the parenting of all children, the day-to-day practice of the principle can look somewhat different depending on the needs of the child. The same is true for psychotherapy.

As I indicated in chapter 1, I comfortably subscribe to the tenets of CBT in my therapeutic work. What resonates most for me with CBT is its emphasis on the present and the client's acquisition of new skills that empower them to take control in the moment. With CBT, clients learn to connect how their present-moment thoughts impact their mood and behavior. Cognitive behavioral therapies are the most empirically supported transdiagnostic interventions. While I know there are some clients for whom CBT is less effective, it's not lost on me that CBT has inspired other more refined, highly effective interventions, including dialectical behavior therapy (DBT) and cognitive processing therapy (CPT) for PTSD, in addition to being adapted for children, couples, workplace stress, and myriad other counseling needs.

When clients are ready for change, CBT elevates their awareness of nonproductive thought patterns. We can all benefit from this peak awareness. And when someone's old cognitive scripts wear off or become harmful, changing their thought process is a solid place to begin. Unfortunately, CBT can't be approached haphazardly for a community of people who are subjected to regular, systemic, and individual mistreatment. While there are circumstances in which direct cognitive restructuring makes sense, there are others where you want to take a more cautious and circuitous route.

So often, the response to reports of mistreatment is that we, as Black people, are "too sensitive" or that the other person "didn't mean it that way," which effectively dismisses our legitimate reality. Even when there are situations to which we seemingly overrespond, that response does not negate the existence and impact of systemic oppression. When there is unfairness in so many aspects of life lurking around too many trauma corners, how sensitive is too sensitive? I digress, but only because this particular elephant in the therapy room—a defensive posture that dismisses a client's reaction, or their assertion of mistreatment, as oversensitivity—is an all-too-common escape hatch and a sure way to undermine effective work with a Black client.

In this chapter, I will walk you through the process of using CBT strategies without minimizing the very real impact of racism and instead embracing the client's cultural preferences. Helping your client shift their pattern of interpreting daily circumstances is foundational to this cognitive work. Nevertheless, you can engage in cognitive work without being skittish about persistent oppression.

Begin at the Beginning

In the first session, you should of course mention your theoretical approach with your new client. Assuming that you primarily adopt CBT principles in your practice, let them know what CBT actually looks like in session, how it works, and the mystery that will unfold. Doing so goes a long way, especially for those who may have been misinformed or are suspicious about therapy. A specific statement might look as follows:

> In the work that I do, we acknowledge that our emotions are connected to our thoughts. When we change our thoughts, we can better manage our feelings and behaviors. As an example, some people minimize the good and positive in their lives. It's not intentional, which is why it's important to first become aware of

our thoughts and how they affect us so that we can make adjustments that have an impact on both our mood and what happens as a consequence of that mood. Taking this approach doesn't excuse disrespectful people or unfair situations around you. Instead, it allows you to take better control of how you're managing potentially stressful situations.

I also love the approach that many CBT-oriented therapists use, which begins with the example of "Imagine you're walking down the street, and you see someone you know and you wave to them, but they don't wave back or respond in any way. What thoughts come to mind?" I haven't met a client yet who couldn't share both their adaptive (i.e., they didn't see me) and maladaptive (i.e., they were ignoring me) thoughts about the situation and connect these thoughts to how they feel. The scenario truly resonates with clients and creates much-needed buy-in. One place that I may deviate from some CBT therapists is that I emphasize the difference between *helpful* and *unhelpful* thoughts, rather than labeling the latter as "cognitive errors" or "maladaptive thinking." I much prefer to avoid pathologizing—and certainly judging—a client's thinking as erroneous.

Though I value thought records and encourage clients to complete them between sessions, I aim to use this chapter to demonstrate how a therapist can use different strategies to elicit thoughts, engage in Socratic questioning for intentional disputation, and produce more helpful or adaptive evaluations, given presumed unfair treatment. I'll do so by revisiting select scenarios from previous chapters. You may have observed in previous chapters that I started down a CBT path of inquiry in the case vignettes but didn't follow through with strategies for the clients. In this chapter, I'll pick up where I left off, beginning with the disturbing shopping scenario, followed by the overwhelmed mom of two, the frustrated renter whose application was denied, and the single mom who was afraid of taking shortcuts.

Cognitive Restructuring with an Unsuspecting Shopper

Remember the 32-year-old shopper from chapter 2? I discussed the situation in the context of the therapist taking time to understand and affirm the client's experience before attempting to "see all sides" when the client was seemingly accused of shoplifting.

If you'll recall, the client asked a presumably rhetorical question of "why can't people just mind their own business?" Since the client had met her therapy goals related to depression and anxiety, she had transitioned to learning anger management skills, which is the focus of this sixth session. When the therapist asks how homework went, the client suggests that it didn't go so well because she got angry in the store. Let's pick up where the client is in recounting her thoughts of the situation:

CLIENT: I should be able to shop in peace without people making racist assumptions about me.

THERAPIST: I agree. That was an awful situation, especially at a time when you needed to do something that would lift your mood in the midst of your heavy workload.

CLIENT: Exactly! But when that happened, I felt so angry! I feel angry now just thinking about it. I wanted to go off on that store clerk and the other shopper.

THERAPIST: What kept you from going off as you wanted to?

CLIENT: I just didn't want to create *more* problems. These are the kinds of situations where people end up calling the police because they feel "threatened." Meanwhile, I was the one who was minding my business. I felt threatened! But no one was there for me. Black people have to put up with this stuff all the time. Those people ruined my peace.

Let's pause for a moment to acknowledge two possible cognitive distortions—one is more explicit while the other is implied. The first is the use of "should," as in "I should be able to shop in peace." Note that the therapist did not respond to this because the timing would have been in poor form. However, making note of the distortion, especially given that the client has awareness of it by session 6, is fair to do.

The second distortion is the seeming magnification the client is making in stating that the store clerk and the other shopper "ruined her peace." Though the therapist must tread lightly, CBT interventions do not have to go out the window in circumstances that are grossly unfair and racist. The goal is to affirm the client and empower them. As I have said before, racism is going nowhere. This is why it is immensely important for a therapist to leverage their rapport with the client to help the client take back their power. On the therapist's own time and in the interest of social justice advocacy, they can send a letter to the store manager or corporate office as a concerned citizen who "overhead a situation at Store #XYZ wherein the clerk was mistreating an African American shopper." (By the way, don't tell the client about your social justice efforts to win favor with them. We'll discuss that in chapter 10.)

THERAPIST: [*pausing*] You said this already and I can see it now—that the frustration about all of it is still with you. You've been doing your best to ignore it, but the pain and frustration are still there.

CLIENT: Yeah . . .

THERAPIST: Is part of your anger that you didn't do or say something else in the moment?

CLIENT: Probably. As I think about this now, it is infuriating that they didn't see the harm that would be done to me by their carelessness. Black people always have to be in defense mode. I deserve to be treated as a human being just like anyone else. And I have to deal with this stuff on top of getting my real work done! It's like having two jobs. And Lord knows I'm too tired and too anxious for two jobs.

At this point, the therapist continues the conversation by first affirming the persistence of the client's struggle and bringing awareness to her effort to counter racism. The therapist also brings the client into the present moment to lower her heightened level of distress.

THERAPIST: You're putting in a good deal of work to navigate the racism and prejudice around you *and* keep your mind intact.

CLIENT: I don't really feel like I have another choice.

THERAPIST: I see that as you describe these infuriating situations. On a scale from 0–10, what would you say is your level of hurt and frustration about this situation?

CLIENT: It's easily a 9.

THERAPIST: That's high. If it's okay with you, I want to pause for a moment to revisit your progressive muscle relaxation.

CLIENT: I haven't been on top of that at all.

THERAPIST: That's fine. This is the type of situation when you would want to use progressive muscle relaxation. We made progress with your anxiety over the last few months, so let's take a few minutes to practice. [*talks client through a series of tensing and relaxing muscles*]

THERAPIST: What would you say is your rating now?

CLIENT: It's about a 5.

THERAPIST: Good. You can try to remember to first lower your feelings of frustration and hurt in those moments when you are most upset . . . [*pausing*] in part, because there is something else that you want to attend to . . .

CLIENT: What's that?

THERAPIST: The thought that you have to be in defense mode (if I heard you right) and the behavior that goes with it may be escalating your anxiety and subsequent fatigue. You mentioned several aspects of the situation that were upsetting—that you wish the other shopper minded their business, that they ruined your peace, that you felt threatened, and that no one was there for you. As you think about the situation at the store, what was most upsetting about it for you?

CLIENT: All of it . . . all of it together was too much.

THERAPIST: That's fair. It was and still is very overwhelming. [*pausing*] When you said the other shopper "ruined your peace," say more about that.

CLIENT: I already see where you're going with this, but in that moment, I was minding my business when this unexpected nosy Karen interrupted my flow. But as I look back, she didn't ruin all of my peace. She did get *a lot* of it though!

THERAPIST: Sadly, these routine experiences of racism mean that each encounter is potentially more painful and more infuriating than the last because they basically pile on top of one another. They aren't individual situations. You feel the *accumulating* burden of racism. [*pausing to let it sink in*]

CLIENT: Yeah. I do. For a moment, I felt consumed by anger at that lady.

THERAPIST: That's understandable. You said you felt consumed . . . for a moment. Did you tell me already how the situation ended?

CLIENT: Ugh. We had a short standoff and then I walked away and out the store. I couldn't say anything because I didn't want to lose my composure, so I left. I sat in my car for a while because I needed to calm down. I was so angry I was shaking. I did some of my deep breathing to help calm myself. Once I stopped shaking, I went back to work.

THERAPIST: You went to work?

CLIENT: Yeah. I still had deadlines.

THERAPIST: After a really very upsetting situation, you redirected yourself to work.

CLIENT: Yes.

THERAPIST: Were you able to make progress on your deadlines?

CLIENT: Some . . . but not much. Honestly, I think I was way too upset.

THERAPIST: That was an honorable thing that you did. In fact, you did several honorable things.

CLIENT: Like what?

THERAPIST: First, you started with excellent intentions for self-care by taking yourself shopping in what was supposed to be a short but restorative time out. In the midst of the chaos, you removed yourself from the situation and engaged in some deep breathing. All of that is important to acknowledge. It didn't go your way, but you were investing in yourself in a way that you probably wouldn't have just three months ago, right?

CLIENT: You're right [*looking somewhat pleased*].

THERAPIST: Also, you said your anger management activity didn't go well, but it sounds like it went better than you gave yourself credit for.

CLIENT: How so?

THERAPIST: Your task was to pay attention to when you get angry and how you manage it so that we can come up with strategies. In the instance you described, you were ahead of the game! You walked away from the situation, you didn't lose control, and you went to your car to use your skills—*away* from people who antagonized you. Given how bad the situation was, I think you handled yourself better than you could have imagined.

CLIENT: You know what? You're right! Another me might have gotten into a shouting match. I hate when I lose control.

THERAPIST: Exactly. How does it feel to give yourself credit?

CLIENT: It feels good.

THERAPIST: There are a couple other things that I want to check in with you about because I think you could give yourself a bit more grace if you address some of your unhelpful thoughts.

CLIENT: Okay.

THERAPIST: You mentioned that the situation ruined your peace.

CLIENT: Yes.

THERAPIST: As you think back to what you were able to accomplish in that very upsetting situation, and give yourself credit for what you did . . . are you able to reclaim a bit of your peace?

CLIENT: I'm not sure.

THERAPIST: The alternative is to say that the clerk and the other shopper have access to your peace. [*pausing*] But how did they get access?

CLIENT: That's an interesting question. I didn't give it to them. And it was their ignorance that made them behave the way they did.

THERAPIST: I agree. They created a situation and tried to steal your peace of mind and your goal for the afternoon. Just a little while ago, you were heated as you thought about it. As you think about it all now, what goes through your mind?

CLIENT: I think about how I bet they felt really small when I left.

THERAPIST: The smallest! And for you, because as you said, "Black people deal with this stuff all the time," if and when you encounter something like this, what do you envision yourself doing?

CLIENT: I'll give them a piece of my mind so they know how ridiculous their racism is, and I'll walk off, go to my car and practice my progressive muscle relaxation, and maybe even reach out to a friend.

THERAPIST: That sounds like a good plan. And if you're in therapy when that happens, we can discuss it here too.

Notice that the therapist arrived at a point where they not only affirmed and normalized the client's anger and pain, but they also highlighted the client's use of skills when the client lost track of them. It is always impactful for the therapist to *amplify* the client's skill use and empower the client. The therapist also doesn't need to rush through these types of conversations. It may be the case that a client never shares an experience of discrimination with their non-Black therapist, perhaps because they do not expect to have a meaningful conversation with a therapist who is presumed not to relate. As an African American person who happens to be a psychologist, I guarantee you that when a therapist can relate to the cognitive and emotional burden of racism, it is quite easy to devote a full session to unpacking a client's racist encounter with a self-deputized store shopper. The eventual goal is to:

- Hear the client through
- Help them understand the myriad ways in which they were affected
- Flush out all their cognitions
- Connect the client's thoughts and feelings to their presenting problem

- Highlight the client's strengths (remember there are always strengths present to acknowledge)

- Leverage skills that the client has learned in therapy and can benefit from in therapy

A Brief Commentary on "Should"

I previously commented on the client's use of "should" as a cognitive distortion. I have a strong aversion to this word, given the unnecessary and added distress that it adds to any situation. I chastise my doctoral student advisees, and especially my clinical students, whenever they say it because if they cannot mindfully substitute the phrase "it would be helpful" in place of "should," then how can they expect their clients to do so? I have never encountered a scenario in which "it would be helpful" wasn't a sufficient substitute to avoid the shame of "shoulding on" oneself or "shoulding on" other people and creating unnecessary resentment. "Should" limits the opportunities for cognitive flexibility.

Philosophically, there *shouldn't* be racism, but the reality is that racism exists whether it should or not. Several years ago, a popular syndicated radio show personality stumped me briefly during an interview. He insisted, "You shouldn't smoke crack, right"? My response (after an extended moment of disarticulation) was that it would be *helpful* if you didn't smoke crack. If we accept that someone smokes crack, we create space to begin to problem solve with the addicted individual. What drove them to smoke crack? How can we remove the dependence from their life? To be sure, I'm not suggesting that we create solutions for racists. On the contrary, we make room for the client to decide how they can protect their emotional health *in spite of* racism rather than getting stuck in a "should pit."

Behavioral Components of CBT for the Mom Who Does It All

Recall the 35-year-old overwhelmed mother of two who I first introduced in chapter 1 and revisited in chapter 5. She presented as "feeling overwhelmed all the time" and eventually got to a point in therapy where she could acknowledge that she was experiencing symptoms of depression. Note that one dimension of her depression is anhedonia—that is, a lack of interest and inability to experience pleasure, including in activities that she once enjoyed. I raise this point because of the behavioral aspect of CBT. This client described being active in a number or organizations due to her belief that she "should" engage in numerous activities, despite the fact that she got very limited joy from doing so.

THERAPIST: Based on what you have shared thus far, it seems a primary driver of what's been going on for you is a lot of investment in obligations that give you limited joy—and maybe not enough commitment to what does bring you joy.

CLIENT: I can see that.

THERAPIST: Is there any part of this description that doesn't quite fit?

CLIENT: Well, all of it is important, so I'm not sure where to start.

THERAPIST: Well, our next step is to figure out where we want to begin. As I understand it, you're having problems falling asleep. You suffer from headaches several days per week and are feeling generally overwhelmed. Is there anything else?

CLIENT: No, I think that's it.

THERAPIST: And how often are these headaches happening?

CLIENT: At least once a week—sometimes twice.

THERAPIST: Okay, let's start to track when your headaches are happening if you don't already know.

CLIENT: They seem random to be honest.

THERAPIST: Okay, when you feel a headache coming on, I want you to make note of the date, the day of the week, the time of day, the circumstances, what your specific involvement is in what you're doing at the moment, as well as what you were doing fifteen minutes before the headache started. That's six things that you'll want to jot down now. You'll have to use a note app in your phone to track.

CLIENT: Yes, I can do that.

THERAPIST: Great. And you'll want to use the same app each time, and we'll discuss it in our next session, okay?

CLIENT: Okay, that works for me.

THERAPIST: Great. Let's shift a bit. What do you do that you genuinely enjoy, just for you?

CLIENT: I like to spend time with friends, but everyone is always so busy.

THERAPIST: Yes, that's understandable, especially if your friends have similar lifestyles to you?

CLIENT: [*chuckling*] Yeah, they all probably need to be in therapy, too!

THERAPIST: Ah, touché! Can you begin by setting a date one month from today for when you and your friends can get together for a happy hour? Does that seem feasible?

CLIENT: Yeah, I can do that.

THERAPIST: Great. What's something you can do right now to ensure that happens?

CLIENT: I can make a note to call one of our favorite restaurants to make a reservation.

THERAPIST: That sounds perfect. Is there anything that would keep you from following through on this plan?

CLIENT: No, I can do this! I'm feeling excited.

THERAPIST: Great. Now, what is something that you enjoy that isn't contingent on other people's schedules or availability?

CLIENT: I like to read fiction.

THERAPIST: That sounds nice. What do you like about reading fiction?

CLIENT: It kind of takes me away from the humdrum of my life.

THERAPIST: That seems like a worthwhile activity. On a 0–10 scale, with 0 being the lowest and 10 being the highest amount of joy you can possibly imagine, how much joy would you say that you get from reading fiction?

CLIENT: I'd say a 9.

THERAPIST: Wow. When was the last time you read any fiction?

CLIENT: Well, last year, I started a book, but I didn't finish it. I don't know what happened. I still have the book.

THERAPIST: Was the book interesting?

CLIENT: I think it had a slow start. Maybe that's why it was easy for me to put it down and not go back to it.

THERAPIST: That's understandable. Do you have a favorite author who you can check to see if they have any new books that have been released? Maybe you can even check now while we're here.

CLIENT: Yes, I can definitely do that.

THERAPIST: Okay, think of some of your favorite authors so you can start your search.

CLIENT: Oh wow, my absolute favorite author has a book that was just released last month! I'm ordering it now.

THERAPIST: That's wonderful to hear. Honestly, I haven't seen you smile like this . . . ever.

CLIENT: I'm really excited about getting the new book.

THERAPIST: I'm happy for you. I also think it's important for you to sit with this feeling you have. You deserve more of this in your life. We didn't do anything magical other than take some time for you to think about what you truly enjoy and find ways for you to get back to those sources of joy. You deserve that.

CLIENT: I agree. It's just so easy for life to take over.

THERAPIST: That's true. And that's why you resist the urge to engage in something you enjoy or do nothing at all. Even if only one friend shows up, will you enjoy the time with her? [*pointing out the client's tendency to engage in all-or-nothing thinking*]

CLIENT: Absolutely. I love my friends.

THERAPIST: I can see how much you smile as you think of them. You have control over what you can control. Take small steps like making a note to schedule a reservation. Then let your friends know that you have a reservation.

CLIENT: I can definitely do that.

THERAPIST: I know you can. And with your book—and anything else you enjoy but haven't committed yourself to doing—take small steps. Think about what barriers have kept you from engaging in the activity. Since we know that "slow" books will stunt your reading, you might want to get your hands on a couple of books that get your attention on the first page so you have one ready to go just in case!

CLIENT: I like that idea. I could also go to the library. I used to love going to the library. I can go and read the first few pages in the Black fiction section and check out the most interesting books so I save money.

THERAPIST: This sounds like a wonderful plan. I look forward to chatting next week about how it goes. By the way, on what day will you go to the library?

CLIENT: Friday . . . I'll go Friday before I pick my girls up from school.

In this scenario, the therapist used guided discovery and 0–10 ratings to highlight the imbalance in the activities the client feels like she "should" be doing and the activities that actually bring her joy. The therapist also helped the client anticipate and respond to any potential barriers that could arise by starting with small, manageable goals in session.

To help further counter the client's tendency to "should" on herself, the therapist could also point out the (unlikely) value of self-sacrificing so much for the community: The client leaves very little of herself to be of use to the community or anyone else. Once the therapist gets better insight into the client's headaches, the therapist may want to revisit the case conceptualization as well. If they discover a particular pattern of stressors, they can target those stressors, thereby creating an even more tailored approach to the client's therapy goals. In all, the strategy that allows the client to improve her quality of life will be most effective in achieving all of her goals.

What About Blatant Racism?

Recall the scenario in chapter 2 where the client found out, shortly before going into session, that his apartment application was denied. The client presumed that this happened because he was Black. Assume that the outcome indeed occurred because the client is Black. In this situation, it is helpful to genuinely affirm the client's experience and use guided discovery to understand the encounter from his perspective, highlighting any notable alternative thoughts. At the end of the day, the goal is for the client to manage his thoughts without having to repress them or triggering panic symptoms.

THERAPIST: Given that the realtor was easygoing and energetic in all of your other communications, I can see how you would deduce that being a Black man was the only reason for her shift in attitude leading to your application being denied.

CLIENT: It's just frustrating because I got through all of the online stages of the application process. There was no new information, and the only thing that changed was her meeting me in person.

THERAPIST: Is it safe to say that if your application was approved, her shift would not have mattered so much?

CLIENT: Well, I would have still wondered why she was acting so differently. I mean, I assumed it was because she was surprised that I was a Black man. It's not unusual. People can't tell my race over the phone. I'm also sure it doesn't help that I'm a big guy. Either way, I wouldn't still be thinking about it, and I'm pretty sure I wouldn't be having this conversation with you if I were approved. I mean, do you think there could be another reason that she was being so standoffish?

THERAPIST: We can't be sure, but it sounds like that thought maybe entered your mind.

CLIENT: Maybe, I don't know. I'd rather put it behind me and not let it fester.

THERAPIST: I see. [*pausing*] But it's festering a bit?

CLIENT: It is!

THERAPIST: That's understandable. You mentioned that you wouldn't be so frustrated if the application had gone your way. That means that you would have drawn other conclusions about how the realtor interacted toward you?

CLIENT: Well, yeah. Maybe she was just having a bad day for some reason. Maybe she was feeling unwell. Maybe she was just surprised that I was a large Black person and she pictured me differently, so it was awkward. That still makes her behavior racist, but I get that all the time. It would be easier to blow off if it didn't have very real consequences for me having a place to live.

THERAPIST: Yes, at the end of the day, your life has been negatively affected by the situation. What's piled on top is that you cannot control who you are and that you may have a case of housing discrimination.

CLIENT: Exactly.

THERAPIST: Is it worth considering legal action?

CLIENT: I hadn't thought of that, but I doubt it. Discrimination is impossible to prove. I don't have the energy for it.

THERAPIST: That's understandable . . . Well, maybe we can think of another way to lighten the load of it all.

CLIENT: How so?

THERAPIST: When you found yourself thinking of the possibility of the realtor having a bad day, how did that make you feel?

CLIENT: Somewhat better. The weight of it all felt less heavy.

THERAPIST: Maybe that's the approach—that when it all feels too heavy, you consider that there may be circumstances of which you are unaware. Doing so might give you time to exhale a bit.

CLIENT: I can try that. At the end of the day, I don't have the apartment and either she or the landlord is racist. But I need to be able to move forward, put in another application, and find a place to live.

THERAPIST: Yes, you still have a big task ahead of you. But in the end, you will likely have less overall anxiety. There was probably a time that you might have had a panic attack associated with this situation. If you find yourself revisiting this other situation, you can reframe your thoughts so you don't get derailed by them.

CLIENT: I can do that.

The therapist effectively acknowledged both sides of the scenario—that the realtor may have been racist and that there may have been other reasons for her behavior. In reality, both could be true. What is most important for the client-therapist relationship is that the client felt heard and was allowed the space to consider his next steps (including possible legal action). From a CBT perspective, he has new tools to navigate both the current and future encounters of racial prejudice and also non-racially instigated situations. Finally, it is notable that the therapist highlighted the client's growth in that he didn't have a panic attack. Clients often overlook their successes. Because the therapist balanced sensitivity to the client's experience with the importance of gaining empowering new tools, they were able to move the needle considerably toward the client's therapy goals.

CBT Can Coexist with Deeply Held Cultural Values

Anecdotally, I have heard African Americans speculate that therapy will make them different (with the difference being more like white people). Given how our lived experiences are often absent from the mainstream at best—or maligned at worst—there is no reason to trust that something developed by white people will have any benefit for those who identify as Black or African American. What we *do* know is that our connection to our community values is the root of how we have survived for generations. There's no reason to give up sources of strength and survival.

Some of the survival strategies, however, can use a bit of tweaking. Others simply need to be affirmed and expanded. As an example, many Black folks insist on sustaining family legacies of sacrifice and hard work. This is a noble enterprise. Family support is absolutely invaluable. However, circumstances have changed for many contemporary families who don't have extended family support. As a therapist, you can affirm the client's devotion to family while also suggesting changes that recognize how the client may have more financial resources but fewer human resources when it comes to childcare. Many would benefit from novel approaches to creating networks of support, but they too often lose sight of this need while struggling alone and managing overwhelm.

For example, in chapter 1, I introduced you to the 41-year-old single mom who felt as if she was failing as a mother. You were reintroduced to her in chapter 5 in the context of the strong Black woman, where the therapist suggested that she take some "shortcuts" with her parenting responsibilities to give herself some breathing room. The therapist also started to question whether she is ungrateful for her life or whether she is simply tired. Here, the therapist continues the conversation by guiding the client to reframe her experience at every opportunity and not taking for granted that the client has her life all figured out:

THERAPIST: Are you ungrateful . . . or are you just tired?

CLIENT: Good question.

THERAPIST: Let's take a step back to consider the big picture. On the one hand, you value your role as a mother—you value all of the sacrifices your mother and grandmother made for you, and it makes sense for you to pay it all forward. On the other hand, you'd like a break but don't see that option.

CLIENT: Yes. I don't get to opt out even if I am tired.

THERAPIST: Tell me more about that.

CLIENT: I'm not sure what you mean. I'm tired, but I can push through. Others have done it, and without complaining.

THERAPIST: I see. And you think they would want the same for you—to push through exhausted and without complaint?

CLIENT: I don't know.

THERAPIST: Let's think about this for a moment. On a 0–10 scale, with 0 being no fatigue and 10 being as much fatigue as you can possibly imagine, how tired would you say you are on an average day?

CLIENT: On an average day, about 7.5.

THERAPIST: Okay, 7.5. So that means that you rarely or never have a day without fatigue, but you definitely have days when your fatigue peaks at 10?

CLIENT: Yes, definitely. By Friday, I'm done, but on Saturday we have piano and soccer to get to.

THERAPIST: Sit with this for just a moment. Think about a typical Friday when you're looking ahead to Saturday and consider how you're feeling. Think about how your body is feeling. [*pausing*] Consider the thoughts that go through your mind. [*pausing a bit longer*] Do you think your mother or grandmother would want this for you?

CLIENT: No. They wouldn't. They would say they worked as hard as they did so that I could have a better life. This isn't really it. I have a lot going for me. I have a good job, but something isn't adding up.

THERAPIST: I think you may be on to something. And what's not adding up is that you may be doing a lot to live up to what was done for you when maybe you have to give yourself permission to do things a bit differently.

CLIENT: I'm not even sure what that looks like.

THERAPIST: Can you begin by not calling yourself a "bad mom" if you do some things differently?

CLIENT: Maybe.

THERAPIST: What would keep you from saying "I'm a mom doing my best to keep my sanity" rather than "I'm a bad mom"?

CLIENT: I just don't want to shortchange my children.

THERAPIST: What would "shortchanging" them look like?

CLIENT: Well, not allowing them to have opportunities that I had.

THERAPIST: I see. One thing that I may not have a sense of is how your family managed your activities when you were growing up. If I recall correctly, you had a lot of aunts and uncles around when you and your brother were growing up in Philadelphia?

CLIENT: We did! And I also feel bad that my kids don't have a lot of cousins around.

THERAPIST: Right. You had a large extended family. And is it safe to say that your family took part in raising you and your brother—that you spent time at their homes and that they helped get you to activities on the weekends?

CLIENT: Yes. And I see where you are going with this. My mom had extended family around to help, but I'm doing it all by myself.

THERAPIST: Well, I wasn't so sure. But it sounds like you've had a realization?

CLIENT: Well, I might be overcompensating for what my children don't have that I had and also trying to do it all by myself. No wonder I'm tired.

THERAPIST: No wonder you're tired. [*pausing*] So maybe we can talk about having your children spend time with other kids and friends and create a community so that you reallocate some of your time to resting. How does that sound?

CLIENT: That sounds really good.

Note that the therapist acknowledges the client's circumstances with guided discovery, using a process of open-ended inquiry and taking into consideration the client's values and therapy goals to gain new insight. Notice that the solution will include creating community. There are likely other moms who are feeling similarly and who could be involved in alternating pickup and drop-off.

The exchanges in each of these scenarios may seem small but will have a considerable impact for the client, who is not only dealing with feelings of worthlessness, worry, anhedonia, and hopelessness but also attempting to maintain sanity in an insane world. The therapist may be tasked with sorting through discriminatory encounters—as well as deeply held cultural beliefs—in order to meet therapy goals. I advise trainees that regardless of what "challenge du jour" your client brings to session, you can find a way to connect it to the concern that first brought them to therapy. If it's not obvious in the moment, the answer will eventually emerge. You can focus on client goals while also giving them opportunities to discuss recent events. CBT provides a useful framework for engaging a client-centered perspective.

CBT Is Not for Everyone

Though modern-day CBT has considerable advantages, especially when compared to first-wave approaches that focused exclusively on behaviors in absence of cognitions, it has some challenges. First, CBT presumes that there is an objective reality with universal truths (Lyddon & Weill, 1997). Too often, it relies on pathologizing the individual and ascribing cognitive deficits to those who fail to embrace "reality." Though there is tremendous opportunity to shape CBT so it has utility regardless of a client's cultural background, it defaults to the Eurocentric, male-dominated cultural worldview. As Lyddon and Weill argue, it is important for CBT practitioners to develop greater appreciation for clients' sociocultural contexts; better account for gender, culture, and other aspects of clients' lived realities; and build empowerment into strategies for change. Rather than generating new ways for clients to conform to an unapproving society, you want to connect them more adaptively to their own cultural milieu.

Second, because CBT is so present- and individual-focused, it often fails to account for underlying or historical causes of mental distress. Despite efforts by scholar-clinicians such as Dr. Jacqueline Persons (2012) to integrate a client's early experiences and social learning history into their case conceptualization, psychosocial factors that contribute to a client's contemporary schema may be minimized or overlooked altogether with CBT. As an example, although African Americans are disproportionately burdened by adverse childhood experiences (ACEs) that warrant culturally informed interventions (Bernard et al., 2021), a client's history of ACEs may be slow to surface in individual therapy. If a client has been in therapy to address present-day challenges and is ready to shift to the deeper work of addressing childhood trauma and dysfunctional environments, CBT may have limited effectiveness. Therefore, once a client has mastered the skill of reframing unhelpful thoughts, tackling deep core beliefs, and making subsequent behavioral changes, they may benefit from transferring to a therapist who can address persistent emotional pain that is tied to childhood events.

Third, the emphasis that CBT places on cognitive restructuring can result in rebound effects, seeing as long-held cognitions can be understandably resistant to change. As a result, other types of therapies such as ACT have emerged, in which the goal is not to challenge unhelpful thoughts but to accept them as part of life. In one of our most transformative client cases, a therapist worked with a woman in her fifties who came to our clinic after having dedicated years to therapy. She was well-versed in CBT vernacular but sought us out because she was unable to navigate her depressive episode with CBT strategies. After three sessions, the therapist concluded that the client could gain relief via ACT, which would permit her unhelpful thoughts to exist with her more adaptive thoughts and without judgment as long as she was living a valued life. Though CBT is effective for some, you must consider other empirically supported approaches for those who have mastered CBT but encounter persistent challenges to their emotional health.

In most cases, though, the benefits of CBT outweigh the challenges, including for African Americans. For example, the research shows that CBT is generally more effective than medication alone (Hofmann et al., 2012); this provides a useful sales pitch for African American clients, given that medical institutions are often associated with harmful systemic racism and that medication isn't trusted in the Black community. CBT is much more accessible.

What Is Culturally Adapted CBT?

A culturally adapted intervention is one that considers "language, culture, and context in such a way that it is compatible with the client's cultural patterns, meanings, and values" (Bernal et al., 2009, p. 362). There are eight dimensions (some of which overlap) for adapting treatment: language, persons, metaphors, content area, concepts, goals, methods, and context. These components provide a framework for the therapist to provide culturally meaningful treatment. The following table provides a summary of treatment adaptations based on the approach outlined by Dr. Guillermo Bernal and his colleagues (2009).

Language	Translating to the speaker's native language as needed (but also using language that reflects regional, inner-city, and relevant subculture) as well as attending to how the client labels their experience so that clinical intervention is most accessible
Persons	Aspiring toward a potential racial or ethnic match between the therapist and client when possible but discussing strategies for working through differences in the absence of a racial/ethnic match
Metaphors	Presenting symbols that resonate with the client—both in therapeutic interactions and in the therapist's physical environment
Content	Providing cultural information associated with the client's beliefs, values, traditions
Concepts	Setting the client's concerns in a manner that is flexible for intervention rather than problematizing cultural values (e.g., interdependence, religious foci)
Goals	Agreeing on therapy outcomes that are clinically meaningful but also consistent with the client's cultural values
Methods	Embracing culturally compatible strategies and techniques for meeting therapy goals
Context	Considering the client's nuanced background, including their educational and economic background, level of assimilation, social support, religious or spiritual beliefs, or beliefs about therapy that inform the client's life experiences

Although research has shown that culturally adapted interventions are efficacious in treating a wide range of mental health concerns in individuals from different racial and ethnic backgrounds (Miranda et al., 2005; Soto et al., 2018), there is no specific recipe for doing so due to the complexity of humans. When it comes to CBT, the primary adaptations I illustrated in this chapter involved the use of culture, which shows up in *language* preferences and specific values in *content*, *concepts*, and *goals*, as well as attention to discriminatory *contexts*.

To effectively adapt psychosocial interventions for your client, you must be able to engage in "dynamic sizing" (Sue, 1998), in which you know when to generalize cultural knowledge about a client versus when to individualize to their experience. You have to know when to integrate your client's unique personality and when to consider broader ethnic, racial, or cultural contexts. Your capacity to engage in dynamic sizing avoids relying on stereotypes. This is why you have to adopt a disposition of curiosity, taking time to understand your client's experience and venturing to test your hypotheses (based on the client's cultural beliefs) along the way. As an example, when I propose that you integrate prayer or community resources in your client's intervention, this reflects an adaptation to the client's therapy. You don't want to ignore important values that could be affecting their thinking patterns and possible solutions. But you also don't want to overattribute culture.

Unfortunately, the research on culturally adapted CBT for Black Americans is sparse. Even more, people who identify with racial and ethnic minority groups are not well represented in randomized control trials that test the efficacy of various interventions. Nevertheless, the available research suggests that tailoring your approach to your African American client is more effective than employing strategies that are not culturally sensitive (Miranda et al., 2005). In the next chapter, I will consider some approaches, but you could benefit from reviewing papers that provide a culturally sensitive perspective, such as Earlise C. Ward and Roger L. Brown's (2015) intervention for Black adults who experience depression symptoms or other texts such as Nancy Boyd-Franklin's (2006) *Black Families in Therapy*. As a licensed mental health professional, you can set your own curricular focus to provide care that is culturally informed.

Chapter 7

Spiritual and Religious Traditions Amplify Therapeutic Work

Black Americans are at a crossroads. The increase in mental health crises coupled with a modest breakdown of mental health stigma has an increasing number of Black people seeking professional help when they find the decision to just "pray about it" insufficient.

I'm glad to see it. At the same time, there is no need to throw the baby out with the bathwater. Religion and spirituality have a solid place in the toolbox of the faithful. I wholeheartedly advocate for sustaining the deep well of resilience that comes from a connection to God, Allah, one's ancestors, or any higher power that has allowed Black people to "make a way out of no way." The religious community can also be the site of strong supportive relationships. Abandoning this source of strength would be a devastating loss—it would leave out a significant component of a culture of perseverance and survival. Instead, it is your responsibility as a licensed mental health professional to integrate spirituality in therapy if it is part of a client's life and cultural identity outside of therapy.

In the previous chapter, I referenced "content area" as one of the eight options to culturally adapt therapy. Spirituality and religiosity are content areas that are not typically included in case conceptualization but that can be very useful for Black and African American clients who believe in a power greater than themselves—a power that is characterized by spirituality. Although I'll sometimes use the constructs of religiosity and spirituality together throughout this chapter, it is important to recognize that the two are related but distinct. There are many in the African American community who would say that they are spiritual but not religious. The reasons vary. Some criticize the Black church for making the community more docile and obedient rather than revolutionary in the face of oppression. Others have been emotionally harmed by religious doctrine and religious leaders. I will discuss this issue later in the chapter, but explicitly asking your African American client about their belief in a higher power will be more effective than presuming religious devotion (or not asking at all).

In my own research, I have found that religion and spirituality are generally adaptive. Anecdotally, I know that the available research does not tell the whole story. There are nuances to how each individual embraces or resists spiritual and religious beliefs, but it is important for you to be intentional about these topics. Given that some people have been mistreated by religious folks, tread lightly in case there is lingering trauma.

Historical Context of Religious and Spiritual Beliefs

A connection to a higher power is part of what it means to be a Black person in the United States and around the world. Spirituality is so ingrained in the ethos of Black culture that it's a bit like breathing air. We breathe without consciously thinking of the many ways that doing so sustains life, oxygenates blood, and removes carbon dioxide so that the body is energized. A common quip in the Black community is that "without God, I would have lost my mind a long time ago." Nevertheless, spiritually isn't consciously or intentionally leveraged as much as it could be.

Perhaps the disconnect is a natural one. That the church is so highly integrated in Black cultural grew out of necessity. African families were guided by a strong faith and a connection to God and their ancestors. Once forcibly brought to the New World, they called upon that faith and connection to survive chattel slavery and Jim Crow. During the tumultuous Civil Rights movement, churches and mosques were safe havens and also hubs for political organizing. The integral role of the Black church in the reality of Black people is well documented (Gates, 2021).

Too many of us have been tricked into thinking that we are fully disconnected from our African heritage because we've "never been to Africa." What we do not realize is the ongoing impact of legalized separation on how we see ourselves as Black people with a unique culture, creatively forcing success despite injustice in almost every aspect of life. From the arrival of the first enslaved African person to the United States in 1619 to the Jim Crow era, to legalized redlining (wherein Black people were only allowed to live in designated areas), to the Civil Rights Act of 1964 and the Voting Rights Act of 1965, Black people were legally fighting for the right to be treated fairly. That's about 346 years. Though the fight hasn't ended, it's only been 60 years or so that we have been granted legal access to our humanity. It doesn't take a genius to realize that it will take more than 60 years to overcome the deep impact of violence and historical injustice, especially when there are efforts to exclude that injustice from history books. Meanwhile, the victims of this history are also duped into acting as if generational trauma didn't happen and doesn't continue to manifest in dangerous ways.

This history is, in part, why we as Black people still see and experience a reality that is different from that of most white people. To survive the brutality of chattel slavery—wherein not just one generation was enslaved but multiple generations were born into and knew nothing but slavery—means that survival mode is ever present, and it is most often powered by spiritual connection. Even today, we live in segregated and unequal societies, but it is manageable. When there is the illusion of inclusion, the legacy of our primarily west African culture that embraces God and ancestors may be needed more than ever. It's actually quite clever if you think about it. Racism is typically unseen and thus easily denied, so having faith in the supernatural can be especially uplifting.

Spirituality and Religiosity— Not for Everyone

The Pew Research Center is an impressive source of statistics regarding religious participation in the Black community. Their findings indicate that, compared to the overall United States population (90 percent), Black Americans (97 percent) are more religious and more likely to believe in God or a higher power. Even more, African and Caribbean immigrants are more religious than Black Americans who were born in the United States (Mohamed et al., 2021).

Though these findings indicate that religious activity in the United States is common, these patterns are beginning to shift. Those born since the 1980s (i.e., Millennials and

Gen Z) are less likely to engage in religious activities, including prayer, than those born in or before the late 1960s (i.e., Gen X and older). Younger generations are also less likely to indicate that prayer is important for their lives, with approximately 20 percent identifying as agnostic or atheist. Though the causes of this religious decline are unclear, it is reflective of trends in the larger U.S. population. That younger generations are less religiously active may be due, in part, to the fact that they're less likely to grow up attending church. In contrast, more than half of Gen Z (64 percent) and baby boomer (83 percent) generations indicate in polling that they grew up in church.

Broader cultural beliefs are also connected to spirituality. For example, compared to 40 percent of the overall U.S. population, 59 percent of Black Americans believe that evil spirits can cause harm. Moreover, approximately 33 percent of Black Americans (compared to 24 percent of the U.S. population) believe that prayer can protect one from harm. The church is also a place where Black people are likely to engage in "call and response," a cultural tradition wherein the congregants respond (often with "amen") to the pastor or speaker-leader. This style of engagement is more common in the Black Protestant Church and provides of sense of familiarity and comfort that isn't experienced in non-Black churches.

Even those who are inactive in the church still believe in God and pray more frequently than those in the general U.S. population. Though there have been shifts in religious practice over the years, this relatively high level of religious participation (which also reveals hints of cultural tradition) is one way in which Black clients' daily lives may be discordant with their non-Black mental health providers.

Religious Belief and Participation Likely Buffer Mental Health Crises

Not only is religion embedded into the history of the Black community, but my research has shown that religiosity serves as a buffer against present-day experiences of racism. For example, in one study, my team and I found that perceived racism was related to thoughts of ending one's own life due to feelings of depression (Walker et al., 2014). While it makes sense that individuals who feel socially disconnected and hopeless about the future would be more vulnerable to suicidal thoughts, we found that those who reported lower levels of religiosity were *uniquely* vulnerable to such thoughts. Those who reported higher religiosity did not report thoughts of suicide, even in the midst of racial discrimination.

In another study, we attempted to unpack specific aspects of what makes religiosity helpful (Walker et al., 2017). We found that those who adopted a more self-directing coping style—meaning they believed they could take care of their problems without God—were more likely to consider suicide as their stress levels increased. Individuals with this self-directing coping style also tended to endorse a more Eurocentric worldview, as opposed to a culturally congruent Afrocentric worldview. Keep in mind that this was a sample of individuals who identified solely as Black or African American and that, as I've said, there is considerable heterogeneity in the community. Nonetheless, these findings speak to the possible impact of embracing a seemingly discordant worldview, which I'll discuss more in chapter 8. Note, too, that suicide is complex and that discrimination and stress are only two possible risk factors among many.

Given the centrality of religion and spirituality in the Black community, the therapist's role may be to balance a client's religious devotion with potential religious hindrance to ensure that their faith is indeed beneficial and amplifies their emotional well-being. At a minimum, religious practice ought not interfere with therapy progress. Since religion and spirituality are so integral to culture and identity, clients may not recognize when their faith, or their confusion about faith coexisting with therapy, can limit their progress.

To illustrate, let's revisit the 52-year-old Black male client I introduced in chapter 2 who presented to therapy primarily due to depression. In your work together, you have uncovered that his depression is due, in part, to unaddressed traumatic stress, and you have conceptualized behavioral activation as the first step in treatment, given that he doesn't get out much and is relatively isolated when he's not at work. In the previous session, you speculated that his prayer and faith practices were interfering with his planned homework. In this session, you reaffirm religion as an important cultural value to the client—working to understand and leverage the ways that prayer has helped him—while also suggesting that therapy can teach him some complementary skills to alleviate his distress:

THERAPIST: Prayer came up in our last session, and to be honest, I wondered if maybe you went to your comfort zone of praying *exclusively* and maybe that's part of why you didn't follow through on that one activity you planned.

CLIENT: I can see why you would think that. Prayer has gotten me through a lot. But honestly, I just couldn't get myself going.

THERAPIST: I see. That's understandable. We can work together to merge your prayer life with new tools, if that helps. Before we do that, I'd like to hear more about how prayer is helpful to you.

CLIENT: Well, I've prayed all my life. I learned as a child to pray to God and to be grateful for my blessings, and especially to ask for help when I need it. Since my mid-20s, I've prayed every night before bed.

THERAPIST: Every night. Since your mid-20s.

CLIENT: Yeah, I survived a bad situation. But my homeboy didn't. I know I still carry that with me—that I survived, and he didn't.

THERAPIST: And so, since that time, you've prayed . . . for continued protection or to express gratitude or something else?

CLIENT: All of the above. I know that God has been watching out for me.

THERAPIST: And you seem to have a sense of peace as you say that.

CLIENT: I do. I hadn't thought of it exactly that way, but I do have a sense of peace. And probably confidence. Whether something goes my way or not, I know God's got my back.

THERAPIST: That must be powerfully reassuring to have that certainty.

CLIENT: It really is. I don't have to worry as much. I still worry a lot, but it helps.

THERAPIST: Would you say God has your back in therapy, too?

CLIENT: I think so.

THERAPIST: [*hesitantly*] Does part of you feel . . . unsure?

CLIENT: Maybe. It's just that we don't talk about therapy at my church. Folks always say to pray and take your problems to the Lord. So I guess I feel confused at times.

THERAPIST: I follow what you're saying. Like maybe if you pray, you wouldn't have to come here.

CLIENT: Right! It's just that I'm tired of struggling and feel like it's time for me to do something different.

THERAPIST: I can appreciate that perspective. I know that there isn't a lot of discussion about mental health in the church. I imagine, however, that the pastor [*or the priest or whoever the leadership is*] would advise their church members to see a doctor for chest pains or a dentist for a prolonged toothache.

CLIENT: I agree 100 percent.

THERAPIST: Well, let's revisit how you can pray *and* follow the steps that we talked about to get yourself going.

Working with your client is always a collaborative process. *They* know how they use faith. *You* are versed in cognitive and behavioral skills. Both may be needed to get your client through a difficult time, but you also must address any uncertainty as you work together to build a comprehensive plan that integrates both behavioral activation and religious practices. The plan can include engaging the client in church-related activities, having them connect socially with others church goers, scheduling time to attend bible study, and so on.

Different Elephant—Same Room

Mental health providers tend not to be very religious (Delaney et al., 2007), which leads me to acknowledge yet another elephant in the therapy room: Most providers aren't trained to integrate spiritual and mental health into their practices. In fact, although 80 percent of licensed clinical social workers believe that their clients would benefit from integrating religious and spiritual values in therapy—and although they reported feeling competent to assess and discuss those values—they simply don't do so (Oxhandler, 2017). What this means, unfortunately, is that a tremendous part of the client's identity (faith and all) gets left at the door. However, part of providing culturally informed care is using resources that the client already has (like their faith) but may not know how to use.

Since professionals tend to be less "religious" than the larger society, it is no wonder that graduate training programs are often secular in nature, with little to no focus on the intersection between mental health and religion. This is a weakness of our training programs, given the compelling evidence on how important spirituality can be regardless of someone's racial or cultural background. Robust studies have found that religion and spirituality have a positive impact on mental and physical health (Koenig, 2009). It is a fascinating elephant that religion and religious practice are associated with health and well-being but aren't systematically included in mental health interventions.

We live in a society where people are so accustomed to hiding their true selves that we as professionals collude in this democratic insanity of hiding, and ignoring, reality. In this instance, we ignore the value of religion and its likely preexistence in many clients' toolkits. As professionals, we must first acknowledge our own values and beliefs. I have had numerous conversations with clinicians in training who are concerned that their religious beliefs could affect their interactions with their client. However, when I ask what that looks like, I often discover that their beliefs have little to no bearing on the client's distress or the clinician's treatment approach. Either way, the first step in addressing the elephant in the room is to begin with an assessment of spiritual values and beliefs.

I like the FICA Method developed by Drs. Christina Puchalski and Anna L. Romer (2000) for assessing the existence and importance of religiosity and spirituality in your client's life. It consists of four basic sets of intake questions to help you learn more about your client's spiritual history. I have found that clinicians use this tool with relative ease. The four question domains include: (1) Faith and belief, (2) Importance and influence, (3) Community, and (4) Address in care. Here, I have adapted the FICA Method for use in mental health practice, as the original text is generated for medical practice.

F: Do you consider yourself to be a spiritual or religious person? What is your faith or belief?

> *If the client answers yes, you can continue with the remaining questions. If they answer no, you might ask:*

What gives your life meaning?

> *Clients sometimes respond to this with answers such as family, close community, and careers.*

I: What importance does faith have in your life? Have your beliefs influenced the way you take care of yourself and your illness? What role do your beliefs play in improving your mental health?

C: Are you a part of a spiritual or religious community? Is this community supportive of you? And if so, how? Is there a group of people you really love or who are important to you?

> *Communities such as churches, temples, synagogues, or masjids can serve as a strong support system for some clients.*

A: How would you like me to address these issues in your mental health care?

> *I especially like this last question, as it facilitates collaboration that is necessary for successful CBT.*

Using the FICA Method for inspiration, Drs. Cassandra Vieten and David Lukoff (2022) developed the SSOPP assessment, which is a clinical interview for assessing a client's spiritual or religious background. It stands for Screening for Religiosity/ Spirituality (R/S) Relevance, Strength of R/S, Organized R/S, Personal R/S, and Problems with R/S. In each area of the SSOPP, which is more expansive than the FICA and designed for mental health settings, the interviewer is prompted to ask and follow up on questions such as "Do you have any beliefs or practices that help you cope with difficulties or stress?" "How do your spiritual and religious beliefs and practices support your mental health?" and "Has what is happening to you with your emotional situation changed your relationship to God or your spiritual and religious practices?"

When professionals first begin to inquire about religiosity and spirituality in their assessments, structured questions can be quite useful. Once a client has shared their perspectives, remember to use the client's own language to reference prayer, special practices, and so forth as you would with any content that is meaningful to the client.

It is notable that conversations about faith may be intimidating for you if you identify as agnostic or atheist. In the same way that you must be honest with your clients and engage in some self-disclosure to establish rapport (see chapter 3), you may have to be upfront about your religious preferences as part of this discussion. Imagine this conversation with a Black client in the first session:

THERAPIST: Thank you for sharing with me what brought you in. Do you have any concerns about working with me?

CLIENT: Well … are you a Christian?

THERAPIST: I'm not. [*Note: You could stop here, but doing so would present as suspicious and closed off.*] I don't subscribe to a religious faith at all. I do, however, support and respect anyone's right to believe in God.

CLIENT: So … you don't believe in God?

THERAPIST: I don't. Are you concerned that my not believing would impact my ability to work with you?

CLIENT: It would just be nice to know that you believe some of what I believe. I just think it would be harder for you to relate to me.

THERAPIST: I can definitely understand that and appreciate you sharing your concern. Open communication like this is a big part of making therapy work. Also, it's important to consider I'm only ever the expert on the skills that I hope to share with you. You are the expert on you—and that includes your faith and your beliefs. This means that we have to work together to figure out what works best. If you want to integrate your beliefs into therapy, I'm happy to help make that happen. I may have to ask you questions to make sure that I understand what we're working through, but I would do that with any client I'm getting to know—and because, even if we were both Christian, your Christianity might look different from mine since people are complex. So, I'd still ask you about how your faith works for you. Does that make sense?

CLIENT: It does.

THERAPIST: Good. What other concerns do you have? [*Note: This is not a close-ended question because you are open to this conversation.*]

CLIENT: I don't think I have any more.

THERAPIST: Okay, please do let me know if any other questions or concerns about this or anything else come up along the way.

An absence of faith and belief in God is one of those topics that many Black people associate with what it means to be white, and it is part of the reason why they may feel like seeing a Black therapist just makes sense. As always, be sure to seek consultation and expertise if you feel out of your depth. While you will collaborate with your client, you also want to be sure that you are doing your part outside of session to address the client's goals, especially when the client's needs could exceed your area of expertise. Your homework could include reading about the basic tenets of your client's faith in case your client is thinking and behaving in ways that are inconsistent with their reported belief system. Reading about religious faith and doctrines goes hand in hand with researching different cultural orientations to generate hypotheses about your client's presenting challenges. If you have strong, antagonistic beliefs about your client's faith, even though the faith isn't harming your client or vulnerable loved ones, you may want to revisit and work through your own beliefs so that they do not undermine your capacity to make progress with your client's therapy goals.

Spirituality and Religiosity Can Foster Mindfulness

As you likely know, mindfulness is the practice of nonjudgmentally and intentionally focusing your attention to the present moment. When it comes to spirituality and religiosity, many African American clients connect mindfulness to the practice of praying and meditating on specific biblical scriptures (Adams Spears et al., 2017). I imagine that the sense of peace and emotional grounding that comes from mindfulness-based activities is synonymous with the comfort that someone gains from praying and connecting with a higher power that is outside of themselves. However, because most clients aren't formally trained in mindfulness-based interventions, it is up to you to make that connection. In doing so, your client can embrace and expand their capacity to respond adaptively to stressful situations and with less emotional reactivity. In fact, mindfulness can provide the type of anchor that is needed for individuals who are at risk for suicide ideation and behavior (Brooks Stephens et al., 2023). Because we think about suicide beyond thoughts, it is important to consider other factors that amplify risk, such as impulsivity. Those who embrace mindfulness as a parallel to their spirituality are less likely to consider crisis-oriented behavior.

Anecdotally, though, I have been advised that some Black Americans interpret spirituality and mindfulness as "anti-God" and perhaps even as a Pagan ritual. I do not know how pervasive this is. However, this possibility is important to consider when introducing "spirituality" as a way of characterizing the client's beliefs. If it seems appropriate, you might ask, "What do you hear me saying when I ask about spirituality?" especially if the client's nonverbal behavior suggests some discomfort. This discomfort could indicate that your client thinks you have some intrinsic beliefs that are different from theirs and that you will judge them (whether the judgment is for being religious, being atheist, or falling somewhere in between). In any case, you'll want to notice how the client responds to any suggestions of mindfulness so you can appropriately clarify and perhaps share insight about (1) what mindfulness entails, (2) how the client can incorporate mindfulness into their routine, (3) and how it can potentially amplify their connection to God, if that is the client's desire.

Consider this case with an African American client who presents to therapy with concerns about task completion and high irritability such that she "snaps" at friends and loved ones when she least expects it. The outbursts seem to be getting progressively worse. In this session, you draw on the client's penchant for gospel music to introduce the idea of music as a mindfulness practice that she can use to ground herself in times of stress:

THERAPIST: You mentioned that you see yourself as a religious person. Have you used scripture or prayer to help keep your thoughts from spiraling downward when you're most upset?

CLIENT: I ask God to help me to not lose my mind and to remove the situations that are stressing me out. Is that what you mean?

THERAPIST: That's part of it. Does it help?

CLIENT: Sometimes.

THERAPIST: That's good to hear. What else do you do?

CLIENT: I listen to gospel music, sometimes.

THERAPIST: Okay, that's good too. And you said *sometimes*?

CLIENT: Yes, when I think about it.

THERAPIST: I see. And how often do you think about it?

CLIENT: Honestly, I could definitely use music more often.

THERAPIST: Okay, let's see what we can do about that right now. Music can help you ground yourself when you are feeling overly stressed and agitated. If you can settle yourself more throughout the day, you may be less likely to "snap" at folks unexpectedly. How does that sound?

CLIENT: I like the idea of that. I'm not 100 percent convinced it'll work, but I'm willing to give it a try.

THERAPIST: Good. Let's see how the next week goes and we can evaluate if you noticed any difference. Do you have an app on your phone, like Spotify or Amazon Music, that you use to listen to music?

CLIENT: I actually do.

THERAPIST: Good—you're already on your way! By chance do you have your music separated based on spiritual music that helps you to feel inspired or that helps you feel closer to God?

CLIENT: I wish I were that organized. I usually download songs when they come to mind, so they're all mixed together.

THERAPIST: I see. Can you pull up your Spotify now and see if there are three songs in there that you can separate out for when you're feeling sad and can use some inspiration?

CLIENT: Yes, I can do that. [*after a few moments*] I'm done.

THERAPIST: Great. Are those songs that you love, that as soon as they come on, your mood shifts?

CLIENT: Yes, every time!

THERAPIST: Okay, that's good to hear. Now, that you have a short playlist ready to go, I want you to play those songs when something upsetting happens or your mood starts to decline for whatever reason. How does that sound?

CLIENT: I can do that.

THERAPIST: Is there anything that would stop you from using this strategy?

CLIENT: None that I can think of.

THERAPIST: Okay, let's see how that goes and we'll check in first thing next week.

Let's pick up the conversation in the follow up session one week later:

THERAPIST: In our last session, we agreed that you would use your playlist when you were in a stressful situation or when your mood started to shift so that you could prevent a downward spiral. How did that go?

CLIENT: It went okay. There was one occasion when I let things get out of hand. I got into an argument with my sister. I was so wound up that my mood was in the toilet for almost an hour when I remembered to start my playlist.

THERAPIST: It sounds like it took you a while to remember, but once you did, you turned on the music and felt better?

CLIENT: Yes, I did. And I was even able to fix things with my sister.

THERAPIST: That's wonderful. Not only did you reverse your mood, but you were able to revisit a difficult conversation with your sister.

CLIENT: Yeah. And in another situation, I remembered my music faster. I was watching a movie and starting to feel lonely. I turned on my playlist. Since I wasn't going out, I took the time to add to my playlist.

THERAPIST: These are all so good to hear. You've really taken this activity and run with it. How are you feeling about this tool for your toolkit?

CLIENT: Actually, I'm surprised how helpful it's been. I don't know why I didn't think of this before.

THERAPIST: Well, all that really matters is that you have it now. Remember when I mentioned that music can help you ground yourself? I know you weren't convinced.

CLIENT: No, I wasn't convinced at all, but I get it now.

THERAPIST: That's good to hear. What I didn't share before is that grounding yourself—when you are completely in the moment and not thinking about the things that are stressing you—is also known as being mindful. Listening to music that brought you into the present moment was a mindfulness activity. If you like, we can work on other mindfulness activities.

CLIENT: Given how well the music worked out, that sounds like a good idea.

THERAPIST: Great—because I'd like for you to work on something this weekend to continue to expand your tools.

CLIENT: [*apprehensively*] Okay . . . ?

THERAPIST: Please be sure to continue to use your music. It works, so we don't want to stop that. But tell me this. Are there scriptures in the Bible that specifically talk about your mind or ways to be focused or to stay in the present so your mind doesn't wander or anything like that?

CLIENT: Yes, I'm sure there are.

THERAPIST: Okay, good. I'd like for you to explore that. Try to find three scriptures that have something to do with keeping your mind focused or staying in the present. Something like that. Save them to your phone. I look forward to discussing them and how we can build them into your mindful toolkit in our next session.

Note that whenever you ask a client to do something, you have to check in about how it went. As you know, some clients are prone to forgetting their homework. If the client can benefit from starting the homework in session, that is advisable. This includes researching scripture in session that could help them. You may conclude that your client would benefit from praying to God for specific help, like remembering to use their skills or guiding them to a perfect scripture. If the client forgets that commitment or some other important assignment, you might ask if they'd like to pray in session. The client may decline, or you may simply feel uncomfortable doing so. Ideally, though, you could make space for the client to bring their whole self to therapy in ways that increase their skillset, and potentially, yours.

At other times, you may have to process troublesome religious beliefs with your client. Recall the SSOPP, in which the last "P" stands for problems with religiosity or spirituality. When faith creates barriers, the goal is to undo those roadblocks to well-being. To illustrate, let's revisit the 20-year-old African American university student from chapter 1 whose mother advised her to go to therapy. By the second session, you assess that she meets criteria for an adjustment disorder with symptoms of depression. She is a biology major aiming to go to medical school, but she has failed two classes and feels like God is punishing her for how she has "strayed away" from her faith.

THERAPIST: In our last session, you said that your faith is important to you but that you might be struggling now because you have "strayed away" from your faith. If it's okay with you, I would like for us to start there.

CLIENT: Well, I was an "A" student all through elementary, junior high, and high school. When I left home for college, I started going to parties and staying out late and drinking. I didn't do that at home with my parents. I was a good kid. Now, I'm failing, and I can't seem to get back on track. It's hard and I don't know what to do!

THERAPIST: And it sounds like you're connecting your failing and getting off track to straying away from your faith.

CLIENT: Yes, and I probably deserve it.

THERAPIST: That's a lot to carry—to feel like you deserve to be failing.

CLIENT: I don't know what else to think. I've been trying to study harder. I just withdrew from one class because I knew I couldn't recover from an "F". I'll have to retake it. It's all so overwhelming. I've been praying, but it's not helping.

THERAPIST: Have you ever gone through anything like this before—where you were having a hard time with classes and couldn't get back on track?

CLIENT: No. This is the first time. That's why I feel like I'm being punished. If I didn't party with my friends and go out drinking and doing things against God, I wouldn't be in this situation.

THERAPIST: It sounds like you feel you're being punished for living life as a young adult, having fun, and maybe even blowing off a little steam?

CLIENT: Maybe, but I know better and now there are consequences.

THERAPIST: Looking back, would you change anything that you did?

CLIENT: Yeah, I wouldn't have gotten drunk at that one party.

THERAPIST: Okay, and what else would you change?

CLIENT: Well, I guess that's it, really.

THERAPIST: Okay, so you would change that one thing if you could do it all over again. Sometimes people do things that they wouldn't ordinarily do because no one is perfect. Right?

CLIENT: You're right.

THERAPIST: Tell me this, is there any part of your faith that talks about forgiveness, or are you supposed to give yourself a hard time indefinitely for mistakes?

CLIENT: It does. [*sighing*]

THERAPIST: Do you think you can forgive yourself and that God can forgive you for making a few mistakes?

CLIENT: Yes.

THERAPIST: Have you prayed for forgiveness?

CLIENT: Honestly, I don't know. I prayed to do well on all of my exams, but that didn't work out so well.

THERAPIST: That's understandable. You've been doing your best to adjust on your own to really very different circumstances. You've been far away from home, tackling a very demanding major, and feeling like God is punishing you. That's a lot.

CLIENT: It is a lot. I just don't know how to fix it all.

THERAPIST: That's okay. We rarely have all the answers in life. But you can give yourself credit for getting yourself here. The other thing that you might want to be mindful of is how your conclusion that God is punishing you may have been emotionally difficult for you, given your faith in God. It may have piled on even more worry and upset. Part of getting back on track will include creating a new interpretation of why it has been hard for you to get back on track.

CLIENT: That makes sense. I definitely don't want to make my situation worse.

THERAPIST: Exactly. The way that I see it, once you got off track, you started to feel depressed. You may not have realized it, but when your sleep was off and you started to disconnect from your friends, and from your faith too, you weren't operating as your full self. You were in emotional quicksand, sinking deeper. Let's create a homework assignment for you to identify scripture on forgiveness—maybe a favorite on how God forgives and on how humans can also forgive. Then you can search online for a sermon or religious presentation on forgiveness—maybe even one from your own pastor. How does that sound?

CLIENT: This works for me. Thank you.

Outside of therapy, the therapist in this case might advise the client to seek support at a faith-based organization or church that offers faith-based mental health services. Available statistics suggest that approximately 23 percent of congregations provide support for mental illness (Wong et al., 2018). Black churches are increasingly offering such support. This is especially true for many of the larger churches, though the specific proportion that offer mental health programming is unclear.

Overall, your goal is to use your client's culturally meaningful strengths and any resource that could be made available to them to improve their emotional and psychological functioning. It's okay if you're not religious. In fact, Dr. David Rosmarin's (2021) work on the intersection between religiosity, spirituality, and clinical practice has found that religiously unaffiliated clinicians seem to be better at delivering his spiritually oriented approach to CBT. When explaining their findings, Dr. Rosmarin and his colleagues speculated that religious clinicians may have had difficulty delivering the intervention as it was intended and that secular clinicians may have been focused on clinical rather than spiritual change. I similarly wonder if secular clinicians were simply more zeroed in on the details of the intervention, whereas those who were religiously affiliated may have been less adherent to the protocol based on their perceived familiarity with the content. In any event, the study findings are notable, especially for clinicians who fear that they will fumble in working with a client to expand their hope, optimism, and capacity to live a productive life. While you may strive for it as a clinician, there is no perfection in therapy. However, you do have a responsibility to tame elephants and invite the client's whole self to the therapy room.

Chapter 8

Identity—the Elephant Not in the Room

If there is an elephant that is comfortably *not* in the room, it is the constellation of cultural, ethnic, and racial identity markers that are infused into the lives of Black people. Identity is like air. It may not be visible with a clearly delineated shape and borders, but it affects how Black people see themselves and how the world sees them, as if identity were a brightly colored garment, precisely because discernible clues—how they carry themselves, their skin color, how they speak—all play a part in how their identity is formed.

Because a client's identity is shaped by their own beliefs and values and those of the generations that preceded them, your client might embrace or intentionally reject it. Some individuals of African ancestry have rejected their Blackness and have low racial identity. Others may wear T-shirts to extol their unapologetic Blackness while rejecting mainstream norms that are deemed "for white people." Many, *many* others exist in the middle, going about their routines and trying to succeed at the game of life, carrying an identity that is both a blessing and a curse. On occasion, life hits them hard. Both George Floyd and Breonna Taylor were murdered by police officers acting in violation of a duty to protect them. Other circumstances are less egregious and seemingly more dismissible, but still impactful.

How your client sees themselves isn't an elephant in the room, but it *is* an elephant. While racism may come up more readily in session, identity is an elephant that is less salient for most. Even if a mom asserts in session that a part of who she is includes running herself into the ground to take care of her children, she may not connect her actions to her values "as a Black woman." This nuanced distinction is useful for you to recognize, as it underscores why the identity elephant is not always in the room. It's more likely tucked away in the attic, but given that this elephant is huge and hard to get around, you might as well invite it to the therapy conversation, or at least to your hypothetical conceptualization of your client's presenting concerns.

Part of what makes identity so big is that it has innumerable functions on different ends of the identity continuum. Positive racial identity is important for well-being. Negative racial identity can be disruptive and even detrimental. In this chapter, I'll consider identity-related heterogeneity in the Black community and provide strategies for improving your client's overall well-being by affirming their cultural values and integrating those values to offset psychological strain.

Reconciling Black Identity

Adolescence is a time of identity formation (Marcia, 1980) during which African American and Black youth receive messaging from every direction about who they are. For example, a tall Black youth might be assumed to play basketball, though in reality he's on the debate team. A Black girl who uses no African American vernacular and who speaks a certain way may be accused of "acting white." For Black youth, part of identity development involves reconciling who they are with societal and familial expectations. Persistent messaging can permeate how those youth see themselves and what they take with them into adulthood.

Everyday Black folks don't talk much about Black identity because it is simply embedded in what we do when we come together. For most Black people, being Black is optional on a day-to-day basis. It doesn't require a label until we're the only Black person in the room or we have to navigate discordant encounters with people who aren't Black. Similar to how you may not ever think about your race, Black people don't walk around thinking about race until it becomes a necessity, like when they are wearing a hoodie, waiting for a friend in Starbucks, taking a nap in a university common room, or doing other random activities that Black people have died from or been harassed by police for doing. I have intentionally digressed, so hopefully you get the point.

For a Black person in a world that often rejects Black people, pro-Blackness is an act of resistance and self-preservation and must be seen as such. With this in mind, I am not confident that I can do justice to talking about the complexities of Black identity. On the other hand, I am confident that you need to be aware that, for your clients, having a positive identity is psychological gold and that having a neutral or negative perspective of what it means to be Black can be kryptonite.

Racial Identity in Theory

There are several different theories of racial identity, the most recognized of which is Dr. William Cross's (1995) Model of Nigrescence. *Nigrescence* references the process of becoming Black in five stages. In the initial stage, the person of African descent doesn't see themselves as Black, but in the second stage, they have an encounter that changes their "frame of reference," making it hard for them to deny their own Blackness. By the fifth stage of the model, the person adaptively integrates a Black identity into their sense of self. Though the model is not without criticism, it speaks to identity as a process.

Imagine a scenario in which your African American client is browsing the sales racks in Saks Fifth Avenue and is abruptly detained by store security for shoplifting. Your client sees herself as an upstanding member of her affluent community and finds the experience emotionally jarring. She identifies as a Christian woman but is shaken up when she realizes that she has been mistreated because she is Black. There is no other conclusion that she can come to after being held for hours, emptying her purse, and assuring the authorities that she is innocent. I have close family members and friends who have been unfairly accused of shoplifting. It is a demoralizing and painful experience that surely shifts a person's perspective if they don't understand what it means to be Black.

While some clients may not talk explicitly about race, remember that it is embedded in how they see themselves (and also in how they choose *not* to see themselves). As a first step, it could be worth it for you to highlight that reality if it peeks out. You can often find these clues woven into your client's implicit or explicit "should" statements. Recall the 41-year-old single mom from earlier chapters who suggested that she'd be taking shortcuts if she did not overdo life for her children. Meanwhile, she is depressed and running herself into the ground. Though she has been able to work through some of her cognitive distortions with her therapist, they have not yet fully unpacked what being a "good" mom means for her. Remember, though, that she did say that when she was growing up, her mom and grandmother made tremendous sacrifices, implying that she "should" too.

In this session, the therapist goes deeper, intentionally connecting the dots of how the client sees herself as a mom to what it means to be a *Black* mom raising *Black* children and acknowledging her approach as a source of cultural strength:

THERAPIST: You said something the other day that I think would be helpful to revisit. You mentioned that your mother and grandmother made sacrifices for you so that you would have a better life. You and I were able to get to a place of reframing those family values and beliefs about the role of the mother figure in order to make life better for you, but I think it could be helpful to unpack that a bit more if that's okay for you.

CLIENT: Okay, what would that look like?

THERAPIST: Well, we probably agree that carrying on family tradition is important, but it's how the tradition is carried that we reframed.

CLIENT: I do realize that now.

THERAPIST: At the same time, you want to recognize the strength in having those values, in passing them on to your children, and in being clear about why those values exist. Where I am going with this, and you can tell me if it makes sense to you, is that part of those values evolved from existing as a Black woman in this society. They are important for your ability to be successful, to get through struggle, and to thrive despite obstacles that come your way.

CLIENT: I hadn't thought about it like that, but yeah, knowing who I am, and claiming my reality as a strong Black woman, means something.

THERAPIST: Yes, and you can be aware of *balancing* when you need to call on your core source of strength and when to resist the pull to overdo it.

The goal for you as the therapist is to (1) facilitate the client's recognition that who she is as a Black woman is powerful and important and to (2) prime your relationship with the client for when the conversation comes up again because she is taking on too much. This begins with seeing the positivity and utility in connecting with what it means to be a Black woman.

One Elephant—Many Shades of Gray

The nature of the identity elephant varies from person to person. Therefore, determining the degree to which your client identifies with their culture of origin will have to be part of your assessment practice. Once you have this insight, you can proceed to integrate their identity-related values in the work that you do together. If you assess ethnic or racial identity early on and for all clients, it flows as part of your intake process. One of the measures that I use in research and that can be integrated in clinical practice is the revised Multigroup Ethnic Identity Measure (MEIM-R; Phinney & Ong, 2007), which asks clients to rate how strongly they agree (with 1 being "strongly disagree" and 7 being "strongly agree") with statements like "I have spent time trying to find out more about my ethnic group, such as its history, traditions, and customs" and "I have a strong sense of belonging to my own ethnic group." Consider reviewing the measure in its entirety if it could be useful for your clinical practice.

Higher scores are indicative of higher ethnic identity. If your African American client indicates that they have relatively high ethnic identity, you might have a conversation with them about whether they would like to be intentional about including their values as an African American person in their therapy. If they report low ethnic identity, you may want to tread lightly, attending to the ways in which their discordant identity may be related to elevated stress and maladaptive coping behavior. Keep in mind that you cannot venture in this direction until you have a strong therapeutic alliance. Otherwise, you risk a breach in your working relationship with your client.

Making sense of identity can be a complex endeavor. Some African Americans prefer the label of "Black," but the reasoning varies by person and perhaps by context. As an academic and professional, I might prefer "Black" on most days and "African American" in more formal conversation. It is truly a personal choice. First- and second-generation individuals may connect more so with their country of origin (e.g., Nigeria, Haiti), in which case they are likely to identify accordingly. For you as a mental health professional, the complexity may begin with understanding the difference between race and ethnicity, which is confusing for most people. Ethnicity is a label that is more closely connected to an individual's cultural values and behavior (e.g., African American, Haitian American), whereas race reflects broader categories of individuals (e.g., Black, Asian, white). As I mentioned in the introduction, not everyone who is Black will identify as African American, in part, because race and ethnicity overlap but aren't the same.

Dr. Robert Sellers and his colleagues (1997) developed the Multidimensional Inventory of Black Identity (MIBI) to assess the importance and meaning of Black identity to Black people. The measure provides an illustration of how multilayered identity can be. Strong agreement with statements such as "I have a strong attachment to other Black people" reflect the *centrality* of a person's identity, or the extent to which someone defines themselves based on race. Since most people have an identity hierarchy, a Black woman might see herself as Black first and as a woman second, while a Black man might see himself as a man first and as Black second. In this instance, race is more central for the Black woman's identity. The scale also measures a person's *regard* for their racial identity—the extent to which they view their race more positively or negatively. Finally, it contains questions to measure *ideology*, which reflects a person's opinions on how Black folks are supposed to act (e.g., aligning with their Blackness versus "minority identity," assimilating to the mainstream, or placing equal emphasis on the humanity of all people).

The work of Dr. Sellers and colleagues is highly regarded and widely cited. Though some of the results have been mixed—with some, but not other, aspects of identity showing an association to mental health—their conceptual framework provides a useful rubric for beginning to understand the complexity of identity. Some might argue that "Black students are better off going to schools that are controlled and organized by Blacks," while others might argue that "Blacks who espouse separatism are as racist as white people who also espouse separatism" (Sellers et al., 1997, p. 815). Beliefs such as these are relevant to your client's therapy to the extent that they impact the client's overall well-being or, more notably, to the extent that they make it more difficult for your client to navigate their identity in non-affirming environments.

Historically, most Black people have adopted and navigated multiple identities for survival purposes. For example, enslaved African people had three options: (1) attempt to escape from the plantation and risk death, (2) fight the slave master and risk death, or (3) identify with the slave master to minimize external and internal conflict (Parham et al., 2015). Imagine generations of captive people accepting inhumane circumstances, relinquishing rich legacies, and embracing their oppressor's worldview and treatment. I don't know that there are words for the psychological impact of such circumstances.

Fast forward to the nineteenth century when W.E.B. Du Bois (1903) captured Black identity in his classic *The Souls of Black Folks*:

> . . . the Negro is a sort of seventh son, born with a veil, and gifted with second sight in this American world,—a world which yields him no true self-consciousness, but only lets him see himself through the revelation of the other world. It is a peculiar sensation, this double-consciousness, this sense of always looking at oneself through the eyes of others, of measuring one's soul by the tape of a world that looks on in amused contempt and pity. One ever feels his twoness,—an American, a Negro; two warring souls, two thoughts, two unreconciled strivings; two warring ideals in one dark body, whose dogged strength alone keeps it from being torn asunder. The history of the American Negro is the history of this strife,—this longing to attain self-conscious manhood, to merge his double self into a better and truer self. (p. 5)

Du Bois wrote this classic text during Jim Crow. Sociopolitically, much has changed since that time, but the post-racial society that many hoped for has yet to arrive. Consequently, many racially and ethnically marginalized individuals struggle to fit in at work, at school, and in some social settings. In my research, I have used the 24-item Social, Attitudinal, Familial, and Environmental Acculturative Stress Scale (SAFE; Padilla et al., 1985) to assess the strain that individuals feel as a result of multicultural dissonance. Though the measure was initially designed for immigrant groups, we tested and felt confident in its validity for Black Americans (Joiner & Walker, 2002). You might consider using the SAFE in your practice. Note that clients don't indicate whether or not specific events occurred. More importantly, they rate the stressfulness of each item that applies to them (with 1 being "not stressful" and 5 being "extremely stressful"). Here is a subset of the statements:

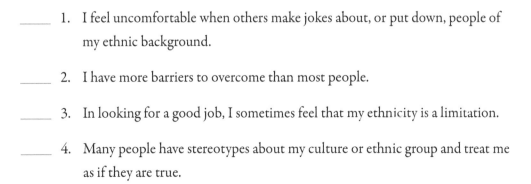

_____ 1. I feel uncomfortable when others make jokes about, or put down, people of my ethnic background.

_____ 2. I have more barriers to overcome than most people.

_____ 3. In looking for a good job, I sometimes feel that my ethnicity is a limitation.

_____ 4. Many people have stereotypes about my culture or ethnic group and treat me as if they are true.

_____ 5. I often feel ignored by people who are supposed to assist me.

_____ 6. Because I am different, I do not get enough credit for the work I do.

Some have understandably referred to racial and ethnic identity as a "double-edged sword" (Yip, 2018). Though positive identity is associated with positive mental health outcomes more broadly, when someone is aware of their own reality as a Black person, it also amplifies their recognition of race-based discrimination and emotional distress.

When Identity Is Stratified

According to the U.S. census, persons who identify with two or more races are approximately 3 percent of the population. The proportion of the population that identifies as biracial or multiracial is said to have doubled from 2010 to 2020. Because census questions have changed, some of this increase is due, in part, to options that permit multiple designations. Nevertheless, the number of persons who identify as both Black and white has grown considerably.

Research on how biracial and multiracial identity impacts well-being is limited, but I have become more interested in this population given findings from one of our national studies, which examined suicide ideation and attempts for more than 200,000 adults (Cheref et al., 2019). There were a number of surprising findings in the data, but one that stood out was the finding for 26- to 49-year-old adults who identified as multiracial, as they were more than three times as likely to attempt suicide than the younger cohort of 18- to 25-year-olds. The age of suicide vulnerability was also somewhat older for multiracial persons compared to Black, Hispanic, and Asian individuals, which leads me to wonder what life circumstances could be different for those individuals.

As is the case for other topics that impact marginalized individuals, much more research is needed. But this is helpful to consider when your biracial client presents with moderate to high levels of anxiety and depression, intermittent thoughts of suicide, and limited friend and social support while feeling like no one understands them.

The Overarching Goal

At the end of the day, the goal is for each individual to connect with their most authentic self without having to assimilate to a sometimes-uninviting society, and without the struggle to embrace an identity that others have deemed inferior. In 1961, author James Baldwin said that to be Black and relatively conscious is to be in a constant state of rage all the time (Baldwin et al., 1961). As a Black woman, this statement resonates with me. If you can understand this as a therapist, this framing affords you a perspective from which to expand how you conceptualize the care of your clients who may feel this rage without the ability to articulate their rageful agitation.

In chapter 2, we encountered a scenario in which the therapist proposed that a 33-year-old Black client send her grandmother to a group home. Given an opportunity to discuss the situation, the client asserted that "Black people don't do that." In this situation, the client was able to acknowledge a cultural more that the therapist had not considered when offering caregiving suggestions. Here, the therapist continues the conversation by brainstorming alternative forms of support for the client (and her grandmother) that are consistent with the client's identity and cultural values as a Black woman:

THERAPIST: I appreciate you being very clear about your values and importantly, your values as part of your community.

CLIENT: Well, yeah, because if you're recommending something that I'm never going to do, that's not helping me.

THERAPIST: That's 100 percent true. So, let's figure out how you can uphold your values and also get some relief. We can start with reviewing your day-to-day responsibilities with your grandmother. By the way, how do you refer to your grandmother?

CLIENT: [*smiling*] She's my nana.

THERAPIST: Okay, what does your day-to-day look like with your nana?

CLIENT: During the day, she watches her favorite TV shows. That's fine because I work from home and prepare her meals. I make sure that she takes her medicine and that she gets her baths. It doesn't sound like a lot, but multiple meals per day starts to add up for me. She had a stroke two years ago, so she doesn't cook or anything, but she does move around okay with her walker.

THERAPIST: I see. Tell me more about your nana. How old is she?

CLIENT: She just turned 70 years old, but she's got a lot of spunk to her.

THERAPIST: Has she changed a lot since her stroke?

CLIENT: She always had a lot of fun and had a lot of energy. When we were kids, she took us to the park on weekends and sometimes we went shopping with her. Until her stroke, she was active in her sorority and several other organizations that coordinated donations for the homeless and the youth. She can't do any of that anymore and it's hard for me to see it. Sometimes she seems like a shell of who she used to be.

THERAPIST: You said before that it's a lot. It sounds like her situation now is probably hard on both of you. It's more than just the level of care but the emotional weight of seeing your nana at this stage of life.

CLIENT: Yes, I feel sad for her. That's another reason that I couldn't dare abandon her in a home.

THERAPIST: That makes sense. Do you feel like she's been abandoned by others?

CLIENT: No. But kind of . . . because her friends used to come over, but then they stopped after a while. I don't know what happened.

THERAPIST: Is it possible to reach out to them? Maybe you can help figure out how to get them to your house to spend some time with her for lunch a few times each week. Maybe they can also figure out other ways to get her involved to help her mood. I know we've talked about how you've been overwhelmed, but it sounds like your nana has also had a lot of loss. Maybe you can help both of you.

CLIENT: I'd like that. And I never reached out to any of the ladies to see why they fell off. I can definitely follow up with them and see if there is a way to include my nana in their outreach efforts. If anyone deserves outreach, she does.

Note that the client's identity connects her and her grandmother to a larger Black community. Identity is what allows us to be connected to similar others. In this case, the "others" are specifically Black senior women who are also part of the community. When someone lacks a sense of identity, finding meaningful support can be a challenge. As you know, social support and meaningful relationships are important for a client's emotional well-being and satisfaction with life. For your Black client, these relationships are most effective when they involve similarly identified others.

Integrating cultural values doesn't have to be that "deep." Once you know what the client's values and identity are, you can help to incorporate what's important in creative ways. If you are a white therapist, know that creativity and collaboration will be far more important in this process than they would be for a Black therapist, who can more naturally access strategies that resonate with the Black community. As I indicated in the last chapter, there is no recipe for adapting your work to every client. Having some understanding of how important race and ethnicity (and by default, culture) are to your client will help to guide you in your collaborative problem-solving.

When *Anti*-Blackness Rules

One reason you can't presume that all your Black clients have the same or similar racial and ethnic identity, or that their cultural values will inform their clinical presentation, is because some Black people are disconnected from, or outright reject, their Black identity. They are more aligned with, and comfortable around, white people than they are with Black people. For some, this misorientation is due to their experience growing up in primarily white communities disconnected from Black people and culture. For others, Black identity is associated with potentially a whole slew of negative associations, especially victimhood.

Being anti-Black may also be a form of survival. Consider this for a moment. We recognize the lifetime impact of ACEs on health and well-being. What do you think the impact is of countless generations of global, adverse lifetime events for millions of adults and children? During the COVID-19 pandemic, we were under social distancing lockdowns for the better part of two years and can track the increase in anxiety and depression and years of academic decline for youth. It was two years. What does 346 years, from the start of the slave trade to the end of Jim Crow, do? Your client and their ancestors learned how to cover up generational scars, but those scars are embedded in their psyche. We will never forget how life changed during COVID. Some are dealing with long COVID, and those with preexisting conditions continue to isolate when possible. Similarly, rather than internalize some form of *long oppression*, some may opt to resist their Blackness.

Self Disorders

Dr. Na'im Akbar (2004) conceptualized anti-self and alien-self as psychological disorders for Black people who adopt belief systems that are contrary to who they are. *Alien-self disorder* is observed among persons who embrace values and behave in ways that are contrary to their culture of origin. They are motivated by materialism and what they can acquire. They are likely to dismiss the realities of racial oppression. It may be unsurprising that these individuals are more likely middle class. Families that are vulnerable to self disorders tend to take pride in living in exclusive neighborhoods where their families may be the only Black family, even though this may adversely impact their children, who fail to develop a positive Black identity. Of course, the family wouldn't label their status as problematic, but it can be helpful for you as the therapist to recognize potential consequences of relinquishing positive Black identity. Though Dr. Akbar used more dated conceptualizations to characterize the intersectional reality of Black Americans who identify as members of the LGBTQ+ community, his classification of the side effects of Black assimilation is no less astute.

In contrast to those who show signs of alien-self disorder, Black people who have overt hostility toward other Black people have *anti-self disorder* (Akbar, 2004). You may have encountered them in varying circumstances. They put down Black people. They may even insist that Black people are naturally dangerous and unintelligent. These individuals are reinforced and embraced by the larger majority. If they go to therapy, they are more likely to see a non-Black therapist. If such an individual is in therapy, they clearly don't have everything figured out. Though they may be overtly resistant to considering their Black identity important to their therapy—so much so that you may get fired on the spot if you say anything about Black identity to them—don't filter yourself from a place of fear. I say this because you may be easily intimidated when a client resists a question or rejects your hypothesis about the role of identity in their distress. Just because the client does not specify race-related issues as why they are in therapy, that does not mean there isn't a race-related concern. It is reasonable to tread cautiously, but if you have good rapport with your client and you suspect there is something about their rejection of their Black identity that could be an issue, it might help to roll the dice in the interest of the bigger picture.

To illustrate what alien-self disorder might look like, imagine a scenario with your 20-year-old Black client who has been coming to therapy weekly for five months to address social anxiety. Her social anxiety has decreased from severe to mild. Too often, it escalates, but it's unclear why the effects of the exposure intervention seem to have plateaued. Here, you gently suggest whether the discordance between her race and the white university she attends may be contributing to her ongoing anxiety:

THERAPIST: Given the unexplained spikes in your anxiety, I wonder if we might consider something else.

CLIENT: I'm using the tools. I don't know why it just feels like they don't work sometimes.

THERAPIST: We haven't ever talked about what it means for you to be enrolled at a primarily white university pursuing a veterinary science degree.

CLIENT: I love animals and this university has the best program in the country.

THERAPIST: That's great that you get to do what you love in such an esteemed institution. I just wonder what it's like for you to be there as a Black woman?

CLIENT: I don't think about it. I've always been around more white people than Black people. It's not a big deal.

THERAPIST: In case it is a big deal, is there any harm in paying attention to who is around you and what you might be thinking in those situations when you feel your anxiety rising? What's the worst thing that could happen?

CLIENT: Nothing, I guess. I just don't want to behave in a way that's racist.

THERAPIST: Well, right now we are simply investigating your anxiety and making the most of your treatment plan. If at any point we have to end this investigation, we will. I don't know where this road could take us, but I'm willing to find out if you are.

In the last chapter, I acknowledged how a more Eurocentric cultural worldview is associated with vulnerability to suicide ideation in the context of overwhelming stress. Rational conversations about culture and race are relatively rare. You have to be willing to take the lead in unpacking your client's sources of stress and creating solutions to manage that distress.

You'll recall the 49-year-old Black man I introduced in chapter 4 who was in middle management at a Fortune 500 company. He had a good number of stress symptoms, including high blood pressure and regular headaches. He also dismissed his anger with his very impressive skill of reframing. The therapist noted that diving deeper into his anger might be necessary to more fully address his stress symptoms. Let's pick up the conversation in the next session:

THERAPIST: In our last session, you shared that you were confused, felt dismissed, and were briefly livid at the conclusion of your conversation with your senior manager. Do you recall our conversation?

CLIENT: I do. You brought up an interesting point about how I had some very strong emotions, but then I bottled them up and they probably showed up in my headache.

THERAPIST: Do you think there was any merit to that?

CLIENT: I could see that. I haven't had any headaches since then, but I have felt very frustrated and sometimes just disconnected from work. I feel like I'm just going through the motions.

THERAPIST: That's understandable. You may be trying to make it all make sense for how best to navigate your work experiences. Have any other thoughts come to mind from our last conversation?

CLIENT: Well, I thought about what you said about things maybe being different for me and basically being unfair because I'm Black. But I still don't know what I'm supposed to do with that! I cannot change who I am. [*getting agitated*] And I definitely don't see myself as a victim. That's what people do when they're playing the race card because they don't have the skills or qualifications to do their job, and that's not me.

At this juncture, the therapist could get defensive about the client's misinterpretation that he needs to change his race. The therapist might feel compelled to defend Black people whom the client has belittled due to his own anti-self disposition. Though the therapist would have noble intentions, neither of these strategies would be as helpful as sharing an open-ended observation.

THERAPIST: It seems like talking about race and how it affects your life . . . well, it's upsetting for you?

CLIENT: No, it's just that I don't see the point in being a victim.

THERAPIST: I see. And it's true that being a victim isn't something that anyone would want. I do want for us to be able to figure out how to manage your stress in light of things that you have no control over. Right now, it seems like you try to repress your upset, but that isn't working.

CLIENT: I agree. It's not, but what can I *do*?

THERAPIST: Stay with me for a moment, okay? We've done a lot of good work with identifying thoughts that could be unhelpful and replacing those thoughts with some that are more adaptive, and we did this without changing who you are. Do you agree?

CLIENT: Yeah, that's true and it's been helpful.

THERAPIST: Okay, we can continue to do that, but we're going to have to examine a different set of thoughts. And those thoughts have embedded in them your thinking about being a Black man in your high-powered company.

CLIENT: Okay, I see what you're saying. I might not like it, but I get it.

THERAPIST: Let's start there—what might you not like about it?

CLIENT: The idea that I have to think about the race card.

THERAPIST: The "race card" means different things to different people, so tell me what it means for you.

CLIENT: It means that I'm using some kind of adversity as an excuse, and that I'm complaining when I'm not.

THERAPIST: I'm glad you said that. As far as I understand, you're not making any excuses for yourself or complaining. To the contrary, you dismiss unfairness that seems to be happening before your very eyes.

CLIENT: But again, what am I supposed to do?

THERAPIST: Well, let's pause. You acknowledge that there is unfairness that is happening?

CLIENT: Well, something must be happening because I *know* I deserve a promotion.

THERAPIST: Okay, and what do you think are the causes of your not getting your hard-earned promotion?

CLIENT: You think it's racism?

THERAPIST: [*smiling*] Well, last I checked, it's not as important what I think as much as what you think.

CLIENT: Okay, let's say it's racism.

THERAPIST: Okay, racism and what else?

CLIENT: [*pausing*] I really can't think of anything else. I've been there for twelve years. Anyone else who has been in a similar situation, and those who have had less-impressive resumes, have been promoted in shorter time . . . Okay, racism is the only thing I can think of.

THERAPIST: [*after a pause*] It seems like that conclusion was very difficult for you to come to.

CLIENT: It was . . . for all of the reasons I said.

THERAPIST: I understand. You're a high-achieving person. You always have been. So, it's hard to acknowledge that something that could be out of your control is affecting your success.

CLIENT: Exactly. And I don't deserve this.

THERAPIST: You're right. You don't. And I hope that you keep that in your mind that you do not deserve to work as hard as you do to be overlooked for any reason, and especially not because of your race.

CLIENT: They don't appreciate me. But I deserve to be appreciated.

THERAPIST: You absolutely do. And I might add, they are fortunate to have you there despite how they have minimized you.

CLIENT: Yes, exactly! I've been stressing myself over how I can do more and better, and they don't even appreciate me or my contributions! I've been making myself crazy and running my body ragged. And for what?

THERAPIST: It sounds like you've gained some new perspective.

CLIENT: I have. I have. I think the next question still is . . . now what?

THERAPIST: That seems up to you. But you do have options—options that you might not have considered until your frame of reference changed to one that acknowledged who you are, your circumstances, and what you deserve.

CLIENT: True. I'm going to map out a plan. I can discretely go on the job market and see what else is out there. I'm sure my skillset would be appreciated elsewhere. Once I have an offer, I can let my senior manager know that I'm leaving and why. They can counter if they want, but it'll cost them.

THERAPIST: You'd tell them that you think you've been underappreciated because of your race?

CLIENT: [*smiling*] I think I'd have to. We don't have any evidence of any other reason.

THERAPIST: [*smiling*] I see what you did there, and that sounds great. In fact, it sounds like you're not concerned about a "race card" or what that means but are acknowledging a situation for what it is.

This session could have gotten derailed quickly. If a therapist forgets they are using CBT to challenge thoughts, or if they feel saddened that a client is hopeless because they can't just be white, the opportunity for restructuring the client's unhelpful thoughts closes. Clients can do that—easily draw us as therapists into their unhelpful thinking patterns when we're not paying attention. Focus is critical.

You have to be prepared to directly or indirectly address your client's maladaptive coping strategies and identify what the client can change (and what is out of their control, including racism). The conversation in this vignette, like many others, was intentionally slowed down so as not to miss any of the multilayered thoughts the client had that were obstructing his capacity to acknowledge his unhelpful thoughts. As you saw, his shift in thinking led to his capacity to reframe his approach to his employment and his manager. The client is a high-functioning individual, so it is of no surprise that he generated new insights from the conversation.

Overall, this chapter has drawn you to the nuanced and parallel realities in which Black people can exist. It is outside the scope of this chapter to articulate the many ways in which identity can impact your client. However, you can use your new insight to generate conversations that set you on a path to best understand your client. Keep in mind that they may not have ready answers to your questions. They only need to know that the questions are worth considering and that you are devoted to discovering the answers with them.

Chapter 9

What Kind of Therapist Are You?

As a disclaimer, I am not an authority on white people, white identity, or white privilege. Over the years, however, I have witnessed the oft-disguised fear in individuals who are uncomfortable with the elephant of racial difference in therapy. I have cajoled grown adults to acknowledge the feared elephant and also shared in the victory of confronting this fear. By now, you are at least cognitively aware of the expectations that await you in the therapy room, even if you remain apprehensive about seeing African American clients. This apprehension is understandable. There is work to do!

Though race often inserts itself as an elephant in therapy, racial differences themselves aren't *the* elephant. The racial elephant is the therapist's strategy of minimizing or tiptoeing around race and racism and how they impact the client's lived experiences—experiences that provide rich opportunities for the therapist to bring their own authenticity in the therapy room. I get that many of us are uncomfortable with authenticity. Offering your authentic self leaves you open and vulnerable. What if you are rejected or worse? To avoid discomfort and unpleasantness, you learn to present the best, safest representative of yourself. As a good southerner, I know how to present well. Like you, I know how to show up to work and other settings with my nicely masked self. To be sure, your Black client is also very comfortable with their masks. They would have no success in life without them. But when we as Black people get to be our authentic selves, a weight is lifted that we didn't know was there. When your Black client can bring their mask-free self to therapy, you'll know. But you will have to de-mask *first*.

This chapter will focus on the necessary work of examining *your* racial identity and how it could impact your capacity to work effectively. Hopefully, the conversation in the last chapter sparked your curiosity about your own racial or ethnic identity. Depending on the extent to which you recognize and connect with your racial identity, the conversation may not have resonated with you at all. While very few therapists would be inclined to acknowledge internalized beliefs that Black people are inferior, this ideology is baked into our society. This chapter will discuss strategies you can pursue as you take responsibility for the biases you may find or already know to be tied to your identity. Simply knowing what a microaggression is will not save you from engaging in microaggressive behavior. However, you can minimize the chances of an errant comment or behavior by being comfortable with your own identity—without shame or apology.

White Racial Identity—Because We All Have a Racial Identity

Dr. Janet Helms (1995) is the pioneer of white racial identity development theory. She suggests that having insight into your own stage of racial awareness can help you on your path to engaging in cross-racial psychotherapy with clients. Similar to how having an awareness of Black and African cultural beliefs and preferences is not sufficient to provide care that will be helpful for your client, you have to dig deeper into what your own racial identity says about who you are.

According to Helms, there are six stages of racial identity development into which a white person might fall. The first is the *contact* dimension, in which someone is naive about race. People with this status assume they don't really have a race and that people are essentially the same. The next is *disintegration*, in which someone is fixated at a low level of racial self-consciousness, seeing racism and racial disparities in our society but rejecting any notion that they directly benefit from our racialized society. In *reintegration*, the third status, individuals adopt feelings of outright anger toward Black people while amplifying white people and an ideology that is perceived to be associated with white people. I doubt you're reading this book if you are in this stage, but you may know or have close personal relationships with some folks who are. You have to decide your tolerance for such ideology as you continue to develop a perspective that does not harm people of other races.

At this point of the book, you may be more in the stage of *pseudo-independence,* wherein you perceive Black culture more on an intellectual level and have an awareness of the role of white racial dominance, but you are still much more comfortable with more assimilated Black people who are perceived as similar to white people. Next is *immersion/emersion,* in which you attempt to connect with and embrace your racial identity while actively working toward being anti-racist. The ideal status (certainly by the time you are seeing clients) would be the final stage of *autonomy,* wherein your white identity doesn't include racial bias or racist beliefs about Black people while you also integrate a positive sense of your own white identity. You're comfortable with interracial encounters and value racial and cultural similarities and differences.

There are several measures of racial identity that are based on Helms's theory. One is the White Racial Consciousness Development Scale-Revised (WRCDS-R; Lee et al., 2007), which asks respondents to rate how strongly they agree to statements on a 5-point scale, with 1 being "strongly disagree" and 5 being "strongly agree," to recreate a racial identity profile. Some sample items include:

_____ 1. I have had little or no contact with Black people other than seeing them on campus. (*Contact*)

_____ 2. I feel torn sometimes between wanting to protect Black individuals from racism and gaining the approval of whites. (*Disintegration*)

_____ 3. Reversed discrimination is a big problem for whites in America. (*Reintegration*)

_____ 4. I support the idea of restitution for Blacks based on the history of slavery and oppression. (*Pseudo-independence*)

_____ 5. Whenever I witness it, I confront people who make racist comments. (*Autonomy*)

Other scholars have developed measures that assess the relationship between white identity development and perceived comfort with Black folks. For example, the Comfort Assessment asks respondents to rate their comfort level with various racial situations such as "driving through a Black neighborhood" or "going to a Black physician" (Claney & Parker, 1989). Comfort is important and can facilitate your openness to your client's perspectives and interpretations—perspectives that a Black therapist who identifies with the community likely already possesses. Note that your client's experiences may be partly due to unhelpful patterns of thinking, but it is critical that you become increasingly capable of balancing their thinking patterns with the very real experience of bias and racial oppression. Since you may not have personal insight, and the client is unlikely to bring it up, you will have to initiate the unpacking of racism in session.

Missed opportunities to address race- and racism-related matters happen for a number of reasons. They could be the result of therapist fatigue or they may occur in response to some random distraction. But they could also be due to color-blindness or your stage of racial consciousness. For example, research has found that white psychologists-in-training who have a poorly integrated racial identity tend to exhibit more color-blind ideology (Gushue & Constantine, 2007). That is, those who lack *autonomy* and confidence with being white are more likely to ignore race and racism. This is why you need to know who you are and the kind of therapist you want to be.

Do you recall your score on the short set of questions related to color-blind racial attitudes in chapter 2? I suggested that if you scored higher than 14 on the seven items, you would benefit from committing to reading about sources of disparities in housing, economics, health care, and social structures in the United States. Hopefully, by now, you are aware of the preschool-to-prison pipeline and the alarming maternal mortality rate for Black women relative to other women in this country. These are a few of many examples of systemic racism that extend beyond police killings of Black people. If you are only aware of widely publicized police violence, why might that be? The time to do the work is now. Any individual who has not reached their most self-actualized racial identity, and who subscribes to the othering of Black people, is at risk for adopting questionable practices in therapy. Knowledge is a prerequisite. There is no skipping steps.

Tame Your Own Self-Talk with Cognitive Restructuring

As part of your work, it is important to use the cognitive and behavioral tools you are versed in to identify and confront your unhelpful self-talk. As you know, CBT focuses on the present, so you may have to go back to your childhood or adolescence to unpack where some of the deep-rooted biases began, but that is for you to decide. In the meantime, that which was learned in the past can be unlearned in the present.

Here are some points to consider:

If you currently have a client who is Black or African American (or have worked with one in the last twelve months), have you introduced their race or cultural identity in any discussion when it was appropriate to do so? If so, how was that for you? Did the client gain new insights? Were you pleasantly surprised? Describe the situation with as much detail as possible.

_____

_____

_____

_____

_____

Let's say you initiated the conversation, and it didn't go so well. What were the circumstances? Was there anything about it that, in hindsight, set you up for failure?

_____

_____

_____

_____

_____

If you have avoided introducing race, what has kept you from introducing it? For example, have you convinced yourself that since your clients don't present with matters of race or racism, it's not worth bringing up? Have you decided that you are unprepared to address race? What are you telling yourself?

_____

_____

_____

_____

_____

List five of your responses here for what you are telling yourself.	Now indicate something you can tell yourself instead.

On a 0–10 scale (with 0 being "little to no fear" and 10 being "the highest level of fear you could imagine"), what would you say is your overall fear of acknowledging racial bias in the life of your client? _____

If your rating is 2 or higher, what evidence do you have for your concerns?

_____

_____

_____

_____

If you have yet to acknowledge race-related concerns with a Black or African American client, list two to three statements you can make to yourself to encourage you to bring up the client's experiences with racism in session. I have listed several throughout the book thus far. Perhaps there are some that resonate with you, or you may have your own.

_____

_____

_____

_____

Now that you had some time to consider your role as therapist who embraces cultural humility, how will you do things differently, if at all? Be as specific as possible.

_____

_____

_____

_____

If you have not had a Black or African American client, how might you volunteer your time to work in settings where Black clients are underserved or where you can promote yourself as someone who can provide culturally meaningful care?

_____

_____

_____

_____

_____

Evaluate Your Effort

Before you hang your shingle to provide care in new settings, consider this: Have you talked about race with anyone who was not the same race as you? Have you talked to someone who identified as Black about their experiences of racism or about living in a racist society? How many hours of TED Talks or YouTube videos have you watched on the topic? If you still have yet to do so, why is that? Hopefully, I don't need to talk to you about avoidance behavior and how ineffective it is. But just in case I do, let's visit the cycle of anxiety and how it works. You begin with a fearful thought. You avoid the situation or circumstances that elicit the fear. In the short term, you feel better because you don't have to confront the anxiety-provoking situation. But your anxiety persists over the long term as a result. The only way to break the cycle is to prepare for, and then confront, the fear. Don't use your client as a guinea pig for practicing cultural humility. First, do your own work on your own fears and apprehensions.

On a 0–10 scale (with 0 being "not comfortable at all" and 10 being "very comfortable"), how comfortable are you with rejecting some of your "conditioning" to establish a solid working relationship with your client, taking risks to acknowledge racial differences and how they might play out in the lives of clients? If your comfort is lower than a 7, you may need to reflect on your racial identity status and any potential resistance you may have.

Those of us who have advanced degrees and higher levels of education may feel that we know more than we actually do. The problem with being authorized as an expert is that you may be even more inclined to miss key messages in this book and in your work with Black and African American clients. Unfortunately, your client may naively assume that your expertise will facilitate their relief from severe emotional disturbance when you are potentially doing harm by ignoring key aspects of their reality. This is why you have to commit to continuing your education beyond the typical diversity CEUs to advance your practice in meaningful ways.

Manage Your Stress Outside of Session so Management Translates in Session

Too often, mental health professionals forget to use their own healthy tools for themselves. If your anxiety is elevated at baseline, the odds are increased that you will take on a topic that is dysregulating for you in therapy. You have to be honest with where you are psychologically. To make sure you are managing your stress level outside of session, think about what you typically do to overcome overwhelming stress.

List your favorite three strategies that require five minutes or less. Next to each strategy, evaluate how effective (e.g., mostly effective, frequently ineffective) they are for curbing your stress level.

_____

_____

_____

Specify a time of day or an occasion when you can engage in your most (or moderately) effective strategies that require five minutes or less. It could be "as soon as the alarm clock goes off" or "at noon" or "at 8 p.m."

_____

_____

_____

List your favorite three strategies that require 30 minutes or more. Next to each strategy, evaluate how effective they are (e.g., mostly effective, frequently ineffective) for curbing your stress level.

_____

_____

_____

Specify which days of the week you can engage in your most (or moderately) effective strategies that require 30 minutes or more. Those days could be Sundays (in anticipation of the new week) or Saturdays (to fully wind down from a week of providing care). You can also decide to engage in a bonus, extended activity on the first Saturday of every month or perhaps quarterly.

It is important for you to know what works and what does not work for you. Depending on the circumstance, I may listen to gospel music or journal about what is most stressful for me in the moment. When I need to get myself together quickly, I focus on my breathing. Each month, I get together with a group of mom friends who are also juggling life's demands. Figure out what works for you to avoid bringing your outside stress into therapy.

It's also important to remember that it's not your client's responsibility to check on how you are doing or console your anxiety in session. Black people are highly adept at placating white people to make sure that you're not uncomfortable. This can be a well-practiced codependent situation that both you and your client shift into by default—your client becoming the comforter when they rightly detect your discomfort with matters of race. If this disposition shows up in therapy, practice deep breathing to quell your anxiety and keep your focus on your therapy goals. Scan your body and release any areas of tension you are carrying. Repeat some affirmations to yourself about your ability to do this work. (You can find some sample affirmations at the end of this chapter.) Use these tools after a client has confronted you on what they perceive as a microaggression. Use them before you ask your client about an experience of barely detectable discrimination. Settle yourself before you forge ahead.

I once advised a student who had a high level of perfectionism that translated well to research and writing. He was a likable person, in part, because he was high on agreeableness. He masked his anxiety to the point that it was only modestly detectable. His perfectionism was a practical strategy that worked well (I dare say he perfected it!) when he didn't need to interface with people. However, when I told him, "You have to begin your next therapy session by acknowledging how you missed an opportunity to check in with your African American client about their potential discomfort with you as a white male therapist," he avoided that assignment for three weeks.

Although I lean toward trusting therapists as they are in the room with the client, in this particular case, the therapist did not want to acknowledge race—ever. I was simultaneously suspicious that race was a factor in why the client tended to present to therapy approximately twenty minutes late each week. In the waiting area, the client was at ease with an African American staff member (displaying the ease that Black people often show one another), but the client shifted noticeably once in the therapy room. I couldn't be sure what was going on, but I insisted that the student therapist could not return to supervision without acknowledging that race was a potential cause of the client's tardiness (unless he had a really good reason).

To increase the student therapist's chances of success (and avoid being banned from supervision if he avoided the conversation again), we practiced a role-play in supervision that went something like this:

THERAPIST: I've been thinking about how we have relatively short sessions because we often don't get to start on time. [*Note that the therapist did not directly blame or criticize the client for their tardiness. Instead, the therapist suggests that their timely start is thwarted.*]

CLIENT: It's hard for me to get here on time. I try every week, but something always comes up.

THERAPIST: Yeah, traffic is always a mess here. We talked about building in time for possible accidents, but it doesn't seem to have worked.

CLIENT: I did try that, but then I was slowed getting out the door because I got an unexpected phone call.

THERAPIST: No doubt there is always something that holds us back from meeting our goals. There is actually something else that I have been wondering about . . .

CLIENT: What's that?

THERAPIST: Well, I wonder if you have been able to get comfortable with me as your therapist. [*pausing*] We live in a world where white men have a lot of privileges, and that can be a huge problem for people who aren't white. If that's true for you and you're still trying to figure me out, I can imagine that you might not be excited about getting to therapy.

CLIENT: [*smiling*] Honestly, I hadn't thought about that. A Black therapist definitely would have been my first choice, but you might be alright.

THERAPIST: I really appreciate your honesty. I want to help you meet your goals for therapy. We'll have to continue this level of openness and honesty. Is that okay for you?

Although this was a role-play, could that scenario have gone poorly when implemented? Most definitely! If the client had felt judged during the conversation, the therapist would have had to repair that breach. Timing is key. You don't want to come in weapons hot, making accusations in the first session, because that is how you will be perceived. You also don't want to miss helping the client problem solve things like getting to session on time. Your client is in therapy for a reason. Evaluate all potential barriers and exhaust the problem-solving before you venture to racial attributions. But then make sure that you are sufficiently versed and comfortable in your privilege to take on this conversation. That's what you do as the therapist—the level-headed person who presumably has their own anxiety, worry, and hypervigilance in check.

Worst-Case Scenario

Let's go down the rabbit hole of the worst-case scenario: You interpret some circumstance that your client is struggling with as racism, but the client disagrees.

THERAPIST: Is it possible that racism is playing a role in how you're being treated?

CLIENT: No, why? Is it because I'm Black?

Let's pause. This is the exact moment of your potential freakout because the truthful response is partly . . . yes! And you're guilty as charged because you are unlikely to ask your white client about being discriminated against due to race. Furthermore, latent white guilt about your own identity and privilege escalates your panic when the client seemingly challenges you. Nevertheless, your client's race is part of the answer, as you have presumably ruled out other possibilities. In case you haven't, just ask.

THERAPIST: It seems we have ruled out most any other reason to account for your mistreatment. Did we miss anything?

CLIENT: No, not that I can think of. I just don't want to assume that stuff is about race just because I'm Black.

THERAPIST: That's fair. And if you can come up with anything else, we can explore that together. But if the situation is about race, we can explore that too. Tell me your concerns.

CLIENT: I don't know. I guess we can talk about it.

If your default is panic, this conversation won't go well, and you'll need to work through the source of your panic. Is it indeed unresolved guilt? Are you in the "contact" phase of racial identity wherein cross-racial interactions are risky? Because if your client has an experience that could be based in racism, it's worth checking in about that. The alternative is to risk showing your client that you don't see them as Black when that is a big part of their identity. And again, I would not expect you to ask about racism until you have ruled out other possible causes with the client.

If there is another worst-case scenario that you have generated for yourself, describe it in detail here.

_____

_____

_____

_____

_____

If that worst-case scenario were to happen, why would it be so upsetting to you? What would that say about you?

_____

_____

_____

_____

_____

Continue down the rabbit hole, considering the worst thing that could happen at each step and what that would mean about you. In the end, are you equipped to handle a worst-case scenario? If it sounds familiar, this is a version of the downward arrow technique. This is a good exercise to practice with professional peers.

Is Your Work Environment Holding You Back?

Over the years, I have conducted countless talks and workshops with mental health professionals about how to conceptualize presenting concerns and provide sensitive, evidence-based care to marginalized communities. Interestingly, what I have found is that among many non-Black practitioners, one of their larger perceived obstacles to providing culturally affirming care is the work environment. They perceive both the management and their co-laborers to prefer the status quo in which race is minimized (either because they have insecurities about how to establish a culturally sensitive environment or they are more comfortable with more assimilated Black people). In any event, ignoring race is the definition of white privilege and is contrary to an evolved white identity.

Consider the following scenario in which a therapist experiences pushback from a peer after they suggest making changes in how they approach mental health care with African American clients:

THERAPIST: I participated in a workshop last week on African American mental health.

PEER: Oh, that sounds interesting.

THERAPIST: It was very interesting! I learned so much about ways we can think more deeply about working with African American clients.

PEER: Well, that sounds nice, but why do we need to do that? We don't even have that many clients.

THERAPIST: That's true, but we do have some clients who are Black, right?

PEER: Well, yeah, but they seem to be doing just fine.

THERAPIST: That might be true, but what if we can be doing more? What if we could be thinking about how race and racism affect them? What if they don't bring up race because they think we are uncomfortable talking about race?

PEER: I just don't know why we have to make a big deal of it.

THERAPIST: Make a big deal of what?

PEER: Racism. They're not coming in for that.

THERAPIST: [*smiling*] It's funny you should say that. The speaker mentioned that in the workshop. Our clients will pretty much never come into therapy with a white person to deal with racism. Like never. That doesn't mean that racism isn't an issue. The speaker gave an illustration of how a client came into therapy for work stress and feeling overwhelmed. The therapist was a white woman. The client came in regularly for months. After some time, the therapist reached out to the speaker, who was a professor in her program, because she felt like she and her client were hitting a wall. Based on the client's presenting problem, the client and the therapist talked about everything related to the client's life *except* her race as a Black woman. The speaker encouraged the therapist to ask the client if she thought race affected her experiences at work. Once the therapist did that, she said her interactions with the client shifted. They talked about race and racism and how it impacted her and they were eventually able to move beyond some stuck points in therapy.

PEER: I can see that, but still, we don't see enough Black clients to make changes.

THERAPIST: I'm a bit confused because it sounds like you're saying that it's not worth thinking differently about how we approach some of our clients from different cultural backgrounds because there aren't *enough* of them?

PEER: You know what I mean. It's just a lot.

THERAPIST: Honestly, I don't know what you mean. As licensed professionals, we are obligated to provide ethical care to all of our clients—each and every one. It concerns me if one of my peers chooses to dismiss a part of a client's cultural background for any reason.

PEER: Okay, so I'm supposed to just walk into a session as if I'm an authority on Black people?

THERAPIST: [*using their clinical skills*] Is that what you hear me saying?

PEER: I don't know, I just feel like you went to one workshop and now you want all of us to make drastic changes.

THERAPIST: We are responsible for our own professional development that we actually *use* in our care for people who trust us. If you don't have training that gives you what you need, you will have to seek it out. Based on the training last week and this conversation now, I realize this is exactly what the speaker was talking about, and maybe we only have a few Black clients because potential clients know that they would have to check part of who they are at the door—at our clinic and many others.

You may have had or can anticipate a future conversation like this. As I think about it, do you really need peers to be on board? I can understand that a team effort would be nice, but why are you waiting for others, allowing them to slow your progress? This is your opportunity to be an ally when doing so might not be popular. If you need a community, start a public Facebook page or a private online group.

The behaviorist in me also wonders how you have been reinforced to avoid discussions of racism. You may practice in a setting that reinforces your fear of addressing a client's racialized realities. Meanwhile, your seeming collusion may have led to psychological harm for individuals in the Black community. It is worth considering all the benefits you have when you sustain the status quo.

Know that if you have avoided race in order to be 100 percent "confident" that you won't say something embarrassing, it is unlikely to happen forever, and it could even be an avoidance strategy. If you've read this entire book, have a graduate degree in a mental health or counseling field, and still don't have a modest degree of confidence, there may be something deeper to examine in you. Your job is not to relate to your client's life story. Your responsibility is to have empathy for pain and to conceptualize a culturally informed treatment plan.

What Kind of Therapist Are You?

As this chapter comes to an end, it's a good time to look back on the self-reflective exercises from chapters 2 and 4, wherein you were prompted to consider your professional identity. I introduced this exercise to eliminate any ambivalence you may have about your responsibility as a mental health provider. Has anything shifted for you at this point?

What does it mean to you to identify as you do? That is, what do you see as your professional responsibilities?

_____

_____

_____

Look over your answers from chapter 4 and make note of what you identified as your single most important professional responsibility. Has your answer changed since then? Be as specific as possible.

_____

_____

_____

On a 0–10 scale (with 0 being "not important at all" to 10 being "very important"), how important to you are your professional responsibilities? _____

Since chapter 4, have you identified any additional notable talents that you hold as a mental health professional? Be sure to indicate those here.

_____

_____

_____

What new barriers to implementing your talents, if any, have you observed since chapter 4?

_____

_____

_____

Based on what you have read thus far, is there anything different you could do to ensure that you're using your talents with your clients consistently?

_____

_____

_____

This exercise is repetitive for a reason. *You will have to do your own ongoing work.* There are no shortcuts. Resist the urge to reach out to your one Black colleague whom you have bantered with on occasion when there is another killing of a Black person by law enforcement. We Black people are as upset as you are and have been carrying this pain for our entire lives, our children's lives, our grandparents' lives, and throughout the family tree. There is literally no room to shoulder your upset.

Take time to consider why you feel compelled to reach out to someone with whom you have a limited relationship. Are you seeking support? What makes you seek support from someone who may also be having a difficult time? What keeps you from talking to your close friends and family? Is it because your Black colleague seems "so strong"? Take time to truly sit with your motivation. Bonus tip: Preempting your support-seeking with "I know you are struggling too" does not help. If your colleague is someone who strongly identifies with the Black community and provides mental health care or occupies some other high-demand space, send them a note letting them know that you're thinking of them and that their commitment to the needs of the community is appreciated. Include a gift card for coffee if you're feeling extra thoughtful.

As a second point, know that until you get out of your comfort zone, the chances are slim that you will engage in any more than a superficial exercise. The difficulty of the work will depend on your racial identity status and your willingness to move forward as the most authentic therapist you can be for you—and subsequently, for your clients.

Bonus tip: If you are ever accused of being racist, you might want to quietly entertain the idea that something you did or said was rooted in racism. Resisting an immediate defensive response is part of the work.

You cannot help your client overcome deeply embedded internal challenges if you struggle with showing up as a therapist who can address matters of race. The ultimate goal is for you to abandon any elephants in the room or, at the very least, commit to engaging elephants in a timely manner. This can be uncomfortable due to the uncertainty of how things will go. Your uncertainty is understandable, but that does not prevent you from having difficult conversations with your client.

Take a moment to close this chapter with statements of affirmation that you can use for yourself. I will list a few. I encourage you to add three additional statements:

- *I can have difficult conversations.*
- *When I feel anxious about a race-related topic, I commit to being fully present in session with my African American or Black client.*
- *My session may not be perfect, but I commit to progress.*

_____

_____

_____

_____

_____

_____

_____

_____

Reflect on your affirmations each morning and each evening.

Do your work.

Chapter 10

What Not to Do

If you skipped the rest of the book to get to this chapter, you may be in trouble. No one is going to leap out of a closet to reprimand you, but skipping may be a clue to your desire for easy answers. There are answers—answers that will advance your skill level and subsequent comfort. But the answers are *not* easy.

Perhaps you have read each chapter to this point and have truly committed to evaluating your biases in addition to watching TED Talks and other resources that amplify cultural realities that are relatively foreign to you. Nevertheless, you remain afraid that you will do *all* the wrong things. I can't be sure, but I surmise that your fear may be about your perceived capacity to develop a strong therapeutic alliance with a Black client. If you have done the work and prepared yourself as best you can, you now realize that there remains an insurmountable reality: You're not a Black therapist who can relate to the Black experience. It is quite possible that the more you have learned as you progressed through these chapters, the more you have discovered what you still do not know.

If so, you may now be convincing yourself that you will reveal your ignorance and perhaps even do harm to your Black client. Resist this thinking. Resist the negative self-talk. If you buy into it, you may worsen an anxiety-provoking situation by overcompensating for your anxiety. That is, as a consequence of your fear of embarrassing yourself, you embarrass yourself. But there are plenty of other contexts in therapy in which we risk embarrassing ourselves—this is just another one. We learn, adjust, and keep working on our competencies.

Throughout this book, I have shared strategies for engaging your client in a manner that embraces the elephant in the room. I have integrated examples of what conversations-gone-wrong look like and discussed how to minimize them. Here, I definitely highlight some not-to-dos. Some warrant more exploration than others. All presume that you aren't beginning here, at the end of the book.

Don't Abandon Your Training and Expertise

Hopefully you have come to this conclusion on your own, but it's worth affirming. Do not abandon your psychotherapy training and expertise. You need your active listening skills. You won't get far without your ability to balance open- and close-ended questions. And you will even have to tap into your clinical judgment. This text is meant to expound on and amplify what you know and who you are as a licensed professional. I get that you have had limited diversity exposure and that available training has failed to integrate practical considerations for Black clients in psychotherapy. If you think about it, however, you are simply doing the work that you learned but with more intentionality and fewer elephants. When you reject that race doesn't matter and resist every elephant that shows up in session, your overall clinical worldview is upgraded. You slow down to be more mindful of your relationship with the client in front of you.

If you think back to the "misdiagnosis" scenario in chapter 5, you'll recall that it was inspired by a real situation in which one of my colleagues suggested a schizophrenia rule-out for a client who had endorsed on a self-report inventory that he was hearing voices. In that scenario, I showed you what it would have looked like if the therapist had taken the time to slowly and deliberately unpack the client's experience. The therapist would have realized that the voices weren't indicative of psychosis but were instead a way that the client maintained a sense of connectedness with his deceased grandmother. In many of the scenarios that I have introduced throughout the book, the therapist has carefully explored the client's thoughts and feelings to get a full understanding of their experience. If this isn't part of your regular practice, you may want to pursue training in this domain of your skillset.

It will always be true that Black people who have a meaningful Black identity will rather see a Black therapist, in part, because of the risk of being *invisibilized* through a white therapist's color-blindness. Whether it is intentional or not, when you keep your client's identity invisible, it adds to their mental strain. A particular scene from *Avatar*, one of my favorite movies for its compelling metaphors, comes to mind as a way to illustrate this point. The fictional main character, Jake Sully, is a paraplegic marine veteran who needs a humanoid avatar to integrate with the fictional Na'vi indigenous people. When Jake first wakes up in his new avatar body, the scientists overseeing his transformation procedure ask him about his basic sensory-motor functioning, but he doesn't attend to them. Instead, he is eager to try out his restored physical functioning. Rather than going slowly through the steps (which includes navigating his now 10-foot body, including a tail), he creates chaos in the room, knocking over equipment before fleeing to try out his restored physical abilities. It is understandable that basic walking and running would be exhilarating for him. However, the chaos he creates could have been avoidable if he would have been willing to begin his new adventure with caution. As long as you acknowledge the elephants, your training can help you avoid needless chaos.

Don't Introduce Race or Racism as an *Issue* in the First Session

This is easy. If your client does not indicate in the first session that racism has brought them to therapy, you don't either. There are no ifs, ands, or buts about it. You have very little, if any, rapport in the first session, so don't start things out by being inappropriate. You will only approach racism as a possibility *after* you have established rapport and have ruled out other possibilities.

But if the client mentions race or racism, you will take a deep breath and explore this possibility with them just as you would any other factor the client introduces, without dismissing their observations and conclusions. In chapter 2, I introduced a 30-year-old client who responded to the question of "What brings you into therapy?" with "I've been hesitant to come to therapy because I couldn't find a Black therapist." I insisted that you have to be prepared and treat the disclosure as a huge opportunity to build rapport. Alternatively, you could botch it by being defensive. A more helpful disposition is one of gratitude that a client doesn't treat you like someone who can't handle a conversation about racism. This would be an ideal scenario.

Don't Go Along with Skipped Homework

I always say that a good client is a client who shows up to therapy and does "homework" or other assigned activities in between sessions. Clients need to complete these between-session assignments to (1) practice important skills to relieve the source of their distress, (2) build adaptive coping strategies, and (3) develop a sense of competency and independence from the therapist so they aren't relying on therapy indefinitely. I address the end of therapy in the next chapter, but suffice it to say, you cannot send your client back out into "the world" if they have not mastered cognitive restructuring or developed strategies for finding more joy in life.

If your client is skipping or "forgetting" homework assignments, you may have to revisit the importance and value of completing these tasks. Too often, therapists fail to communicate to clients what they think is driving and sustaining their maladaptive behavior. As a result, clients don't buy into the therapist's conceptualization of their issues and subsequently fail to see the value of homework. If the homework assignment is something that the client has bought into but simply failed to complete, have the client practice the assignment at the beginning of the session. If they have a pressing concern about the activity, you can discuss it after they have completed the assignment. Have you heard the saying "I can show you better than I can tell you"? The immediate priority is for them to benefit *experientially* from the task. But if there is lingering uncertainty, you can address that directly.

Assuming that the homework is appropriate, you are not being racially insensitive if you insist that your client complete the task. You are not an oppressor who is forcing your client to do something that they don't want to do. You may need to work harder to problem solve their difficulty in completing the assignment, but you cannot enable their resistance. Your own hesitance to problem solve is problematic because you are essentially pretending to do therapy when very little therapy is taking place. Eventually, your client will stop coming to session, saying that "Therapy didn't work" or "That's why I need a Black therapist!" Most clients don't know what to expect and have built-in apprehension about going to therapy. They may not know what "counts" as therapy, but you do. They may think they are "doing therapy" even in the absence of completed homework. Little do they know that *you* are avoiding an elephant in the room by failing to bring it up.

Don't Prematurely Impose Your Values on Your Client

In chapter 2, I introduced a scenario where the therapist suggested that the 33-year-old client put her grandmother in a group home to relieve the stress of being in the sandwich generation. As you'll recall, the therapist's caregiving suggestion represented an unfortunate misstep because, as the client said, "Black people don't do that." But what do you do if *your client* brings up a potentially ill-advised suggestion—one that seems discordant with their cultural beliefs and worldview? Even if you do not initiate the conversation, you don't want to go along with a potentially problematic plan even if your client brings it up. They may be thinking of what they "should" do without fully exploring their own values.

Consider this scenario with a 45-year-old mother of two who is overwhelmed with managing her daughters' needs as well as taking care of her mother, who is experiencing increasing levels of dementia:

CLIENT: The situation at home just feels like it's too much. I'm responsible for my mom, and my 4-year-old, and my 6-year-old. It's a lot.

THERAPIST: If you could wave a magic wand, what would you do to get out from under the feeling of being overwhelmed?

CLIENT: I don't know. My supervisor at work mentioned that they had to put their mother in a home.

THERAPIST: That sounds like it would give you some relief?

CLIENT: It would . . . I just don't know.

If a client is expressing ambivalence, the therapist absolutely must explore that ambivalence. The ambivalence could be culturally laden or not, but the therapist doesn't have to be distracted by potential cultural tenets. What is most salient is the client's uncertainty. Attend to the uncertainty.

THERAPIST: It sounds like you're not so sure about the nursing home idea.

CLIENT: I'm not. It just doesn't feel right.

THERAPIST: So, on the one hand, you can imagine feeling less overwhelmed, but on the other hand, something about the nursing home seems wrong.

CLIENT: Yeah, I know it sounds crazy.

THERAPIST: The situation probably *feels* crazy, in part, because you're overwhelmed. We can work through this together. Let's start with what would be wrong with putting your mom in a nursing home. I think I have some ideas from our work together so far, but tell me from your perspective.

Here, the therapist doesn't have to act as if they don't have any insight into the dilemma, but they also want to prime the client to think about her own perspective:

CLIENT: This is my mother. She's the reason I'm here. She raised me and my brother. She worked two jobs. [*crying at this point*] I should be able to sacrifice for her the way she sacrificed for me.

THERAPIST: [*definitively but empathically*] This is really weighing on you.

CLIENT: [*after some silence and continued tearfulness*] It's too much. I can't do that to her.

THERAPIST: The more that you think about what your mother sacrificed for you, the more impossible it seems to put her in a nursing home.

CLIENT: I couldn't bring myself to do that.

THERAPIST: Okay, that's fair. We can work on two things today. The first is, what would your life and circumstances have to look like for you to seriously revisit this conversation? And second, what are some ways you can get some relief to avoid that time becoming a reality?

CLIENT: Okay. What my life would have to look like?

THERAPIST: Yes, so on the one hand, you started the session by talking about being overwhelmed. But perhaps you're not so overwhelmed that you want to put your mom in a nursing home right now. You feel like you can get by. Is that safe to say?

CLIENT: Yes, I think I can get by.

THERAPIST: Okay, so at what point do you know you are no longer getting by and the situation is no longer feasible?

CLIENT: That's a good question. Some days, I feel like I'm already there, but then the next day is better. Other days, I think I might have a mental breakdown.

THERAPIST: Okay, so how many days can you tolerate feeling like you're having a breakdown?

CLIENT: If it's maybe three days in a row. At that point, someone would be putting *me* in a home.

THERAPIST: Okay, so we'll say if you have two days in a row of feeling like you're on the verge of a breakdown, it is time to make substantial change. If you wait to decide until day three, you may be paralyzed with your overwhelm, right?

CLIENT: Yes, that's true.

THERAPIST: Okay, so at the two-day point, what do you do? You need to have a plan in place to get some relief for two days. Maybe you can research options and we can discuss it next week—a certain plan for relief for two full days. It might involve other family members, or people you know, or even a strategy to develop a community if you don't feel like you have that.

CLIENT: You're right . . . because at the moment, I don't know what that would look like.

THERAPIST: That's okay. We're working on this for when you need it. In the meantime, let's talk about what you can do each day to give yourself some relief so that you don't need that emergency plan.

As the therapist who can see the client's bigger picture, you have to help problem solve and affirm the process rather than jump to solutions that may not be feasible. Clients get so stuck in their hopelessness that they often forget they have a record of creating solutions for all types of problems and occasional crises. They can create solutions for this problem as well—solutions that adhere to their values and sustain their sense of resilience.

Don't Let Comments About "Being Crazy" Go Unaddressed

Too often, I hear about Black folks avoiding therapy because they think going to therapy means that they are crazy or weak or that something is wrong with them. The fear of being crazy is one of those unspoken barriers that you don't want to leave unaddressed. Your client has been feeling crazy for some time. If you let such outward comments go unaddressed, you leave room for your client to continue such musings and to assume you agree! As someone who is culturally minded, you can have as a goal to normalize how your client is feeling. Help them see that they are being courageous by getting the help they need. Evaluate, too, whether they are holding themselves to some unreasonable standard.

To illustrate, let's continue the conversation with the 45-year-old mother of two who is considering putting her mother into a nursing home:

THERAPIST: Earlier, you mentioned that your confusion about putting your mother in a nursing home sounded crazy. Can we check in about that?

CLIENT: I guess so . . .

THERAPIST: You're going through a tough situation. I just want to be sure that you're not unintentionally piling on by telling yourself that how you're handling it is in some way unreasonable. Your situation might feel crazy, but you're not crazy. [*pausing*] Tell me what you hear me saying.

CLIENT: My situation is crazy. I'm not crazy. My situation is.

THERAPIST: Good. What else?

Remember to always get all of the client's thoughts. Even if a client responds with great insight, ask for more. Keep asking until they tell you they don't have any more to say. Having them disclose all of what they hear allows them (and you) to ensure that they fully comprehend what you're saying—and with their own interpretation so the message sinks into their conscious awareness.

CLIENT: I don't have to beat myself up about this. That won't help me.

THERAPIST: Yes! In fact, you're working through your situation so you can begin to create solutions that will help you rather than prolong your struggle. This isn't to say that you can come up with a plan overnight. This situation has built over time, so a quick solution isn't realistic. However, you *can* work toward a manageable solution for yourself and your family.

As a therapist, you have a responsibility to dispel the stigma that therapy is only for people who are "crazy" or "weak," especially among Black clients who carry the added burden of having been systematically mistreated and oppressed for simply living in this world. The therapy room should not be another place where they have to navigate the feeling that something is wrong with them.

Don't Rely on Your Client to Do Your Work!

Transparency is good, but making comments like "I don't know anything about Black people" is something that I hope you never say. If you do, go back to chapter 1. You can ask questions so that if your client introduces something that you do not understand, you can say, "I want to make sure that I follow you. When you say [*fill in the blank*], can you tell me what you mean?"

Don't Ask Your Client If They Enjoy Rap Music

Asking questions based on stereotypes is always ill-advised, but it is especially so at the beginning of the therapist-client relationship. Even if you love rap music and are endeavoring to make connections with your new Black client, there is no basis for this question outside of race-based assumptions that put your credibility immediately in question.

A friend once asked me if it was okay that her new therapist asked her if she liked rap music. My friend was put off by the question but wanted to give the therapist the benefit of the doubt. My friend likes rap as much as she likes jazz and R&B. I advised her that if she felt uncomfortable, that was her honest experience and that it was her right to honor that. She could conclude that the therapist had failed at connecting with her. She could return for a second session and let the therapist know that it was inappropriate, or she could return and say nothing if it wasn't too off-putting, or she could simply find another therapist. In case you're curious, she didn't say anything and eventually stopped seeing the therapist. I deduced that the connection just wasn't there and the question about rap music was the first indicator.

It is likely an adaptive response for some African Americans to question their own feelings in order to give a misguided individual the benefit of the doubt. Even if your client needs a music-related behavioral activation exercise, you can ask, "Do you like to listen to a particular type of music?" Unless they walked into session with a T-shirt that reads "I love rap music," you have no reason to infer their music preference—no reason at all. Black people know how awkward non-Black people can be when trying to make connections or present as more informed than they are. Try not to end up looking like Jake Sully as a first timer in his avatar.

Don't Let Your Angst About Discussing Suicide Take Over When a Client Quickly Dismisses Thoughts of Suicide

When discussing issues related to confidentiality in chapter 3, I introduced you to a 30-year-old male client who denied having current thoughts of suicide but who admitted to having thoughts about how he would die (e.g., driving his car off the road) several months before the session. Even though the client was no longer having such thoughts, the therapist still walked him through the process of developing a safety plan so he could avoid getting to the point of feeling hopeless and paralyzed regarding his situation again.

Most clients are apprehensive of suicide-related conversations, but African Americans can be especially leery about it. Younger generations, including millennials, may be less skittish about suicide, but in all, a thorough suicide risk assessment and safety plan are necessary, particularly when clients reveal moderate to severe psychological distress.

Don't Make It About You

On social media, I have observed critiques of perceived "look at me" comments, where someone seems to "one-up" someone else's post by indicating how their experience deviates from everyone else's. The goal, presumably, is to show how unique they are.

A different brand of "look at me" might show up in therapy when you highlight that you, too, were first in your family to go to college or that you can relate to discrimination due to your Jewish ancestry. You might feel compelled to share that when you were a child, your "great-grandmother told painful stories of how she was subjected to racial slurs in Poland," or perhaps how you were taunted at a rural convenience store while on a cross-country road trip. Ask yourself: How do your experiences enhance rapport-building or treatment planning for your client who experiences chronic microaggressions or whose neighbor was killed by police?

While you may have experienced some of the strains of being marginalized, you cannot relate to the experience of your visibly Black or African American client. Resist inserting your personal experiences into their emotional pain. Rather than announcing your heritage or saying, "I can understand because . . . ," consider whether you have an experience of pain that would allow you to access a deeper level of empathy for your client's circumstances. If so, let your pain drive your questions. That is, quietly tap into the pain, isolation, and helplessness that you or a loved one felt during a personal mistreatment so you can respond accordingly to your client.

Think back to a painful experience that you encountered in life. Describe the situation using just the facts and with as much detail as possible (e.g., Were you alone? What time of day was it?).

_____

_____

_____

_____

What thoughts went through your mind during and after the situation?

During:

_____

_____

_____

_____

_____

After:

_____

_____

_____

_____

_____

As you revisit the situation, what feelings come up for you now?

_____

_____

_____

_____

_____

How did the situation end?

_____

_____

_____

_____

_____

What would you have wanted someone to say to you at the time?

_____

_____

_____

_____

_____

The feelings that come up for you in recounting this situation may approximate those that emerged for your client in their disturbing situation. One difference could be that they don't have the words to capture it, or they wonder if what they feel is warranted. To help your client work through their pain, ask how they would have wanted someone to support them at the time. Then make sure that you provide that support in real time.

Don't Make It About Your Advocacy Either

Recall the scenario in chapter 2 where the 32-year-old client was accused of shoplifting? I advised that the therapist acknowledge in session that the situation was grossly unfair. I also advised that the therapist might independently write a letter to the store's manager or corporate office, reporting that they "overheard" a situation in one of their stores wherein a clerk mistreated an African American shopper. The purpose of the "overheard" part is to protect the client's anonymity and not reveal the client's status as a client. Presumably, the therapist could sign their name and perhaps even sign off with their credentials.

In any case, writing to complain is a reasonable action given the ubiquitousness of racism. Social justice advocacy will always be needed. However, there is no need to disclose actions such as these to a client, as there is no breach of confidentiality. There is also no need to win favor with a client by pulling a "look at what I did!" By now, you realize that there are other ways to increase rapport. Sharing some external action you took can be risky if the client interprets it as an attempt to "prove" you're a good person. Even worse, they may wonder if you risked breaching their confidentiality. In sum, it is okay to advocate absent an audience.

Don't Participate in Your Client's "Shoulding"

"Should" is such a problematic and emotionally costly cognitive distortion. Like I mentioned in chapter 6, I typically avoid using terms like "distortion" and "maladaptive cognition" because it seems more appropriate to label *helpful* and *unhelpful* thoughts, but I make an exception for "should." When invoked, "should" brings forth feelings of guilt and distorts reality. Many assume that "shoulding on themselves" motivates them to engage in some behavior. The reality, however, is that there is a reason that they haven't engaged in that behavior (or have discontinued it altogether).

As someone who wears the hats of PhD, psychologist, and African "Americanist," I have concluded that "should" is ingrained in the African American vernacular. We say things like "I should be able to take care of everyone else even if I'm not doing so well," "I should be able to handle these folks at work who ignore my boundaries" and "I shouldn't be so upset about this recent violence against Black people, given there is violence everywhere." Too often, we convince ourselves that we're not supposed to experience emotional pain. Doing so limits meaningful evaluation of the situation. Whether or not the client *should* feel pain isn't the issue. The issue is that they *do* experience complex emotions that are brought on by realities that surround them. It is worth spending time processing your client's distressing thought together rather than colluding with them in pretending it doesn't exist.

Don't Be Coy About Answering Questions

When you can answer a question directly, answer it. Understandably, there are important inquiries in therapy that do not have straightforward responses. As you know, "How long will I need to be in therapy?" is one of them. Be as honest as you can. In the case of this question, let your client know that the amount of time varies by client, how much difficulty they are managing, and so on. Let them know that a rare few people can work through their concerns in eight weeks or less, but others find that they need more time. Though consistency and attendance are also factors, you don't want to mention those in the first session to avoid the risk of insinuating that the client may be inconsistent or not punctual.

On occasion, your clients will also ask, "What do you think I should do?" when they are experiencing considerable conflict and would prefer to get another opinion. Some clients presume that a therapist's purpose is to give advice, which means that if you fail to do so, you may be perceived as intentionally withholding support. Keep in mind, though, that we as therapists are not tasked with giving advice. That role is for friends and family. At the same time, you also don't want to look like a sadist who is withholding useful insights. The goal is to communicate to your client that you can share your opinion, but one goal of therapy is to help them trust themselves in ways that they may not have in the past. You don't want to shortchange their opportunity for growth.

Alternatively, you can let them know that you're more interested in where their mind is leading them and that it would be more helpful for them in the long run if they can use a decisional balance approach, where they weigh the advantages and disadvantages of a decision (Janis & Mann, 1977).

Don't Be Psychotic—Acting Like Your Black Client Ain't Black

Remember the client in chapter 2 whose apartment application was denied? Although the client expressed their belief that race was a factor, the therapist proposed that there are all kinds of reasons someone might not get an apartment—reasons that, in the therapist's view, mattered as much as race to their distressed African American client. In instances like this, do not repeat the same mistake by assuming that your client is being paranoid or "overly sensitive" about race. Proceed as if their perception of racial discrimination is not a form of pathology but a valid source of their distress.

If you've read through this book to this point and taken part in your personal work, then you are at least beginning to recognize your default responses to the mention of race, and you are working on your avoidance—enhancing your ability to listen without judgment and provide supportive responses. This work must include situations where the client mentions race—and more commonly, in situations where the client does not mention race but that you recognize that race could possibly be a factor. In the scenario of the client being denied an apartment, while there may be lots of reasons for being denied, the only one that matters in your particular dynamic is race.

Don't Forget to Apologize

Be sure to prioritize apologizing when the situation warrants it. When there is a potential breach in the therapeutic alliance, including when you say something offensive or off-putting, or something that runs contrary to your client's cultural traditions, an immediate apology is the best course. If you are trying to build rapport but bungle your attempt, acknowledge your mishap and apologize. If you fail to address an elephant, say so.

If after the session, you realize your mishap when replaying an interaction with the client in your head, apologize when (or if) you next see them. If the client no-shows for their next session and you have permission to leave a voice mail, leave a short apology message:

> Hi [client name]. *I'm sorry we weren't able to have our last session. I was hoping to revisit our conversation from the previous session. As I replayed it in my mind, I realized that I may have communicated something that wasn't at all helpful. Let me know if we can reschedule. Either way, I hope you have the opportunity to meet your important goals in the near future.*

Don't Be Misguided by Your Fears

You had an initial session with an African American client several years ago, and they failed to return to see you a second time—you're certain you botched the session. Rather than assuming that the client had logistical challenges, you presumed you did something wrong. Maybe you did, but you'll never know.

You now find yourself prepared (at least, cognitively) to see your first Black client since that time. You've read more, listened to recommended podcasts to gain better insight into the lived experiences of Black people, and engaged in your own self-reflection. Your new client presents with familial and work-related stress. She reports seeking therapy because her capacity to deal with all of it is getting to be too much, and her doctor is concerned about her emotional eating.

Midway through the intake session, the client asserts, "I know they treat me the way they do in that doctor's office because I'm a Black woman." Rather than support her in the moment, your fear of looking "ignorant" or offending your client takes over. What if she stops coming to therapy? In turn, you fail to address the perceived racism and don't circle back in the next session to all the ways you can unpack her thinking. Missing an opportunity to help your client work through racism-related frustration is unacceptable. Your client will continue to endure (rather than escape) her frustration if you fail to put the conversation in a context that empowers her.

Above All Else . . . Don't You Dare Cry

This sounds like the opposite of empathy coming from me as a therapist. However, as a Black woman, this is the unapologetic part. Black folks have endured a lot. We persist through mistreatment, through folks insisting that we're too sensitive or take things the wrong way, through death and near death at the hands of police *and* medical professionals, through folks telling us where we cannot live and what careers we cannot pursue despite our brilliance. Facing issues of race in session is your opportunity to push through in the way that your client has had to push through. This is your professional moment of triumph as a prepared listener who can handle the uncomfortable and provide support for hardships you may not be able to relate to. Don't spoil it by crying.

It is understandable if you get teary when a new client shares details of their trauma history, but if you're still developing rapport, tears could be problematic. A sad or difficult moment in session is when you must be the embodiment of anti-white fragility. Black people expect "white tears" but do not trust these tears. So take a deep breath and see the conversation through to the end with dry eyes focused on your client.

Chapter 11

It's Hard to Say Goodbye—Planning for the End of Therapy

Over the years, I have observed that many clients, including African American clients, show a hint of relief in the first session when therapists assert that "The goal of therapy is to not be in therapy." The main point is to communicate that we are not invested in binding clients to therapy indefinitely. Instead, we want them to have what they need to navigate life's challenges. I do not know if this idea provides some reassurance that they are "stopping by" temporarily to pick up a few tools, or if they simply appreciate the therapist's affirmation that they are sane enough to eventually end therapy. The alternative could be something much more practical. That is, who has the time and resources to indefinitely invest in years of weekly sessions? Some do, but many do not.

You may be the only white person your client has ever encountered with whom they feel comfortable. After you've taken the time to develop rapport in a way that your client might not have ever expected with a non-Black person, ending therapy might seem daunting for both of you. They may have few people in their life with whom they can have a real conversation, so talking to you is especially rewarding. If this is the case, you may want to work with them on extending their network of support. In sum, you have to be intentional about bringing therapy to an end at the appropriate time.

Too often, the end of therapy is left to chance, leaving you and your client unable to coordinate when and how it will occur. This uncertainty can create a different kind of elephant. Your client may hope that the topic is delayed for as long as possible. In other instances, the end of therapy happens unexpectedly (e.g., when the client no-shows and stops responding). In an ideal world, you help the client meet their goals and therapy ends mutually.

There doesn't have to be an awkward "breakup." Some sadness may accompany the last session, but your client (and you) are capable of doing sad things. Consider that looking ahead to the client's future can offset some of this sadness. You can also model how to appropriately end an activity that persists past its time. That is, your client can and will continue to benefit from continually reevaluating their life for behaviors that may have served them well at one point but that they eventually need to cease so they can achieve more in life. Continuing in therapy can inadvertently communicate that your client has not mastered new skills (when, in reality, they have)!

The End Is Ethically Mandated

The end of therapy is commonly known as "termination." Although our professional organizations acknowledge termination procedures in their ethical codes, they leave the interpretation of these procedures somewhat fuzzy. For example, according to the American Counseling Association (2014), "Counselors terminate a counseling relationship when it becomes reasonably apparent that the client no longer needs assistance, is not likely to benefit, or is being harmed by continued counseling" (p. 6). Similarly, the APA (2017b) notes that "prior to termination, psychologists provide pretermination counseling and suggest alternative service providers as appropriate" (p. 15). Understandably, our ethical codes cannot specify how to accomplish such procedures. When exactly is it "reasonably apparent" that it is time to end therapy if a client has achieved their initial goals but continues to present with something new each week? In addition, if you have any guilt about setting expectations with your African American client, you may feel compelled to continue therapy as long as they continue to show up. The end may never come.

To help make this determination, Dr. John Norcross and colleagues (2017) surveyed 65 experts across multiple therapeutic orientations, including CBT, psychoanalytic, multicultural, and humanistic therapy. They found a 90 percent or better consensus in certain termination behaviors, which include supporting the client's progress, adhering to ethical codes for pretermination planning, ensuring that the client does not feel abandoned, and setting a specific plan for ending therapy.

In the scholarly literature, however, the successful end of therapy is a surprisingly unaddressed topic. More often, premature termination and therapy dropout are addressed, despite the fact that clinicians search for information related to termination more than any other topic on the APA's website (Hilsenroth, 2017). When it comes to the importance of successful termination, a gymnastics competition metaphor comes to mind. A gymnast can execute an amazing routine wherein they complete a series of skillful jumps and turns, but if the dismount isn't right, the gymnast loses points. Catastrophic injuries are rare, but they can occur at any point in a routine, including the dismount. To solidify the gains made in therapy, the dismount must be right. Thus, preparation is key.

Consolidation Rather Than Termination

Years ago, I detected a stuck point for therapists in training when they were nearing the end of therapy. Therapists avoided it like the plague. For one, it never seemed fair to remove the client's presumed safety net. Perhaps doing so was perceived as harmful and, thus, against the ethical code. Second, "termination" sounded so final, adding to the theme of doing harm. Who would want to *terminate* a client? No one—that's who. I eventually collaborated with Jessica Maples, an advanced doctoral student at the time, to address what I saw as an implicit weakness in the termination process.

As part of our investigation, Jessica discovered that the use of the label "termination" seemed to be based on a misinterpretation of Freud's original writings. Freud is said to have more likely referred to the end of therapy as "finite" or *finally* coming to an end rather than being "terminable" (Leupold-Löwenthall, 1988). The misunderstanding that Freud characterized the end of therapy as terminable led to the use of the term "termination." More dramatic interpretations of Freud's original writings might have concluded with "finale" as the end of therapy. With this knowledge, we outlined where scholars and clinicians went wrong with the label of "termination," and Jessica and I organized a comprehensive approach for ending therapy called "consolidation." Ultimately, consolidation is the enterprise of shifting psychotherapy content to "life outside the therapeutic context" (Maples & Walker, 2014, p. 107), which is a process *you* are responsible for as the therapist.

Therefore, as we wind down our work together, let's discuss consolidation—for your work with your client and also for you. There are five strategies for consolidation, which aren't numbered by specific sessions because the exact timing of the strategy can vary. It is, however, expected that the strategies occur in sequential order. With this in mind, let's walk through each consolidation strategy.

Consolidation Strategy 1: Establish Therapy Goals

Clients often present to therapy feeling overwhelmed and seeing therapy as a last resort. However, they haven't necessarily had a conversation with themselves about what exactly needs to be different. It is your responsibility to first establish the goals and then regularly evaluate your client's progress.

While a client's goals will often shift and increase in clarity over time, they must always be concrete. This is how the first strategy of consolidation is initiated. You always need to tie goals to the question of "How will your life be different on the other side of therapy?" Your client will appreciate that there is a vision in mind for the end of therapy. Alternatively, when you proceed without an end in sight, the client might infer that there is something irreparably wrong with them. Having a working plan of the endgame allows you and the client to know what the end of therapy looks like. The inherent understanding is that once goals are met, therapy ends.

Consolidation Strategy 2: Ask About Ending Therapy When There Is Evidence of Goal Attainment

When the client has demonstrated three to four weeks of sustained progress toward their therapy goals, consolidation may be imminent. It is at this time that you are expected to check in on their thoughts about ending therapy. This check-in occurs some time before the last day of therapy and includes a discussion of how many sessions will be needed to consolidate.

This initial conversation may be jarring for the client, but it isn't terribly surprising, as you pick up this discussion at a time when they have had considerable symptom relief and decrease in emotional strain. Some clients will be pleased, while others who have less confidence in their capacity to sustain goals will be apprehensive. However, your avoidance of the client's apprehension will not serve the therapy well. If you wait until the client is "ready," you delay consolidation. If your decision to begin consolidation is based on anything other than your client's decreased scores on symptom inventories and their continued behavior change, you delay consolidation. It is okay to normalize both the positive and negative emotions associated with ending therapy. Nevertheless, it must end once the client has met predefined goals or when they have plateaued in their progress.

THERAPIST: You have had several weeks of maintaining relatively low symptoms of depression. Have you noticed that?

CLIENT: I do feel much better, that's for sure.

THERAPIST: So given that, it's a good time to start thinking about consolidating your therapy.

CLIENT: [*after a momentary look of surprise*] Like ending therapy? You think so?

THERAPIST: I would say yes, based on your goal of wanting to decrease your irritability and get more joy out of life by spending your time engaging in activities for yourself, but I'd like to hear your thoughts.

CLIENT: Well, I guess you're right.

THERAPIST: It is understandable that you would have some apprehension. We have accomplished a lot together. I also imagine that you appreciate these opportunities to focus on yourself and your needs.

CLIENT: That's true. I guess I don't feel ready to lose that.

THERAPIST: To be sure, I'm not suggesting at all that today is our last session. There are some specific details that we want to first address. We need to review what you have accomplished in therapy and also what hasn't worked. We also need to discuss what would have to be going on in your life for you to decide later on that you want to resume therapy. Perhaps we can also talk about what you need to do to create a support system that replaces therapy to some degree?

CLIENT: I would like that. Okay, what's our next step?

THERAPIST: Let's talk about how many more sessions we need to develop a plan to take care of those details.

Again, ending therapy isn't easy. It is a much smoother process when it has been introduced at the beginning of therapy. The therapist has to make sure to communicate that the end of therapy is as intentional as other phases of therapy. When you observe that the client's goals are met and have been sustained for several weeks, it is time to commence consolidation.

Consolidation Strategy 3: Summarize the Client's Accomplishments

A primary goal of the third phase of consolidation is to review the new insights and skills that the client has gained. The client may also want to identify ways to expand on their therapy success. Another important goal is to identify barriers that will prohibit or undermine the client's capacity to maintain their goals. This is key so that you can collectively problem solve how best to navigate barriers when the client is no longer in therapy.

Consolidation Strategy 4: Empower the Client to Review New Skills and Tools

This strategy, which often occurs simultaneously with strategy 3, is about encouraging your client to lead conversations about their therapy progress. The client may not recognize how far they have come or how their effort can pay off (or has paid off) in multiple areas of life. For the client to feel most accomplished, you must ask them to take the lead. As an example, imagine that you have helped a client overcome her fears about asserting herself at work, which has led to an accompanying increase in her ability to be more assertive at home in expressing her needs. In this phase of therapy, you can help your client "connect" the dots of her success.

THERAPIST: Okay, do you remember our primary goal for today? [*prompting the client to begin the session right away*]

CLIENT: Yes, and I've already thought about it. We have to talk about what might keep me from maintaining my therapy progress.

THERAPIST: Okay, great. So what did you come up with?

CLIENT: I can see the possibility that I might fall back into my old routine with my family, though I've been doing better and they see it. My youngest has commented that I seem happy. I almost started crying when he said that. He's 6!

THERAPIST: Wow. How did you feel about your 6-year-old child noticing your happiness?

CLIENT: [*crying*] I don't know why I'm crying. It just hit me so hard. Even my child was used to me being unhappy so much that it was new for him to see me happy. My goodness. My children deserve a happy mom.

THERAPIST: They do. And that's pretty powerful. [*pausing*] One thing that I find fascinating is that you came to therapy primarily because of struggles at work. But you are also happier at home . . . ?

CLIENT: I don't think I realized that things were so tough at home. Everything feels so much lighter.

THERAPIST: Say more about that.

CLIENT: I've turned so much around in my life. I don't have all of the stress weighing me down. I mean, everything's not perfect, but I'm a lot better. I did that.

THERAPIST: You did. And I'm so glad you said that *you* did that.

CLIENT: Yes, I had to do the work. You guided me along the way, but I did the work.

THERAPIST: Exactly. Now I do want us to revisit one other thing because a little while ago, you said that your family has noticed your happiness. As you sit in front of me, you seem happy and maybe even proud of yourself, but do you think you could fall back into old patterns?

CLIENT: Yeah. I know that it took a lot for me to get here. And if I don't have accountability, I can fall into old habits. It was those habits that probably brought me to therapy.

THERAPIST: That's an important insight that you just shared. Old habits probably got you to therapy. So what is something you can do to prevent yourself from falling into old habits and to ensure accountability?

CLIENT: I can create a list of things that signal I've started to slip, like when I start snapping at my children at home?

THERAPIST: Okay, yes, and what else? And also, what is your accountability?

CLIENT: I can ask my 19-year-old to point out when I start to resemble my old self—when I'm snapping at them and not as happy.

THERAPIST: Okay, that sounds good. Is this a plan that you're comfortable with?

CLIENT: Yes, I can definitely follow through on this. My oldest is an adult who has started his own career, though he is still living at home. I'm comfortable with him helping with this.

As a therapist, you want to guide your client to their goals but prompt them to create their own solutions. One such goal is to sustain therapy progress. One way to do this is to facilitate the client's sense of empowerment. This can be particularly important for clients who feel disempowered in many aspects of their lives. Importantly, it might coincide with their value of being able to "handle anything" that comes their way. It's a win-win.

Consolidation Strategy 5: Make Plans to Return to Therapy as Needed and Prevent Relapse

In the final phase of therapy, you want to be sure to identify when your client might need to return to therapy. I do not advise that clients return at the first hint of a "relapse," but if several weeks of trying skills fail, then it may be time to go back to therapy. Once they are in the middle of a crisis, they have less resources to problem solve. Therefore, they will benefit from both a preidentified threshold that indicates they need to return to therapy and a recap of strategies they can use when they find themselves backsliding.

As an example, your client may find that she doesn't want to get out of bed on workdays. This is something that she recognizes from when her mind previously spiraled. The difference is that she has new strategies she can use.

THERAPIST: Well, today is our last session. [*smiling . . . and after a momentary pause*] What do you think about that?

CLIENT: After our last session, I feel good about what I do know, so I feel more ready.

THERAPIST: That's good to hear. What was it about last session that was most helpful?

CLIENT: Just being able to reevaluate that I have more tools than I know. I was taking them for granted because I use them regularly. But after summarizing them, I feel like I'm ready to end therapy. When you first mentioned it a few weeks ago, I got nervous. I was feeling better, but I didn't think I was ready to end our sessions.

THERAPIST: You've made so much progress to this point, but it sounds like it was most helpful for you to sit with the actual list of what you do differently and how you accomplished your goals.

CLIENT: Exactly.

THERAPIST: Did any additional thoughts come to mind since last time?

CLIENT: I did have a little worry about what will happen if I forget to use my skills.

THERAPIST: I'm glad you raised that because that's what I want us to talk about today. You can always resume therapy if you feel you need to. It might not be helpful to rush back at the first sign of trouble because you want to give yourself time to use your skills, but let's talk about what would signal to you that your skills may not be working as you need them to.

CLIENT: Well, I guess if I start sleeping too much, or if I start snapping at my children for no reason.

THERAPIST: Yes, you definitely want to attend to that. How long do you think that would have to occur unchecked for you to conclude there is a problem?

CLIENT: Maybe if I have two to three weeks of going backward, and I can't seem to get myself back on track, *and* I've talked to my sister about it for accountability, it's time to come back and see where adjustments are needed.

THERAPIST: This all sounds good. I think we're on the same page about your strategy.

It is helpful for the therapist to create space for the client to revisit previously agreed-upon goals and highlight exactly what the circumstances would be to return to therapy. Once the client confirms that they feel good about the plan, they can say goodbye.

When Potential Consolidation Fades into a New Goal

Although these five consolidation strategies might progress smoothly in an ideal world, it has been my observation over the years that when your client does not want to experience the loss of therapy, they will introduce new issues to resolve. They could have other motivations, but at the end of the day, they are not motivated to consolidate their work. This is why it is your responsibility to evaluate their progress and their thinking on what work remains to be done.

Recall the 32-year-old client from chapter 2 who initially met criteria for an adjustment disorder with mixed anxiety and depressed mood following the death of her younger brother due to COVID-19. I return to this case because the client presumably benefited from the therapy that addressed her initial adjustment-related anxiety and depression and perhaps her prolonged grief. However, she continued therapy to address reported anger issues. It was the anger issues that she was navigating when another shopper in a store suggested that she was shoplifting.

Here, we consider how this dialogue might have taken place in a manner that acknowledges the client's improved anxiety and depression symptoms but allows for the therapist and client to collaboratively assess next steps and transition into a new goal regarding anger:

THERAPIST: When we first began our work together, we agreed that we would address your thoughts about your brother's death and find ways to help you manage your emotions. Along the way, we monitored your anxiety and depression. Today is a good day to evaluate how things are going from your perspective.

CLIENT: Yes, it started out rough, but I really feel like it's been going well for the last few weeks. I don't feel as wound up, and I definitely feel better about doing more than just going to work.

THERAPIST: This all sounds good. I noticed the same in recent weeks. You know, whenever we try something new, getting started is challenging for all sorts of reasons. What's important is your ability to stick with it and integrate the new strategies to help meet your goals.

CLIENT: I did! I still have work to do, but I see how far I've come.

THERAPIST: I'm so happy to hear this. If it's okay with you, I'd like for us to talk about where you are with your goals and what could be remaining. You mentioned that there is more to do.

CLIENT: I'm feeling okay about what we've done. I feel like I can sustain it. But one thing that I hadn't brought up is how angry I still feel sometimes. I don't even know if I have a right to feel angry. I just do.

THERAPIST: What I hear you saying is that while you feel less depressed and less anxious, you have some anger that comes up for you—anger that you're not sure where it comes from?

CLIENT: Yeah. It's not like when those folks at work get on my nerves. I know why I get angry with them. It's more like, I feel the anger in my body and want to fight but there's no one to fight.

THERAPIST: How often would you say this happens?

CLIENT: It's at least once a week.

THERAPIST: Do you recall the last time this happened?

CLIENT: I was in the grocery store. Ha! There must be something about me and stores! But I was in the store and this woman who had a cart full of groceries jumped in an empty line ahead of me and I only had three things. I mean-mugged her until she checked out. I know she wasn't even thinking about me, but I was furious.

THERAPIST: On a scale from 0–10, with 10 being as much anger as you can imagine, how angry were you?

CLIENT: I was at a 10!

THERAPIST: Wow. You were really upset.

CLIENT: See? That's what I'm telling you. And after the fact, I was like "Why was I so upset?" Maybe that lady had to get those groceries home to her children and here I was all upset. I wasn't even in a big hurry.

THERAPIST: Well, do you see how you were able to use your reframing . . . but it just took you a little while?

CLIENT: Yes, that's a good point. But it took me waaaaay longer to get there than I would have wanted.

THERAPIST: I tell you what, let's continue to monitor when these angry feelings come up. Be sure to document them on a thought record so we can discuss them. Perhaps we can work on this for a couple weeks and reevaluate if we need to make adjustments to your treatment plan. This could be a manifestation of your adjustment difficulties and depression.

Keep in mind that your client's level of distress is unlikely to get to zero, especially if they presented with an exceedingly high level of overwhelm at the start of therapy. It is your responsibility to focus on the decrease that allows them to be fully functioning rather than chronically dysregulated. Pursuing a goal of being symptom-free or anxiety-free could delay consolidation. If they have been sitting with "mild" symptoms for six weeks or more, that might be the ceiling for their success.

No-Shows to Avoid Ending Therapy

Another barrier to consolidation can occur when clients stall the end of therapy by no-showing or canceling at the last minute to avoid the actual end. This is an elephant that is not to be left undisturbed. Assuming that you have permission to leave a voice message, you can say something like this:

> *I'm sorry we've missed our last two sessions. As we begin to consolidate the impressive work that you have accomplished, I hope that we have an opportunity to truly understand how your success has empowered you to live your life on your own terms. It'd also be great to talk about how to maintain your progress. I have our regular appointment time on the books for Friday at 10 a.m. If I don't get to see you, I'll understand that this may no longer be a good time for you. Please follow up if another time could be better for at least one more session.*

Anecdotally, I estimate that at least half of clients make it to one more session if you let them know upfront that is all you're asking. Either way, you are too far along in the game to invite new elephants. Understandably, both you and the client may want to avoid the end of a wonderfully productive working relationship. It's hard to say goodbye!

Premature Termination

Finally, what do you do if your client needs to return to therapy but working with you isn't an option? Perhaps the client has moved, or you've moved, or they need to find another therapist for some other reason. As you consolidate, you don't want to leave anything to chance, which is why you need to be proactive and problem solve through this possibility *before* it occurs.

THERAPIST: Let's talk about what happens if you decide that you need to return to therapy, but you would like to work with a different therapist, or you prefer to work with me, but I'm not available for whatever reason.

CLIENT: Oh, I hadn't thought of that.

THERAPIST: It may not be the case, but it's good for us to consider these scenarios. If you find yourself in a spot, it could be overwhelming to think about the details of finding a new therapist.

CLIENT: That makes sense.

THERAPIST: I have a list of local therapists I can share with you, but if you're out of state or that list doesn't work, you'll need another plan. Remind me of how you found me.

CLIENT: I found you on the psychologytoday.com website.

THERAPIST: Would you be content to create a list of three or so therapists who could be an option?

CLIENT: Yes, I can do that this weekend.

You may find that this conversation is more helpful for clients who have unpredictable lives and high levels of distress, but less important for those who are managing acute challenges and unlikely to return to therapy. Perhaps you carry a heavy caseload that can make it impossible to quickly resume care. In any case, it can be helpful for clients to have as complete a plan as possible, recognizing that it's challenging to foretell all possible scenarios.

Conclusion

Your Own Consolidation

In the same way that you help your client assess their progress and readiness to use their tools out in the world on their own, you might find it helpful for you to think about your goals toward cultural humility and your readiness to prioritize curiosity over "expertise."

Throughout this book, you have gained new insights—not just about working with Black and African American clients but also, and more importantly, about yourself. You have come to recognize and confront your fears and blind spots. You have decided to be part of the solution in our inadequate mental health care systems—systems that disenfranchise individuals who endure unnecessary emotional health challenges.

As this book comes to a close, reflect on what your expectations were for this book.

_____

_____

_____

_____

_____

_____

_____

_____

_____

_____

What have been your key takeaways from this book? Be as specific as possible.

_____

_____

_____

_____

_____

_____

What new strategies have you committed to implementing?

_____

_____

_____

_____

_____

_____

In what circumstances would you regress to ignoring the elephants in the room?

_____

_____

_____

_____

_____

_____

Are there other circumstances that would prevent you from implementing your goals?

_____

_____

_____

_____

_____

_____

If you could wave a magic wand, what types of trainings would you pursue to reinforce what you've learned and better address your remaining blind spots and points of greatest anxiety?

_____

_____

_____

_____

_____

_____

You have made tremendous progress and gained key insights. Providing emotional health care in a society that is replete with injustice is no small feat. This is even more notable when mental health providers can be complicit in ignoring elephants. You may have mishaps along the way, but your self-awareness will keep you on track. Commit to ensuring your own accountability by coordinating reading groups and collaborating with peers. As the African proverb says, "if you want to go fast, go alone. If you want to go far, go together" (Goldberg, 2016).

Cultural Formulation Interview (CFI)

Supplementary modules used to expand each CFI subtopic are noted in parentheses.

GUIDE TO INTERVIEWER	INSTRUCTIONS TO THE INTERVIEWER ARE *ITALICIZED*.
The following questions aim to clarify key aspects of the presenting clinical problem from the point of view of the individual and other members of the individual's social network (i.e., family, friends, or others involved in current problem). This includes the problem's meaning, potential sources of help, and expectations for services.	*INTRODUCTION FOR THE INDIVIDUAL:* I would like to understand the problems that bring you here so that I can help you more effectively. I want to know about *your* experience and ideas. I will ask some questions about what is going on and how you are dealing with it. Please remember there are no right or wrong answers.

CULTURAL DEFINITION OF THE PROBLEM

CULTURAL DEFINITION OF THE PROBLEM
(Explanatory Model, Level of Functioning)

Elicit the individual's view of core problems and key concerns. *Focus on the individual's own way of understanding the problem.* *Use the term, expression, or brief description elicited in question 1 to identify the problem in subsequent questions (e.g., "your conflict with your son").*	1. What brings you here today? *IF INDIVIDUAL GIVES FEW DETAILS OR ONLY MENTIONS SYMPTOMS OR A MEDICAL DIAGNOSIS, PROBE:* People often understand their problems in their own way, which may be similar to or different from how doctors describe the problem. How would *you* describe your problem?
Ask how individual frames the problem for members of the social network.	2. Sometimes people have different ways of describing their problem to their family, friends, or others in their community. How would you describe your problem to them?
Focus on the aspects of the problem that matter most to the individual.	3. What troubles you most about your problem?

CULTURAL PERCEPTIONS OF CAUSE, CONTEXT, AND SUPPORT

CAUSES
(Explanatory Model, Social Network, Older Adults)

This question indicates the meaning of the condition for the individual, which may be relevant for clinical care.	4. Why do you think this is happening to you? What do you think are the causes of your [PROBLEM]?

Note that individuals may identify multiple causes, depending on the facet of the problem they are considering.	*PROMPT FURTHER IF REQUIRED:* Some people may explain their problem as the result of bad things that happen in their life, problems with others, a physical illness, a spiritual reason, or many other causes.
Focus on the views of members of the individual's social network. These may be diverse and vary from the individual's.	5. What do others in your family, your friends, or others in your community think is causing your [PROBLEM]?

STRESSORS AND SUPPORTS
(Social Network, Caregivers, Psychosocial Stressors, Religion and Spirituality, Immigrants and Refugees, Cultural Identity, Older Adults, Coping and Help Seeking)

Elicit information on the individual's life context, focusing on resources, social supports, and resilience. May also probe other supports (e.g., from co-workers, from participation in religion or spirituality).	6. Are there any kinds of support that make your [PROBLEM] better, such as support from family, friends, or others?
Focus on stressful aspects of the individual's environment. Can also probe, e.g., relationship problems, difficulties at work or school, or discrimination.	7. Are there any kinds of stresses that make your [PROBLEM] worse, such as difficulties with money, or family problems?

ROLE OF CULTURAL IDENTITY
(Cultural Identity, Psychosocial Stressors, Religion and Spirituality, Immigrants and Refugees, Older Adults, Children and Adolescents)

	Sometimes, aspects of people's background or identity can make their [PROBLEM] better or worse. By **background** or **identity**, I mean, for example, the communities you belong to, the languages you speak, where you or your family are from, your race or ethnic background, your gender or sexual orientation, or your faith or religion.
Ask the individual to reflect on the most salient elements of his or her cultural identity. Use this information to tailor questions 9–10 as needed.	8. For you, what are the most important aspects of your background or identity?
Elicit aspects of identity that make the problem better or worse. *Probe as needed (e.g., clinical worsening as a result of discrimination due to migration status, race/ethnicity, or sexual orientation).*	9. Are there any aspects of your background or identity that make a difference to your [PROBLEM]?
Probe as needed (e.g., migration-related problems; conflict across generations or due to gender roles).	10. Are there any aspects of your background or identity that are causing other concerns or difficulties for you?

CULTURAL FACTORS AFFECTING SELF-COPING AND PAST HELP SEEKING

SELF-COPING
(Coping and Help Seeking, Religion and Spirituality,
Older Adults, Caregivers, Psychosocial Stressors)

Clarify self-coping for the problem.	11. Sometimes people have various ways of dealing with problems like [PROBLEM]. What have you done on your own to cope with your [PROBLEM]?

PAST HELP SEEKING
(Coping and Help Seeking, Religion and Spirituality, Older Adults, Caregivers, Psychosocial Stressors, Immigrants and Refugees, Social Network, Clinician-Patient Relationship)

Elicit various sources of help (e.g., medical care, mental health treatment, support groups, work-based counseling, folk healing, religious or spiritual counseling, other forms of traditional or alternative healing). *Probe as needed (e.g., "What other sources of help have you used?").* *Clarify the individual's experience and regard for previous help.*	12. Often, people look for help from many different sources, including different kinds of doctors, helpers, or healers. In the past, what kinds of treatment, help, advice, or healing have you sought for your [PROBLEM]? *PROBE IF DOES NOT DESCRIBE USEFULNESS OF HELP RECEIVED:* What types of help or treatment were most useful? Not useful?

BARRIERS
(Coping and Help Seeking, Religion and Spirituality, Older Adults, Psychosocial Stressors, Immigrants and Refugees, Social Network, Clinician-Patient Relationship)

Clarify the role of social barriers to help seeking, access to care, and problems engaging in previous treatment. Probe details as needed (e.g., "What got in the way?").	13. Has anything prevented you from getting the help you need? *PROBE AS NEEDED:* For example, money, work or family commitments, stigma or discrimination, or lack of services that understand your language or background?

CULTURAL FACTORS AFFECTING CURRENT HELP SEEKING

PREFERENCES
(Social Network, Caregivers, Religion and Spirituality,
Older Adults, Coping and Help Seeking)

Clarify individual's current perceived needs and expectations of help, broadly defined. *Probe if individual lists only one source of help (e.g., "What other kinds of help would be useful to you at this time?").*	Now let's talk some more about the help you need. 14. What kinds of help do you think would be most useful to you at this time for your [PROBLEM]?

Focus on the views of the social network regarding help seeking.	15. Are there other kinds of help that your family, friends, or other people have suggested would be helpful for you now?

CLINICIAN-PATIENT RELATIONSHIP
(Clinician-Patient Relationship, Older Adults)

Elicit possible concerns about the clinic or the clinician-patient relationship, including perceived racism, language barriers, or cultural differences that may undermine goodwill, communication, or care delivery. *Probe details as needed (e.g., "In what way?").* *Address possible barriers to care or concerns about the clinic and the clinician-patient relationship raised previously.*	Sometimes doctors and patients misunderstand each other because they come from different backgrounds or have different expectations. 16. Have you been concerned about this and is there anything that we can do to provide you with the care you need?

References

Chapter 1

American Psychological Association. (2016). *2015 APA survey of psychology health service providers*. https://www.apa.org/workforce/publications/15-health-service-providers/report.pdf

American Psychological Association. (2022). *Demographics of the U.S. psychology workforce* [Interactive data tool]. https://www.apa.org/workforce/data-tools/demographics

Gold, J. (2021, March 19). We need to talk about Black therapist burnout. *Forbes*. https://www.forbes.com/sites/jessicagold/2021/05/29/we-need-to-talk-about-black-therapist-burnout/?sh=2f2864a25d60

Joiner, T. E., Robison, M., Robertson, L., Keel, P., Daurio, A. M., Mehra, L. M., & Millender, E. (2022). Ethnoracial status, intersectionality with gender, and psychotherapy utilization, retention, and outcomes. *Journal of Consulting and Clinical Psychology*, *90*(10), 837–849. https://doi.org/10.1037/ccp0000726

Nielsen (2022, February). *How Black audiences are engaging with audio more than ever.* https://www.nielsen.com/insights/2022/how-black-audiences-are-engaging-with-audio-more-than-ever/

Substance Abuse and Mental Health Services Administration. (2015). *Racial/ethnic differences in mental health service use among adults*. (SMA-15-4906). https://www.samhsa.gov/data/sites/default/files/MHServicesUseAmongAdults/MHServicesUseAmongAdults.pdf

Terrell, F., & Terrell, S. L. (1981). An inventory to measure cultural mistrust among Blacks. *The Western Journal of Black Studies, 5*(3), 180–184.

Chapter 2

Constantine, M. G. (2007). Racial microaggressions against African American clients in cross-racial counseling relationships. *Journal of Counseling Psychology, 54*(1), 1–16. https://doi.org/10.1037/0022-0167.54.1.1

Dana, R. H., Behn, J. D., & Gonwa, T. (1992). A checklist for the examination of cultural competence in social service agencies. *Research on Social Work Practice*, *2*(2), 220–233. https://doi.org/10.1177/104973159200200208

Hansen, N. D., Randazzo, K. V., Schwartz, A., Marshall, M., Kalis, D., Frazier, R., Burke, C., Kershner-Rice, K., & Norvig, G. (2006). Do we practice what we preach? An exploratory survey of multicultural psychotherapy competencies. *Professional Psychology: Research and Practice, 37*(1), 66–74. https://doi.org/10.1037/0735-7028.37.1.66

Hook, J. N., Farrell, J. E., Davis, D. E., DeBlaere, C., Van Tongeren, D. R., & Utsey, S. O. (2016). Cultural humility and racial microaggressions in counseling. *Journal of Counseling Psychology, 63*(3), 269–277. https://doi.org/10.1037/cou0000114

Lui, P. P., & Quezada, L. (2019). Associations between microaggression and adjustment outcomes: A meta-analytic and narrative review. *Psychological Bulletin, 145*(1), 45–78. https://doi.org/10.1037/bul0000172

Neville, H. A., Awad, G. H., Brooks, J. E., Flores, M. P., & Bluemel, J. (2013). Color-blind racial ideology: Theory, training, and measurement implications in psychology. *American Psychologist, 68*(6), 455–466. https://doi.org/10.1037/a0033282

Neville, H. A., Lilly, R. L., Duran, G., Lee, R. M., & Browne, L. (2000). Construction and initial validation of the Color-Blind Racial Attitudes Scale (CoBRAS). *Journal of Counseling Psychology, 47*(1), 59–70. https://doi.org/10.1037/0022-0167.47.1.59

Owen, J., Tao, K. W., Imel, Z. E., Wampold, B. E., & Rodolfa, E. (2014). Addressing racial and ethnic microaggressions in therapy. *Professional Psychology: Research and Practice, 45*(4), 283–290. https://doi.org/10.1037/a0037420

Pierce, C. M., Carew, J. V., Pierce-Gonzalez, D., & Wills, D. (1977). An experiment in racism: TV commercials. *Education and Urban Society, 10*(1), 61–87. https://doi.org/10.117/001312457701000105

Plaut, V. C., Thomas, K. M., & Goren, M. J. (2009). Is multiculturalism or color blindness better for minorities? *Psychological Science, 20*(4), 444–446. https://doi.org/10.1111/j.1467-9280.2009.02318.x

Salvatore, J., & Shelton, J. N. (2007). Cognitive costs of exposure to racial prejudice. *Psychological Science, 18*(9), 810–815. https://doi.org/10.1111/j.1467-9280.2007.01984.x

Sue, D. W., & Torino, G. C. (2005). Racial-cultural competence: Awareness, knowledge, and skills. In R. T. Carter (Ed.), *Handbook of racial-cultural psychology and counseling: Training and practice* (Vol. 2. pp. 3–18). John Wiley & Sons, Inc.

Sue, D. W., Capodilupo, C. M., Torino, G. C., Bucceri, J. M., Holder, A. M. B., Nadal, K. L., & Esquilin, M. (2007). Racial microaggressions in everyday life: Implications for clinical practice. *American Psychologist, 62*(4), 271–286. https://doi.org/10.1037/0003-066X.62.4.27

Tervalon, M., & Murray-García, J. (1998). Cultural humility versus cultural competence: A critical distinction in defining physician training outcomes in multicultural education. *Journal of Health Care for the Poor and Underserved, 9*(2), 117–125. https://doi.org/10.1353/hpu.2010.0233

Yeo, E., & Torres-Harding, S. R. (2021). Rupture resolution strategies and the impact of rupture on the working alliance after racial microaggressions in therapy. *Psychotherapy, 58*(4), 460–471. https://doi.org/10.1037/pst0000372

Chapter 3

Wharton, T., Watkins, D. C., Mitchell, J., & Kales, H. (2018). Older, church-going African Americans' attitudes and expectations about formal depression care. *Research on Aging, 40*(1), 3–26. https://doi.org/10.1177/0164027516675666

Weldon, T. L. (2021). *Middle-class African American English*. Cambridge University Press.

Chapter 4

Clark, R., Anderson, N. B., Clark, V. R., & Williams, D. R. (1999). Racism as a stressor for African Americans: A biopsychosocial model. *American Psychologist, 54*(10), 805–816. https://doi.org/10.1037/0003-066X.54.10.805

Hoyert, D. L. (2022). *Maternal mortality rates in the United States, 2020*. National Center for Health Statistics: Health E-Stats. https://dx.doi.org/10.15620/cdc:113967

Hoffman, K. M., Trawalter, S., Axt, J. R., & Oliver, M. N. (2016). Racial bias in pain assessment and treatment recommendations, and false beliefs about biological differences between Blacks and whites. *Proceedings of the National Academy of Sciences of the United States of America, 113*(16), 4296–4301. https://doi.org/10.1073/pnas.1516047113

James, S. A. (1994). John Henryism and the health of African-Americans. *Culture, Medicine, and Psychiatry, 18*(2), 163–182. https://doi.org/10.1007/BF01379448

Lu, D., Palmer, J. R., Rosenberg, L., Shields, A. E., Orr, E. H., DeVivo, I., & Cozier, Y. C. (2019). Perceived racism in relation to telomere length among African American women in the Black Women's Health Study. *Annals of Epidemiology, 36*, 33–39. https://doi.org/10.1016/j.annepidem.2019.06.003

Mercer, S. H., Zeigler-Hill, V., Wallace, M., & Hayes, D. M. (2011). Development and initial validation of the Inventory of Microaggressions Against Black Individuals. *Journal of Counseling Psychology, 58*(4), 457–469. https://doi.org/10.1037/a0024937

Ross, J., & National Journal Magazine (2014, May 27). African-Americans with college degrees are twice as likely to be unemployed as other graduates. *The Atlantic*. https://www.theatlantic.com/politics/archive/2014/05/african-americans-with-college-degrees-are-twice-as-likely-to-be-unemployed-as-other-graduates/430971/

Selby, D. (2021, February 5). 8 facts you should know about racial injustice in the criminal legal system. *Innocence Project*. https://innocenceproject.org/facts-racial-discrimination-justice-system-wrongful-conviction-black-history-month/

Smedley, B. D., Stith, A. Y., & Nelson, A. R. (Eds.). (2005). *Unequal treatment: Confronting racial and ethnic disparities in health care*. Institute of Medicine: Committee on Understanding and Eliminating Racial and Ethnic Disparities in Health Care. The National Academies Press.

Utsey, S. O. (1999). Development and validation of a short form of the Index of Race-Related Stress (IRRS)—Brief Version. *Measurement and Evaluation in Counseling and Development, 32*(3), 149–167. https://doi.org/10.1080/07481756.1999.12068981

Walker, R. L., Wingate, L. R., Obasi, E. M., & Joiner, T. E., Jr. (2008). An empirical investigation of acculturative stress and ethnic identity as moderators for depression and suicidal ideation in college students. *Cultural Diversity and Ethnic Minority Psychology, 14*(1), 75–82. https://doi.org/10.1037/1099-9809.14.1.75

Winerman, L. (2021, October 7). For Black students, unfairly harsh discipline can lead to lower grades. *American Psychological Association*. https://www.apa.org/news/press/releases/2021/10/black-students-harsh-discipline

Chapter 5

American Psychological Association. (2017a). *Multicultural guidelines: An ecological approach to context, identity, and intersectionality*. http://www.apa.org/about/policy/multicultural-guidelines.pdf

Bailey, R. K., Mokonogho, J., & Kumar, A. (2019). Racial and ethnic differences in depression: Current perspectives. *Neuropsychiatric Disease and Treatment, 15*, 603–609. https://doi.org/10.2147/NDT.S128584

Baker, F. M. (2001). Diagnosing depression in African Americans. *Community Mental Health Journal, 37*(1), 31–38. https://doi.org/10.1023/a:1026540321366

Butcher, J. N., Graham, J. R., Tellegen, A., & Kaemmer, B. (1989). *Manual for the restandardized Minnesota Multiphasic Personality Inventory: MMPI-2*. University of Minnesota Press.

Carter, R. T. (2007). Racism and psychological and emotional injury: Recognizing and assessing race-based traumatic stress. *The Counseling Psychologist, 35*(1), 13–105. https://doi.org/10.1177/0011000006292033

Early, K. E., & Akers, R. L. (1993). "It's a white thing": An exploration of beliefs about suicide in the African-American community. *Deviant Behavior, 14*(4), 277–296. https://doi.org/10.1080/01639625.1993.9967947

Jarvis, G. E. (2012). Changing psychiatric perception of African-Americans with affective disorders. *The Journal of Nervous and Mental Disease, 200*(12), 1031–1040. https://doi.org/10.1097/NMD.0b013e318275cf43

Morrison, L. L., & Downey, D. L. (2000). Racial differences in self-disclosure of suicidal ideation and reasons for living: Implications for training. *Cultural Diversity and Ethnic Minority Psychology, 6*(4), 374–386. https://doi.org/10.1037/1099-9809.6.4.374

Pew Research Center. (2019, April 3). Most Black adults have negative views about the country's racial progress. https://www.pewresearch.org/social-trends/2019/04/09/race-in-america-2019/psdt_04-09-19_race-00-10/

Richardson-Vejlgaard, R., Sher, L., Oquendo, M. A., Lizardi, D., & Stanley, B. (2009). Moral objections to suicide and suicidal ideation among mood disordered Whites, Blacks, and Hispanics. *Journal of Psychiatric Research, 43*(4), 360–365. https://doi.org/10.1016/j.jpsychires.2008.03.008

Rockett, I. R. H., Wang, S., Stack, S., De Leo, D., Frost, J. L., Ducatman, A. M., Walker, R. L., & Kapusta, N. D. (2010). Race/ethnicity and potential suicide misclassification: Window on a minority suicide paradox? *BMC Psychiatry, 10*(35). https://doi.org/10.1186/1471-244X-10-35

Walker, R. L., Lester, D., & Joe, S. (2006). Lay theories of suicide: An examination of culturally relevant suicide beliefs and attributions among African Americans and European Americans. *Journal of Black Psychology, 32*(3), 320–334. https://doi.org/10.1177/0095798406290467

Williams, M. T., Printz, D. M. B., & DeLapp, R. C. T. (2018). Assessing racial trauma with the Trauma Symptoms of Discrimination Scale. *Psychology of Violence, 8*(6), 735–747. https://doi.org/10.1037/vio0000212

Williams, M. T., Metzger, I. W., Leins, C., & DeLapp, C. (2018). Assessing racial trauma within a DSM–5 framework: The UConn Racial/Ethnic Stress & Trauma Survey. *Practice Innovations, 3*(4), 242–260. https://doi.org/10.1037/pri0000076

Chapter 6

Bernal, G., Jiménez-Chafey, M. I., & Domenech Rodríguez, M. M. (2009). Cultural adaptation of treatments: A resource for considering culture in evidence-based practice. *Professional Psychology: Research and Practice, 40*(4), 361–368. https://doi.org/10.1037/a0016401

Bernard, D. L., Calhoun, C. D., Banks, D. E., Halliday, C. A., Hughes-Halbert, C., & Danielson, C. K. (2021). Making the "C-ACE" for a culturally-informed adverse childhood experiences framework to understand the pervasive mental health impact of racism on Black youth. *Journal of Child & Adolescent Trauma, 14*(2), 233–247. https://doi.org/10.1007/s40653-020-00319-9

Boyd-Franklin, N. (2006). *Black families in therapy: Understanding the African American experience* (2nd ed.). Guilford Publications.

Hofmann, S. G., Asnaani, A., Vonk, I. J. J., Sawyer, A. T., & Fang, A. (2012). The efficacy of cognitive behavioral therapy: A review of meta-analyses. *Cognitive Therapy and Research, 36*(5), 427–440. https://doi.org/10.1007/s10608-012-9476-1

Lyddon, W. J., & Weill, R. (1997). Cognitive psychotherapy and postmodernism: Emerging themes and challenges. *Journal of Cognitive Psychotherapy, 11*(2), 75–90.

Miranda, J., Bernal, G., Lau, A., Kohn, L., Hwang, W. C., & LaFromboise, T. (2005). State of the science on psychosocial interventions for ethnic minorities. *Annual Review of Clinical Psychology, 1*, 113–142. https://doi.org/10.1146/annurev.clinpsy.1.102803.143822

Persons, J. B. (2012). *The case formulation approach to cognitive-behavior therapy*. Guilford Press.

Soto, A., Smith, T. B., Griner, D., Domenech Rodríguez, M., & Bernal, G. (2018). Cultural adaptations and therapist multicultural competence: Two meta analytic reviews. *Journal of Clinical Psychology, 74*(11), 1907–1923. https://doi.org/10.1002/jclp.22679

Sue, S. (1998). In search of cultural competence in psychotherapy and counseling. *American Psychologist, 53*(4), 440–448. https://doi.org/10.1037/0003-066X.53.4.440

Ward, E. C., & Brown, R. L. (2015). A culturally adapted depression intervention for African American adults experiencing depression: Oh happy day. *American Journal of Orthopsychiatry*, *85*(1), 11–22. https://doi.org/10.1037/ort0000027

Chapter 7

Adams Spears, C., Houchins, S. C., Bamatter, W. P., Barrueco, S., Stewart Hoover, D., & Perskaudas, R. (2017). Perceptions of mindfulness in a low-income, primarily African American treatment-seeking sample. *Mindfulness*, *8*(6), 1532–1543. https://doi.org/10.1007/s12671-017-0720-3

Brooks Stephens, J. R., Lebeaut, A., Jewell, R. D., Zegel, M., Walker, R. L., & Vujanovic, A. A. (2023). Living in the present moment: The role of mindfulness in the association between impulsivity and suicidality among Black emerging adults. *Mindfulness, 14,* 1790–1803. https://doi.org/10.1007/s12671-023-02180-x

Delaney, H. D., Miller, W. R., & Bisonó, A. M. (2007). Religiosity and spirituality among psychologists: A survey of clinician members of the American Psychological Association. *Professional Psychology: Research and Practice*, *38*(5), 538–546. https://doi.org/10.1037/0735-7028.38.5.538

Gates Jr., H. L. (2021). *The Black church: This is our story, this is our song*. Penguin.

Koenig, H. G. (2009). Research on religion, spirituality, and mental health: A review. *The Canadian Journal of Psychiatry, 54*(5), 283–291. https://doi.org/10.1177/070674370905400502

Mohamed, B., Cox, K., Diamant, J., & Gecewicz, C. (2021, February 16). Faith among Black Americans. *Pew Research Center*. https://www.pewresearch.org/religion/2021/02/16/faith-among-black-americans/

Oxhandler, H. K. (2017). Social work field instructors' integration of religion and spirituality in clinical practice. *Journal of Social Work Education*, *53*(3), 449–465. https://doi.org/10.1080/10437797.2016.1269706

Puchalski, C., & Romer, A. L. (2000). Taking a spiritual history allows clinicians to understand patients more fully. *Journal of Palliative Medicine, 3*(1), 129–137. https://doi.org/10.1089/jpm.2000.3.129

Rosmarin, D. H., Salcone, S., Harper, D. G., & Forester, B. (2021). Predictors of patients' responses to spiritual psychotherapy for inpatient, residential, and intensive treatment (SPIRIT). *Psychiatric Services, 72*(5), 507–513. https://doi.org/10.1176/appi.ps.202000331

Vieten, C., & Lukoff, D. (2022). Spiritual and religious competencies in psychology. *American Psychologist, 77*(1), 26–38. https://doi.org/10.1037/amp0000821

Walker, R. L., Salami, T. K., Carter, S. E., & Flowers, K. C. (2014). Perceived racism and suicide ideation: Mediating role of depression but moderating role of religiosity among African American adults. *Suicide and Life-Threatening Behavior, 44*(5), 548–559. https://doi.org/10.1111/sltb.12089

Walker, R. L., Salami, T. K., Carter, S. E., & Flowers, K. C. (2017). Religious coping style and cultural worldview are associated with suicide ideation among African American adults. *Archives of Suicide Research, 22*(1), 106–117. https://doi.org/10.1080/13811118.2017.1289871

Wong, E. C., Fulton, B. R., & Derose, K. P. (2018). Prevalence and predictors of mental health programming among U.S. religious congregations. *Psychiatric Services, 69*(2), 154–160. https://doi.org/10.1176/appi.ps.201600457

Chapter 8

Akbar, N. (2004). *Papers in African Psychology.* Mind Productions.

Baldwin, J., Capouya, E., Hansberry, L., Hentoff, N., Hughes, L., & Kazin, A. (1961). The Negro in American culture. *Cross Currents, 11*(3), 205–224.

Cheref, S., Benoit, J. S., & Walker, R. L. (2019). Refining psychological, substance use, and sociodemographic predictors of suicide ideation and attempts in a national multiethnic sample of adults, 2008–2013. *The Journal of Nervous and Mental Disease, 207*(8), 675–682. https://doi.org/10.1097/NMD.0000000000001026

Cross, W. E., Jr. (1995). The psychology of nigrescence: Revising the Cross model. In J. G. Ponterotto, J. M. Casas, L. A. Suzuki, & C. M. Alexander (Eds.), *Handbook of multicultural counseling* (pp. 93–122). Sage Publications.

Du Bois, W. E.B (1903). *The souls of Black folk.* A.C. McClurg and Company.

Joiner, T. E. Jr., & Walker, R. L. (2002). Construct validity of a measure of acculturative stress in African Americans. *Psychological Assessment, 14*(4), 462–466. https://doi.org/10.1037/1040-3590.14.4.462

Marcia, J. E. (1980). Identity in adolescence. *Handbook of Adolescent Psychology, 9*(11), 159–187.

Padilla, A. M., Wagatsuma, Y., & Lindholm, K. J. (1985). Acculturation and personality as predictors of stress in Japanese and Japanese-Americans. *Journal of Social Psychology, 125*(3), 295–305. https://doi.org/10.1080/00224545.1985.9922890

Parham, T. A., Ajamu, A., & White, J. L. (2015). *Psychology of Blacks: Centering our perspectives in the African consciousness* (4th ed.). Psychology Press.

Phinney, J. S., & Ong, A. D. (2007). Conceptualization and measurement of ethnic identity: Current status and future directions. *Journal of Counseling Psychology, 54*(3), 271–281. http://doi.org/10.1037/0022-0167.54.3.271

Sellers, R. M., Rowley, S. A. J., Chavous, T. M., Shelton, J. N., & Smith, M. A. (1997). Multidimensional Inventory of Black Identity: A preliminary investigation of reliability and construct validity. *Journal of Personality and Social Psychology, 73*(4), 805–815. https://doi.org/10.1037/0022-3514.73.4.805

Yip, T. (2018). Ethnic/racial identity—A double-edged sword? Associations with discrimination and psychological outcomes. *Current Directions in Psychological Science, 27*(3), 170–175. https://doi.org/10.1177/0963721417739348

Chapter 9

Claney, D., & Parker, W. M. (1989). Assessing White racial consciousness and perceived comfort with Black individuals: A preliminary study. *Journal of Counseling & Development*, *67*(8), 449–451. https://doi.org/10.1002/j.1556-6676.1989.tb02114.x

Gushue, G. V., & Constantine, M. G. (2007). Color-blind racial attitudes and white racial identity attitudes in psychology trainees. *Professional Psychology: Research and Practice*, *38*(3), 321–328. https://doi.org/10.1037/0735-7028.38.3.321

Helms, J. E. (1995). An update of Helms' White and people of color racial identity models. In J. G. Ponterotto, J. M. Casas, L. A. Suzuki, & C. M. Alexander (Eds.), *Handbook of multicultural counseling* (pp. 181–198). Sage.

Lee, S. M., Puig, A., Pasquarella-Daley, L., Denny, G., Rai, A. A., Daltape, A., & Parker, W. M. (2007). Revising the white racial consciousness development scale. *Measurement and Evaluation in Counseling and Development*, *39*(4), 194–208. https://doi.org/10.1080/07481756.2007 .11909798

Chapter 10

Janis, I. L., & Mann, L. (1977). *Decision making: A psychological analysis of conflict, choice, and commitment*. Free Press.

Chapter 11

American Counseling Association. (2014). *ACA code of ethics*. https://www.counseling.org /resources/aca-code-of-ethics.pdf

American Psychological Association. (2017b). Ethical principles of psychologists and code of conduct. https://www.apa.org/ethics/code/ethics-code-2017.pdf

Hilsenroth, M. J. (2017). An introduction to the special issue on psychotherapy termination. *Psychotherapy*, *54*(1), 1–3. https://doi.org/10.1037/pst0000106

Leupold-Löwenthal, H. (1988). Notes on Sigmund Freud's "Analysis Terminable and Interminable." *The International Journal of Psychoanalysis*, *69*(2), 261–272.

Maples, J. L., & Walker, R. L. (2014). Consolidation rather than termination: Rethinking how psychologists label and conceptualize the final phase of psychological treatment. *Professional Psychology: Research and Practice*, *45*(2), 104–110. https://doi.org/10.1037/a0036250

Norcross, J. C., Zimmerman, B. E., Greenberg, R. P., & Swift, J. K. (2017). Do all therapists do that when saying goodbye? A study of commonalities in termination behaviors. *Psychotherapy*, *54*(1), 66–75. https://doi.org/10.1037/pst0000097

Conclusion

Goldberg, J. (2016, July 30). It takes a village to determine the origins of an African proverb. *NPR*. https://www.npr.org/sections/goatsandsoda/2016/07/30/487925796/it-takes-a-village -to-determine-the-origins-of-an-african-proverb

Acknowledgments

I am immensely grateful for the amazing team at PESI Publishing, with extra special thanks to my editor, Dr. Jenessa Jackson. Thank you, Jenessa, for your unwavering confidence in this project and your capacity to see its significance above and beyond what I could have imagined. Even more, thank you for sharing your tremendous editing talents. The conversation in these pages needed your expertise and discerning eye! Huge thanks also to the team effort led by Emily Dyer for the graphic design. The book title immediately "comes to life" on the cover.

Tremendous thanks to Dr. David Franklin, who convinced me that this was the time to write this book. Even with Jenessa's enthusiasm, I didn't fully see the light without your encouragement and vision when I had other ideas in mind to pursue. This has been an amazing journey because you helped me take the first steps.

I am always and forever indebted to Gina Carroll, my writing coach who keeps me on task and true to my word. Thank you for your gentle nudges, your patience, and your insightful guidance. I am also grateful to have Laurie Fickman, a communications aficionado, in my corner to help me meet audiences' needs through media. Very early on, you recognized my knack for delivering complex messages in ways that would change long-standing beliefs and behavior.

Like many, I avoid asking for help, so it's wonderful to have trusted colleague friends who make it easy for me to do so. Thank you, Dr. Peter Britton, for your enthusiastic feedback, including how early drafts of specific texts helped you with challenging conversations. Knowing that the content was helping "in real time" renewed my excitement when the project was near completion. I'm also immensely grateful to Dr. Robin Weill, for sharing her expertise in cognitive behavioral science. It's easy to overlook nuances in the research, so thank you for helping me flesh out my ideas in meaningful ways.

I am fortunate to have brilliant scholar friends who understand both our discipline and our community. Thank you, Dr. Leslie Bessellieu, for assuring me that I could address topics that are complicated for us in the community but that desperately need to be discussed with therapists who are outside of the community. Thank you, Deborah Kai Kai, for helping me stay grounded and on the right path since grad school days. I trust you when you remind me of the "necessariness" of this work.

To my sister, Kristie, who does it all behind the scenes, from giving me feedback on whether a single sentence sounds odd to updating me on my social media mentions to reminding me of my "why." I can't thank you enough.

Finally, I am deeply grateful for my husband, Dr. Ezemenari Obasi, and our son, Kamau. Ezemenari, you support me in all aspects of life, from technical assistance on computers and gadgets to making sure we have dinner and the kiddo gets to his games. Thank you for all you do! And of course, I am blessed that I get to be called "Mom" by my sharp-witted son. Thank you, Kamau, for tolerating when I'm immersed in my "writing zone" and also for finding the humor in all things. Laughter is the best medicine. I couldn't do any of this if I didn't have a soft place to land with my guys at home. And I am beyond blessed.

About the Author

Rheeda Walker, PhD, is an award-winning professor of psychology at the University of Houston, licensed clinical psychologist, and influential scholar who has published more than sixty scientific papers on African American adult mental health from a culturally meaningful perspective, suicide risk, and psychological resilience. Dr. Walker is also the author of the highly acclaimed *The Unapologetic Guide to Black Mental Health*, which makes sense of cultural tensions and lays out practical strategies for improving psychological well-being in the Black community. Dr. Walker is a fellow in the American Psychological Association, the leading scientific and professional organization of psychologists in the United States.

Dr. Walker's expertise has been cited in countless media outlets, including *The Washington Post*, *The New York Times*, *The Los Angeles Times*, and *The Houston Chronicle*. She has been a guest expert psychologist on *Good Morning America*, *NPR*, *The Breakfast Club*, and *The Talk* on CBS as well as *Red Table Talk*, to name a few. She has trained and mentored clinical psychology doctoral students toward independent clinical and research careers since 2003 and is well known for engaging keynotes and workshops that address emotional wellness and culturally informed interventions. Dr. Walker is a Georgia native who now claims Houston, Texas as home with her husband and teenage son. Visit her online at www.drrheedawalker.com.